PRAISE FOR *HIKING THE WONDERLAND TRAIL*

"*The* book for Wonderland hikers, whether planning a day trip, weekend, or the full circuit. This beautiful guide is full of all the details every hiker needs to know ..."

—WASHINGTON TRAILS ASSOCIATION

"As guidebooks go, Tami's will get the reader from point A to point B better than other books, but it is the genuine love of the outdoors found on the trail between those points that comes out in her pictures and in her prose."

—*SEATTLE BACKPACKER* MAGAZINE

"Hits all the bases you need to cover in preparing for your own circumnavigation of Rainier."

—*NATIONAL PARKS TRAVELER*

"*Hiking the Wonderland Trail* takes the mystery out of planning such an involved trip.... Buy the book and maybe you won't be putting off this dream circuit of Mount Rainier for another year."

—*THE OREGONIAN*

"A larger format and engaging photos elevate Asars's work beyond guidebook to a perfect coffee table adornment for both Wonderland hikers and dreamers."

—*TACOMA NEWS TRIBUNE*

"*Hiking the Wonderland Trail* will lure you to the 90-plus-mile trail that circumvents Mount Rainier."

—*EVERETT HERALD*

T0280115

HIKER TESTIMONIALS

"This book is the best I've seen. Particularly helpful were the details of the backcountry camps in each section, and the distance table between camps that helps you plan for a fun and enjoyable trip. A necessary companion for your planning and trip."

—LISA ELLIOTT

"A fantastic resource on the Wonderland Trail. If you have ever wanted to hike the WT in sections or as a complete loop, you need this book. It is the most comprehensive guide for planning the adventure available. Each time I prepare for this trail I return to this book for planning purposes and for inspiration."

—LINDEN MONTGOMERY

"*Hiking the Wonderland Trail* really helped guide our decisions on which camps to select. Highly recommend this book for anyone preparing for a full circuit or even segments of the trail."

—LEIGH ANNE HANCOCK

"When I contacted Tami, she encouraged me to just start planning—take one step at a time, as hikers say. So with Tami's book under my arm, I took a big gulp and off we went. I wholeheartedly encourage you to 'take the gulp' and start planning. Your copy of this book will be dog-eared by the end of it."

—ROBERT MAULDEN

"As a relatively new backpacker, I decided to tackle the Wonderland Trail to celebrate my fiftieth birthday. Thanks to *Hiking the Wonderland Trail* by Tami Asars, I thoroughly enjoyed the backpacking trip of a lifetime. The suggested itineraries and detailed information about mileage and elevation between camps, as well as tips about water sources, were critical to my success. Tami's writing is fun and inspiring, with plenty of practical tips on handling everything from hiker etiquette to the critters, large and small, you might encounter on the trail or in camp."

—BECKY JACOBSEN

"From suggested itineraries to invaluable resources, this book has it all. It is one of my go-to books for many reasons. Such useful info right at your fingertips."

—LORI CARLSON

HIKING THE
WONDERLAND TRAIL

The Complete Guide to Mount Rainier's Premier Trail

2ND EDITION

TAMI ASARS

MOUNTAINEERS
BOOKS

MOUNTAINEERS BOOKS is dedicated to the exploration, preservation, and enjoyment of outdoor and wilderness areas.

1001 SW Klickitat Way, Suite 201, Seattle, WA 98134
800-553-4453, www.mountaineersbooks.org

Printed in China
Distributed in the United Kingdom by Cordee, www.cordee.co.uk
First edition, 2012. Second edition, 2024.

Design and layout: Melissa McFeeters
Cartographer: Lohnes+Wright and Mike Schley
All photographs by the author unless credited otherwise
Cover photographs, front: A deer wanders through meadows near Reflection Lakes as the sun sets on the mountain; back: Expansive Indian Bar; spine: Red-breasted sapsucker

Library of Congress Cataloging-in-Publication Data is available for this title at https://lccn.loc.gov/2023058839. The ebook record is available at https://lccn.loc.gov/2023058840.

Mountaineers Books titles may be purchased for corporate, educational, or other promotional sales, and our authors are available for a wide range of events. For information on special discounts or booking an author, contact our customer service at 800-553-4453 or mbooks@mountaineersbooks.org.

Produced with support from the Port of Seattle Tourism Marketing Support Program

Printed on FSC-certified materials

ISBN (paperback): 978-1-68051-646-3
ISBN (ebook): 978-1-68051-647-0

MIX
Paper | Supporting responsible forestry
FSC
www.fsc.org
FSC® C188448

An independent nonprofit publisher since 1960

CONTENTS

OVERVIEW OF THE WONDERLAND TRAIL

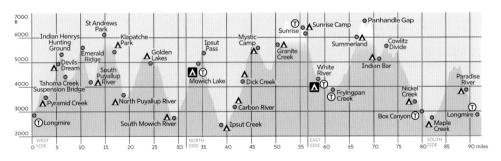

Elevation profile of the Wonderland Trail

MOUNT RAINIER, NATURE'S MASTERPIECE

The Wonderland Trail is a spectacular loop that encircles the base of Mount Rainier, gaining and losing about 22,000 cumulative feet along more than 90 miles. It runs through fragrant subalpine meadows, raging river valleys, and mossy forest floors, leaving your head spinning and your eyes longing for more. Around each turn is something new, unique, and unusual. Nature is the masterpiece on display in the gallery that is the Wonderland Trail.

At the center stands Mount Rainier at 14,410 feet. A Northwest icon and legend to mountaineers, Rainier has dozens of prominent glaciers, along with permanent snowfields and highly eroded slopes. The Wonderland wraps around Rainier, moving up and down, showcasing the many expressive faces of the volcano. From some vistas, Rainier appears decrepit, powerless, and crumbly, while from others she appears savage, forceful, and strong. The Wonderland Trail is also variable. In some places the trail is wide and cushioned with decaying pine needles; in others it's brushy, narrow, and exposed, where a fall would have serious consequences. Mount Rainier is the trail's ultimate sculptor, and each year as the mountain's landscape changes and bridges and sections of the trail wash out, its location shifts, keeping the Park Service and early season hikers on their toes.

The throngs of achy-backed, weary-muscled backpackers who've hiked the trail will tell you that the Wonderland is not easy by any stretch of the imagination. Its ups and downs put a roller coaster to shame: it gains elevation as quickly as some high-rise elevators, and the downhills—oh, the downhills. Even if your knees are good and strong, you'll find them complaining on the steep descents.

But for as much challenge as the Wonderland Trail throws down, it gives back in the form of landscapes so magnificent they might make you cry. This trail is worth every single step of demanding hill climbs and each strand of protesting muscle. Your memories of this epic journey will linger long into the chills of the coming winter, and you'll have stories to tell your grandchildren as they fall asleep.

Rosy spiraea dots the edge of the trail near Indian Henrys Hunting Ground.

HISTORY OF THE MOUNTAIN AND TRAIL

Long before Mount Rainier became a national park on March 2, 1899, people had a deep history with the beautiful and challenging mountain. Five Native American tribes—the Nisqually, Muckleshoot, Yakama, Puyallup, and Taidnapam (or Upper Cowlitz)—are known to have lived around the mountain, claiming various areas in the present national park as their hunting and berry-picking grounds. In fact, Native Americans used many of the same paths that make up today's Wonderland Trail to travel to their harvesting grounds.

Native American legends swirled around Takhoma (deemed Mount Rainier in 1792 by George Vancouver, a name officially accepted by the US Board on Geographic Names in 1890), the most feared of the Pacific Northwest volcanoes, with an angry spirit that inhabited the lake of fire in the summit crater. One Native American in particular, Sluiskin, whose true identity is somewhat shrouded in mystery, made history by acting as a climbing guide to the first party of white men to stand upon the mountain's summit. Since he strongly respected and believed in the legend of the fire lake, he became nervous and uneasy as the climbing party approached the base of the mountain and refused to travel farther. The night before the big summit bid, he pleaded with the white men to abort their mission, claiming that if they did not, they would be punished by demons. The next day, Hazard Stevens and P. B. Van Trump reached the summit and stopped briefly to enjoy the warmth of the steam vents, which they suspected to be Sluiskin's mistaken fire lake. Sluiskin, who had assumed the men were dead, hailed them upon their return by shouting, "Skookum tillicum! Skookum tillicum!": a phrase meaning "strong men with brave hearts."

In 1888, legendary Sierra Club founder John Muir climbed the mountain, using rented horses on his approach. His original intention was to visit and write about the area, but seeing Rainier filled him with exuberance and he decided he simply had to reach the top. While he enjoyed the summit views, he claimed that the best views were from below. Muir's words and writings tempted people who were just hearing of this amazing land and wanted to see it for themselves.

The dawn of a new era was upon America, and roadway construction was feverish. Middle-class families were trading in horses and buying vehicles for transportation, itching to hop in them and see the world. Visitors flocked in droves to see the country's new national park playgrounds, prompting visions of access roads through the parks. In the early 1900s, road work at Mount Rainier National Park was supervised from Seattle by Major Hiram Chittenden of the US Army Corps of Engineers, who suggested building a 100-mile road that would circumnavigate the mountain and flirt with the toe of each glacier.

The idea met with controversy. Conservation groups objected to roads because they jeopardized the goal of preserving wilderness areas. The long-lasting tension between preserva-

EIGHT FUN FACTS ABOUT MOUNT RAINIER

1. **Mount Rainier has many names.** Named by the British explorer George Vancouver for Rear Admiral Peter Rainier, it was also called "Mt. Regniere" on the Lewis and Clark Expedition. It's been widely rumored that Native Americans called the mountain "Tahoma," but writer Theodore Winthrop (of the Winthrop Glacier namesake), wrote that the Natives called it "Tacoma." Yet other accounts say it was called "Tacobet," or "Pooskaus." Native peoples living near Mount Rainier have many names for the peak, including xʷaq̓ʷ and təq̓ʷubəʔ as it is known in Lushootseed. And in recent years, tribal members, particularly members of the Puyallup Tribe, have proposed restoring one of its original names: *Ti' Swaq'*. When you see it, you'll probably also call it "beautiful."

2. **Mount Rainier has twenty-five major glaciers and countless unnamed snow and ice patches.** The largest is the Emmons Glacier (visible from the Sunrise area), with a surface area of 4.3 square miles. The Carbon Glacier, found on the northwest side of the mountain, has the lowest terminus altitude of all the glaciers in the contiguous forty-eight states.

3. **There are more than 150 waterfalls in the park.** Though many are difficult to access, a few legendary ones, such as Comet Falls, are day-hiking favorites. You'll see many cascades along the Wonderland, including Carter Falls, Martha Falls, Sylvia Falls, Ipsut Falls, and Garda Falls.

4. **Owls give a hoot. The most common in Mount Rainier are barred owls,** which have vertical brown stripes down the white fluff on their chests and horizontal stripes on their backs. Their hooting call has been noted to sound like "who cooks for YOU?" with a slight trill on the word "you." If you hear an owl, it's likely this guy. You'd be really lucky to see the endangered spotted owl, which biologists are actively monitoring in the park. They look similar to barred owls but are slightly smaller, and their chest and backs generally have spots, which can appear like white dots or horizontal bands.

5. **Just shy of ten thousand people attempt to climb Mount Rainier each year,** and approximately half of those who attempt it reach the summit.

6. **Over nine hundred plant species grow in the park, including over one hundred exotic species.** Among the most common wildflowers are lupine (purple), paintbrush (red or coral), Sitka valerian (white), heather, western pasqueflower (and its wonderful furry seedpods), and Jeffrey's shooting star. In springtime, look for the unique calypso orchid (purple) in the forest duff and the unusual white ghost pipe growing on the floor of the moist, damp forest.

7. **The park has 260 miles of hiking trails,** including the 93-mile Wonderland Trail.

8. **Reptiles live in the park!** It's home to one variety of lizard, the northern alligator lizard, and two varieties of snakes, the rubber boa and the garter snake (including three subspecies).

A barred owl peers out from the safety of evergreen boughs.

tion and conservation versus land use and economic development was beginning. The lack of automobiles in the backcountry would end up defining wilderness areas in America. Chittenden's suggested road around Rainier was never built. However, the Wonderland Trail meanders along the road's preliminary survey lines and, as Chittenden dreamed, you can nearly touch the toe of the glaciers as you travel its path.

In 1915, three crews of fifteen men each worked for three laborious months to complete the around-the-mountain trail. The trail was originally created to allow rangers to patrol for poachers, vandals, and wildfires. In late July and August of 1915, nearly ninety people from The Mountaineers Club, along with their pack train of fifty horses, used the brand-new trail for their annual outing.

In the 1920s, visitation to the park skyrocketed, and the Wonderland Trail gained its inspiring name. Before long, it dawned on the Park Service that what they had created originally as a ranger-access tool had become one of the most highly prized recreational opportunities in America. During the next two decades, the Park Service put some finishing touches on the trail, including rerouting and lengthening it to make it more accessible. Today the Wonderland Trail is a cultural landmark and, with approximately ten thousand backpackers requesting permits to complete the majestic loop each year, it is one of the most treasured trails in the world.

THE DESTRUCTIVE POWER OF STORMS AND VOLCANOES

Eighteen inches of rain fell in thirty-six hours from November 6 to 7, 2006, changing Mount Rainier National Park forever. The park had seen its share of weather challenges and flooding, but nothing in its 107-year history had been as devastating as the floods of 2006. It's hard to visualize eighteen inches of rain. A simple yardstick measurement of heavy precipitation is often deceiving, as rain impacts land dynamically and leads to much more damage than just adding eighteen inches of water to creeks and streams. As a comparison, eighteen inches of rain is roughly equivalent to fifteen feet of snow. And the record snowfall in the United States for a twenty-four-hour period is just six feet. The amount of rain that fell on Rainier in this two-day period in November 2006 is more than the states of Utah, Wyoming, Montana, Colorado, New Mexico, and North Dakota get in an entire year.

The 2006 storm centered itself like a destructive missile over the park, with hurricane-force winds and warming temperatures for ammunition. The warm tropical air caused the snow level to rise above 10,000 feet, just 4410 feet shy of the top of the mountain. With the majority of the precipitation falling as rain, the mountain's snow cover melted quickly, sending even more water into rivers, creeks, and streams. All that water had nowhere to go

Every year, the Wonderland Trail is rerouted in the river valleys that surround the mountain, like the area near Kautz Creek shown here, as winter storms reshape the terrain.

and a short time to get there. Flowing downhill, the water uprooted trees and boulders and sent them into waterways, causing giant logjams and sending water in all directions.

The damage was catastrophic. The debris-ridden water took out park roads, campgrounds, and utilities and undermined park structures, rendering vast areas of the park unstable and unsafe. Landslides and mudflows wiped tourist attractions off the map or destroyed them beyond recognition. When the water finally receded, the Park Service had no other option than to close the park for an unprecedented six months. The storm had taken out nearly every footbridge along the Wonderland Trail and made a mess of various hillsides, collapsing or destroying sections of the trail. The trail was closed, and permits were not issued the following summer.

Other park trails suffered damage as well. Wind ripped the roofs off two historical fire lookouts, and bridges on trails over hazardous waterfalls were destroyed. One car campground in the park, Sunshine Point, was wiped out completely, and others suffered the loss of several campsites. In the northwest corner of the park, the roadway to Ipsut Creek Campground was so severely damaged by the Carbon River's flooding that the park closed the roadway indefinitely. A historical log patrol cabin in this area was undercut so severely that it had to be taken apart and moved to a safer location outside the park for restoration. It is now back at its home near the Ipsut Creek Campground, looking perfectly rebuilt.

The mountain rises high above the devastated Kautz Creek area.

Volunteer support came pouring in from all over the country. Many corporations and private citizens spent countless hours and dollars on recovery efforts. Culverts were installed and roads repaired. Backcountry bridges were rebuilt and trails rerouted. Major campgrounds were reopened and buildings were restored. Ten months after the 2006 storm, the park held a celebration on National Public Lands Day to commemorate the triumphant recovery and to thank volunteers.

Years later the park is still recovering, and the damage is evident almost everywhere you look, especially as you travel the Wonderland Trail. Near Carbon River a portion of the Wonderland was washed away, and the trail was rerouted to a portion of the Northern Loop Trail. In Stevens Canyon, the Wonderland crosses a landslide area made up of mostly shale and sand. Many bridges were replaced and other trail damage overhauled. When all was said and done, the price tag for repairs was a staggering $27 million.

The 2006 storm was the worst disaster of its kind to hit Rainier in recent memory, but the mountain is no stranger to bullying storms. In October 1947, nearly six inches of rain fell on the south side of the mountain near Paradise in just twenty-four hours. A storm cloud parked itself on Kautz Glacier and sent water straight down onto it. Blocked by the glacier's drainage system, all that rainwater sat deep within the bedrock and ice. When the pressure became too great, the glacial dam gave way, and within hours, Kautz Creek had become a churning cement mixer of mud and rock.

Twenty hours later, the flood had left its mark. The massive strength of the ice clawed loose from the center of the Kautz Glacier, combined with mud and water, had carved a gorge 60 feet deep that extended 2.5 miles. Large trees and boulders the size of buses were scattered in a showcase of volcanic power. The few trees that still stood upright were choking on the silt and debris piled high around their roots. The bridge on the park's main roadway near the Nisqually Glacier was gone, and at least a half mile of roadway was deemed unusable.

Mount Rainier is the highest of fifteen recently active volcanoes in the Pacific Ring of Fire. Considered a stratovolcano (also sometimes called a composite volcano), Rainier has been built up by many layers of hardened lava, volcanic ash, tephra, and pumice. Inspiring uplifting poetry and foreboding fear, it provides an awe-inspiring backdrop for Seattle and surrounding cities along with a world-class recreational playground.

Yet the thought of this volcano unleashing its explosive strength is never far from conscious thought. Mount Rainier is listed as active but has not erupted since the first half of the nineteenth century, and experts say the odds of it doing so in our lifetime are low. The bigger risk is massive slides or powerful volcanic mudflows, known as lahars. Scientists studying sediment layers have discovered that ancient lahars from Rainier's flanks have slid as far down as the Puget Sound lowlands. If Mount Rainier were to unleash that kind of massive lahar today, the flow could move up to 50 miles per hour, covering towns, cities, and the homes of up to two hundred thousand people. Because of the serious consequences of such flows, the United States Geological Survey (USGS) monitors Rainier daily for signs of volcanic activity and lahar flows.

Despite these wild weather and geological hazards, rest assured that your Rainier rodeo is unlikely to be a twisting, kicking ride. Instead, any memories of explosions will likely be of vivid wildflower profusion, with sunsets straight out of a Hollywood movie.

HOW TO USE THIS BOOK

As one park ranger told me, most people who tackle the Wonderland Trail have no idea what they're in for. This guidebook is designed to help you plan, organize, and unravel the details that make up the Wonderland. With the trail's eighteen wilderness camps, a couple of frontcountry campgrounds, a complex permit system, and a slew of other challenges and potential hazards, having a dependable guide to tell you what to expect will prepare you for your Wonderland journey.

Chapter 1, The Wonderland's Moody and Sunny Sides, introduces you to the trail's character and inhabitants, including weather and critter concerns and the backpacking season. Chapter 2, Preparing for Your Adventure, tackles Wonderland logistics, from getting your permit and caching your food to packing your gear and training for the trail.

Chapter 3, Backpacking the Wonderland Trail, is the heart of the book: the trail data, such as trailheads and other factors, that affect your hiking plan. This chapter parses Wonderland's overall mileage and route, details trailhead options, and describes the pros

MAP LEGEND

⛺	frontcountry campground	⤙	waterfall	㊵	state route
⛺	wilderness campsite	开	picnic area	——————	paved road
Ⓣ	trailhead	) (	mountain pass	××××××××	unpaved road
Ⓒ	food cache	=	bridge	— — — —	trail
⚑	ranger station	～	river or creek	·············	other trail
■	point of interest	〰	lake	‒‒‒‒‒‒‒‒	closed trail
▲	mountain peak		glacier	–·–·–·–	park boundary

and cons of traveling clockwise or counterclockwise. Chapters 4–7 take you around the mountain clockwise, with camp-to-camp trail descriptions, mileage, and elevation gain and loss. A handful of bonus day trips from some camps offer you backstage VIP access deeper into the park trails. These day hikes are some of the very best the park has to offer and are easily accessed from the Wonderland, though you may want to plan an extra day at their camp of origin to avoid feeling rushed.

For this second edition, some particularly memorable areas along sections of the trail are called out as Blue Ribbon Areas, worthy of more time to explore and fully appreciate all that they have to offer. A bear icon 🐾 indicates places you are more likely to spot wildlife. You may see goats, deer, or other critters—not necessarily a bear—but a bear is an easy one to remember. And since taking your pack off while you take a break is important, and eating is decidedly delightful, I've included optimal spots along the trail for doing just that. They may be great places to sit and soak in some grand views, or simply spots to plunk down on a relatively level surface and bust out the peanut butter.

Chapter 8, Sampling the Wonderland Trail, is a bonus, with suggestions for hiking segments of the Wonderland if the entire route is not in your game plan just yet.

Finally, the appendixes are loaded with trail stats and resources to help you plan your dream trip or perhaps several dream trips over the years. Appendixes A and B, with clockwise and counterclockwise itineraries of seven to thirteen days, will be especially useful.

Whether your backpacking adventures lead you to experience the Wonderland all at once or in sections, you won't be disappointed. Not for the faint of heart, this trail is for the adventurer and explorer who lives in all of us. This is your chance to travel in the footsteps of the few and join them in saying, "Yes, I've backpacked the Wonderland Trail!"

CHAPTER 1

THE WONDERLAND'S MOODY AND SUNNY SIDES

One time on the Wonderland Trail, I heard a hiker huffing up a hill exclaim, "This ain't no Disneyland!" I had a good laugh and then realized that truer words had never been spoken. The wildest ride in the wilderness is not a theme park roller coaster: it's loud thunder that has you sprinting through hail to the shelter of the nearest large tree. Experienced backpackers know that preparing for everything from weather to elevation gain and loss to encounters with wild animals is key to making wonderful memories on the trail.

A band of mountain goats looks a little worse for the wear while shedding their winter coats near Sunrise.

WEATHER AND TRAIL CONDITIONS

Very few people are fortunate enough to hike the circumference of the Wonderland without a story about eventful weather for a souvenir. When you're planning your trip, you picture yourself walking through flowered meadows with open vistas as the warm July sun shines on your shoulders. The reality can be very different. Mount Rainier is so big that she often makes her own weather, and the clouds can't resist stopping and gathering at her summit. Those of us hiking around the base often get a sample of what's going on at the top. So the big question is always, Which month to hike the trail?

Hiking season. The optimal timeframe for backpacking the Wonderland Trail is generally late July, August, and September. Depending on snowpack, the optimal season varies from year to year, but the trail is rarely in optimal shape before mid- to late July. By late July, the majority of the snow has usually melted in the high country, with the exception of permanent snowfields that linger all year. By August, the ground is generally free of snow, the weather is warmer, and wildflowers are opening up to the sun. Plus, the Park Service has had a chance to remove blowdowns and repair bridges. September can also be a great month, with fewer people in camp and the opportunity to eat your weight in berries.

Planning your trip outside of these months poses considerable hazards. In summer, the trail can be a place of refuge and peace, but in the other three seasons, you may face dangerous weather and trail conditions. I understand the trail fever of folks champing at the bit in June or early July, but early season hazards such as swollen rivers, damaged bridges, and steep snow can be hazardous. Hiking in October or later poses many of the same hazards, combined with much colder temperatures, fewer hours of daylight, and fewer rangers in the backcountry should you run into trouble.

Regardless of when you plan to do your trip, the only thing consistent about Mount Rainier's weather is, well, that it's reliably inconsistent. Late July can be warm and wonderful; or it can be snowy chaos. August can occasionally be a swampy mess, with rain and freezing temperatures. On one trip my hiking partner and I experienced five consecutive days of continuous downpour. On another trip we sat in our chilly tent in mid-August with the thermometer reading 38 degrees Fahrenheit, while mixed rain and snow blew hard against our shelter. September may toss in an early season snow or freezing rain. Even worse, autumn's relentless rainy season may begin.

It's anyone's guess what the weather will do when you're on your trip, but don't despair. Some of my trips have proved glorious, with twelve days of bluebird skies and warm places to perch while snacking or catnapping. Shoot for the season when the trail is in good shape and deal with what might fall from the sky when the time gets closer. In the meantime, learn a trusted sun dance and practice it to perfection.

A shy Mount Rainier hides from the paparazzi in layers of clouds near the Sunrise Visitor Center.

WONDERLAND BINGO

Just for giggles, challenge the other members of your group, to see who will be the first to get five in a row.

HOARY MARMOT	RAINY WEATHER	SMELLY BACKCOUNTRY PRIVY	WESTERN PASQUEFLOWER SEEDPOD (mouse on a stick)	BLOWDOWN (fallen tree)
LUPINE	SHELF FUNGI (Hint: look for large, protruding growths on evergreens)	NERVE-WRACKING SUSPENSION BRIDGE	WATERFALLS	FOOD HANGING ON BEAR POLES
GOLDEN-MANTLED GROUND SQUIRREL	TRAIL REROUTE IN RIVER VALLEY	GROUCHY KNEE(S)	SITKA VALERIAN (wildflower)	BACKCOUNTRY PARK RANGER
GRAY JAY (Canada jay, whisky jack, camp robber)	DOUGLAS SQUIRREL	WASHED-OUT OR BRUSHY SECTION OF TRAIL	PATROL CABIN (bonus if you get to see inside)	MOUNTAIN GOATS
WESTERN CORALROOT	AN OWL'S HOOT	BLISTER OR HOT SPOT	BLACK BEAR	ELEPHANT'S HEAD FLOWER (Hint: look near Mystic Lake)

Weathering the Rain

There's almost nothing more difficult than trying to stay dry when backpacking through consecutive days of rain, and the Wonderland is famous for throwing down the challenge. One time, after five days of deluge, a hiking partner and I considered building a canoe out of downed wood to paddle the trail back to Longmire. Thankfully, the skies brightened,

Watch where you pitch your tent if the forecast calls for rain.

and we came away with a great story, a couple of rusty spots on our elbows, and a few mushrooms growing in our hair. These simple tips will help if you get caught in raindrops.

Bring waterproof and breathable raingear. Don't get caught in the rain without a lightweight, waterproof, breathable jacket and pair of pants. Some hikers believe waterproof shoes are necessary in rain or dew, while others argue they don't breathe well and take too long to dry. If the forecast calls for rain, I hike with nonwaterproof trail running shoes and a light pair of waterproof socks. Test out both before you go and decide for yourself—at worst, you'll end up with an extra pair of kicks to wear around the neighborhood when you walk the dog.

Invest in a backpack cover. For years, I fought the need to spend thirty bucks on this piece of gear, but now that I own one, I'm grateful to have it at the ready when the first sprinkle hits. If you don't want to carry a pack cover, you could purchase a pack with a water-repellent fabric, such as Dyneema. Or if your wallet is feeling a little light, you can always line the inside of your pack with a trash compactor bag, a popular and frugal choice. No matter which option you choose, you will be prepared for that unexpected cloudburst.

Keep your sleeping bag and clothing dry. Use a couple of small, ultralight, waterproof stuff sacks for your sleeping bag and clothing.

Consider packing a tarp. A small, ultralight tarp or spare tent rainfly with a small amount of cord can create a protected space for gathering, cooking, and even changing clothes, making for a much more pleasant experience in the rain. Since backpacking tents are generally itty-bitty, a tarp will offer you some space to move around, even in inclement weather. Of course, carrying a tarp will add to your pack weight. Unless the weather forecast calls for a soupy mess, you probably don't need one.

Towel it off! Tiny, superabsorbent backpacking towels are perfect for wiping water off everything, including your body after a sponge bath. You may even want to cut one in half to save weight.

Choose your tent placement carefully. Avoid setting your tent up in a potential drainage route or puddle. Look for evidence of previous puddles, such as ground debris or depressions in the soil. Many of the level, most appealing tent locations happen to be right where water gathers. Look above you, too, because tree edges drip; avoid placing your tent under a "tree gutter."

Stake it out. Stake out your tent completely, with your tent fly taut as a drum. You may need extra cord to achieve the desired result. Doing so will make the tent slightly tense—instead of you!

Stow your gear and clothes before bed. Stow everything in a dry, covered place before you climb into your tent each night. Rainstorms can come on quickly, even if the sky is full of stars.

Sleep in. On rainy mornings, wait as long as you can before breaking camp, in hopes of the weather showing a little mercy. If the rain just keeps coming, do everything you can while still inside your tent before facing the deluge: Pack up all of your gear. Get dressed fully in your raingear. Once outside, break down your tent, shake it, and try to fold the rainfly and ground cloth dry side in, wet side out (if there's a dry side left). Slide the wet mess into a pack pocket, or strap it on the outside of your pack if possible (outside your pack but under your pack cover).

Take a break. When the rain finally stops, take a break and try to dry out your tent's rainfly and ground cloth. Of course, you can do this at your next camp, but sometimes it may be raining again by the time you get there. Drying out your tent even a little bit can offer a huge benefit if the foul weather continues.

Snow in August

One year at Mowich Lake, the temperature was 38 degrees Fahrenheit inside the warmth of my tent—in mid-August. Up near Spray Park, snowfall had started and was collecting on the trail, making routefinding a challenge. My hiking partner and I did our best rendition of "Jingle Bells," drank some hot cocoa, buried ourselves in goose down, and toughed it out. Although rare, snow is a possibility on the Wonderland Trail, even in summer, especially at higher elevations.

The key to staying warm and preventing hypothermia is staying dry and warm. When you stop for a break on the trail, don't wait until you feel chilly to throw on a jacket—put on a warm layer as soon as you stop. Wind and cool temperatures can zap warmth from your body very quickly. Once you reach camp, remove wet or sweaty hiking clothes immediately and change into dry clothes. Avoid cotton, including underwear and socks; synthetic, silk, or wool fabrics retain warmth when wet. Wear a warm hat, and dress in layers. No one will laugh at you if you look like the abominable snowman in midsummer—I promise.

Two photos taken on the same date in different years show how the trail can vary.

Dehydration, overexertion, and eating too little food can all contribute to your risk of developing hypothermia. Watch for these symptoms: uncontrollable shivering, slowed or slurred speech, memory lapses or incoherence, exhaustion, drowsiness, stumbling, fumbling hands, and immobility. Get the victim out of any wet clothing immediately, and give him small amounts of warm, nonalcoholic drinks, and high-energy foods. Set up a tent to get the victim out of the elements. Wrap the victim in sleeping bags to warm him. If the hypothermia has reached a critical stage, keep the victim awake and send a companion or passing hiker for help.

Suddenly, I Can't See for the Fog

Along the Wonderland, fog can roll in from valleys to hilltops in the blink of an eye. Should visibility become tough, continue hiking only if you feel it is safe to do so. For the most part, the trail is well marked and routefinding isn't a concern, but on the higher hills and in the parkland areas, hikers occasionally get off course.

In the high areas, especially around Indian Bar, Spray Park, and Panhandle Gap, cliffs and hazardous areas may not be visible in inclement weather. If you think you've lost the trail—or if you're confused—stop, seek shelter, and wait for the storm to pass before you attempt to continue. You may be surprised to find out where you are when you finally have a better view of the landscape.

Cell phone coverage on the Wonderland Trail is much better than it has been in years past, but depending on your carrier, you may only get service on higher hills near Sunrise or Summerland or closer to the Paradise area. In emergency situations, having a personal locator beacon or two-way messaging device is a giant advantage (see First Aid and Other Safety Concerns in chapter 2).

If you do get lost, the Park Service has a fleet of experienced backcountry rescuers who will search for you. While you may not feel like singing and dancing, rest assured that you are in good hands, and do your best to stay positive and optimistic. Use your time waiting to daydream about the delectable meal you'll enjoy once you get out of your precarious plight. Or make meticulous notes and take plenty of pictures for the *New York Times* bestseller you'll write about your experience once it's all over.

Sunshine Isn't Always Bliss

In late June 2021, a record-breaking heat wave pushed the temperature to 105 degrees Fahrenheit at Longmire, while the snowy summit of Mount Rainier was a balmy 63 degrees. Such extreme temperatures are very unusual. With any luck, you'll have nice weather for your Wonderland trip, and all you'll need to stay comfortable on the sunny slopes is a little sunscreen and a good pair of sunglasses. If you get lucky, you'll be grateful that most of the big hill climbs on the trail are in the shaded comfort of the forest. Wind will also be your friend, as a gentle breeze can do wonders to cool you off in the summer heat. Sunny days on Mount Rainier are most often very pleasant with low humidity—more bliss than burden.

In hot weather, drink plenty of water or powdered sports drinks with electrolytes. Take frequent breaks to hydrate and renew your energy, especially when climbing. Wear lightly colored, lightweight, loose-fitting clothing. I enjoy stopping at creeks and splashing my

Fog can blanket the river valleys around the mountain as seen from an aerial viewpoint.

face, hat, and shirt with cool water when the temperature rises. They dry quickly on hot days, and the cool water feels amazing when you are slightly overheated.

When you encounter sunny hillsides and exert yourself with vigorous climbing, keep a close eye out for signs of heat exhaustion and heatstroke. Heat exhaustion, a precursor to heatstroke, will usually present the first troubling symptoms: headaches, muscle cramps, fatigue, dizziness, nausea, and vomiting. Be sure to catch these early symptoms because heatstroke can be life-threatening.

If symptoms are present, get the victim out of the sun and have her rest quietly in the shade. If the victim feels dizzy, have her lie flat on her back with her feet elevated. Make sure the victim is well-hydrated; you can administer rehydration supplements or recovery drinks. Remove any clothing that may prevent the victim's body from ventilating, and wet the person down if possible. Keep the victim calm and allow them to rest. Once your ordeal is over, be sure to buy the sufferer a well-deserved ice cream cone.

A Long History of Wildfires

Records show that more than 90 percent of the forests around Mount Rainier have suffered fires. Accounts from early explorers and expeditions have countless references to smoke, fire, and smoldering trees. Wildfires are not all bad, however. In fact, they can be beneficial to the park's ecosystem, removing dead wood and shifting key nutrients back to the soil to support healthy plant growth.

There have been fourteen major fires in the park (the last one was in 1934), and all occurred during seasons of drought and dry conditions. It's nearly impossible to control the spread of fires during a drought. There is dry timber on nearly every slope in every direction, and access is challenging for firefighters. For this reason, campfires are prohibited in the backcountry at Rainier; backcountry travelers are limited to camp stoves.

In late July 2009, a thunder and lightning storm roared through the park. Lightning touched down in ninety-four places in less than twenty-four hours, starting a multitude of small fires. Twenty-three small fires began spreading and one, near Grand Park, grew to twenty acres. Firefighters worked diligently to contain the blazes, preventing damage to property and harm to people.

The park's number-one priority is keeping the public safe, and backcountry rangers are knowledgeable about any fire hazards that may come up during your Wonderland adventure. After thunder and lightning storms, keep your eyes open for wildfires. Use common sense and turn back if conditions seem unsafe.

The Bridges of Wonderland Country

You'll cross so many bridges along the Wonderland Trail that you'll lose count. It seems that all watercourses, and even some dry creeks, have a footlog or old stock bridge. The Park Service does a fantastic job of replacing bridge washouts as quickly as possible, but all it takes is a good rainstorm or heat wave (which increases snowmelt runoff) and the bridges will be gone faster than green grass through a goose.

The footlogs are often attached to long metal cables so that trail crews can recover the logs when they're swept downstream. Before this practice, footlogs would constantly float away and decorate the downstream riverbanks. No matter how thoughtful the Park Service is about placing the logs over defined river channels, with solid ground on each end, they invariably wash away year after year. In wet or hot years, the Park Service may have to replace a single bridge more than ten times. As you hike, keep an eye out for battered footlogs, some up to thirty years old, that have come to their final resting place downstream from the new crossing.

Years ago, retired trails foreman Carl Fabiani shared an unfortunate bridge story with me. In the Stevens Canyon section of the Wonderland Trail, a big, beautiful wooden bridge

Primitive bridges, like this one near the South Mowich River, are replaced frequently, depending on how the rivers shift from year to year.

once graced a gorge crossing not far from Martha Falls. One year, the wooden bridge failed, and the trail was rerouted to a makeshift crossing. When funds became available to replace the bridge, the Park Service decided to build it out of durable steel. Steel bridges are costly, so they're only used in areas that have stable bedrock on both ends for anchors and where the possibility of water damage is slim. This particular water crossing was across a high gorge, with big trees and solid stone edges, making it a perfect candidate for steel.

Trail crews worked feverishly that summer, and the bridge was completed by late September, just as fall set in. The excitement was building for Wonderland Trail hikers to enjoy the bridge the following summer. But come that next spring, when trail crews went out to inspect the bridge, they were shocked and saddened at what they found. A highly unusual avalanche had come careening down an adjacent hillside, smashing the bridge into pieces. Not only was the bridge destroyed, but its steel remnants were an eyesore, littering the water downstream. Much to everyone's disappointment, the mangled steel had to be flown out and disposed of before any hiker ever got to cross the great structure.

Despite facing challenges like these, backcountry trail crews work hard to keep the Wonderland open and enjoyable for everyone. Be sure to thank them, should you pass them on the trail. It's a tough job and they do it day after day, no matter the weather, to make your trip the best it can be.

Tricky Water Crossings

If you happen to reach a river where a bridge has washed out, be extremely cautious—don't attempt to cross if your instincts are telling you to wait. Many of the waterways that come from the glaciers above are brown with sediment, and often you can't see the bottom or gauge how deep and/or fast the water is flowing.

If you must cross, look for downed logs you might use and gingerly walk or crawl across. Focus your gaze on the log, or the opposite riverbank, as looking down into a swiftly moving water can cause vertigo. Use caution—you can do a triple toe loop on a wet log just as easily as you can on ice.

Before crossing, unbuckle the hip belt on your pack for an easy exit strategy in case you accidentally go for a swim. If you're backpacking solo, wait for other hikers to come along before you attempt to cross.

If the water is high and crossing is not safe, wait until early morning, when the water flow usually slows, and assess the situation again. Nothing is more important than your safety—don't risk your life. If all else fails, enjoy the view from the riverbank for a day or two until park personnel get a chance to make repairs.

Bridges, like this important one near Indian Bar, take a beating from storms and feet.

Shifty Landslides

Although rare on the Wonderland Trail, landslides can occur after torrential rains or significant seismic activity. They happen most often near river gorges or on steep hillsides, where there is already gentle erosion or waterfalls. If a landslide occurs across the trail, attempt to cross only if you decide that it is safe to do so.

Probe the debris with a trekking pole or long stick to assess its stability. As you cross, gently kick in steps to keep your weight centered above your feet. If an area seems unsafe, turn back. Park Service personnel generally will respond to landslides within a day or two and inform travelers of their options.

Speaking of seismic activity, did you know it's normal for Mount Rainier to have several small, high-frequency earthquakes every day? Hot fluid circulating inside the mountain is to blame, according to geologists. Before you cancel your wilderness reservation, consider that the odds of feeling a shake or seeing any effects are slim. Most earthquakes at Mount Rainier are shallow, small on the Richter scale, and located near sea level deep within the mountain. That said, if a larger earthquake occurs, it may trigger lahars or flooding, so move uphill and away from river valleys.

Lahars, an Intimidating Threat

Because lahars are the biggest threat to Mount Rainier and the surrounding Puget Sound area, they are worthy of some ink. Lahars are mudflows that consist of volcanic material, sediment, clay, sand, water, ice, and rocky debris. Throw in a few trees, and you have a destructive, muddy cocktail. Lahars have the consistency of concrete, with similar cementlike properties, and can bury everything in their path. Moving up to 50 miles per hour, they have the strength and speed of a Mack truck and often develop with little notice.

Lahars occur when rainfall, volcanic activity, or warming temperatures cause glaciers or glacial dams to break and shake material loose. The energy and force of all that debris and water shoots downhill into the river valleys below. As the flow moves along, boulders, soil, and other glacial components may pick up hitchhiking trees, campsites, bridges, or even whole hillsides.

Most lahars cause significant landscape destruction. Approximately 5600 years ago, a mudflow ten times larger than anything else in recorded human history poured down the mountain. As it cruised by what is now the White River Campground, this ancient lahar was 500 feet deep and covered an area of 130 square miles. It flattened hills, swallowed valleys, diverted rivers, and covered bogs and saltwater marshes near Puget Sound. Nowadays, cities and towns exist atop this old mudflow, and farmers work the rich volcanic soil to grow crops. While scientists warn that a lahar of this magnitude could happen again, such a risk is not imminent. Smaller debris flows, however, occur on the mountain with some regularity. Mount Rainier spits out a lahar every three to five years, some with devastating consequences. Only a handful of mountains in the world are considered as dangerous when it comes to lahars.

Watch for these signs of lahars and be extra aware of your surroundings in river valleys: shaking ground, a strong gust of wind coming down the mountain, rapidly rising water, changes in water coloration, a strong and sudden smell of earthy soil, or a deep, guttural, roaring noise. There are lahar sirens near visitor areas in the park, such as Longmire, Cougar Rock Campground, and the Nisqually Entrance. If any of these warnings occur, get to higher ground immediately. Once you are at least 160 feet above the valley floor, you should be in the safety zone. There have been many documented sightings of lahars over the years, but thankfully no fatalities.

THE DANCE OF THE PLANTS

Mount Rainier is home to an abundance of wildflowers, shrubs, and trees, both of coniferous and deciduous varieties. In the optimal season of the Wonderland Trail, see if you can identify some of the most popular varieties. Some of the most common subalpine wildflowers in the park are the pasqueflower or western anemone, American bistort, Sitka valerian, mountain bog gentian, and broadleaf lupine.

Also nicknamed moptop, towhead baby, mouse-on-a-stick, and old man of the mountain, the beautiful pasqueflower or western anemone changes so much over the season, it hardly looks like the same flower from bloom to seedpod. In late spring and early summer, the flower starts as a fuzzy yellow bud that then opens up into a delicate white flower with a yellow center. After blooming, the seedpod looks like an eighties rock star hairband with fluffy, long white wisps folded in a large, layered clump. You'll feel like running your hands down them and saying "I could do so much with this hair."

Other notable subalpine flowers that feature blossoms on single stems are the American bistort, Sitka valerian, and mountain bog gentian. American bistort, which grows in meadows, features a single, oblong white-headed bloom that is as soft as the fur on a kitten's ear. Of the buckwheat family, it was an important food plant for Native Americans who used the roots, seeds, and leaves. Sitka valerian, which grows in moist subalpine meadows, features a bloom with many small white or light pink flowers, each under a centimeter in size. Mountain bog gentian, which grows in clusters in wet, boggy areas, is a native perennial featuring a tubular, bell-shaped dark blue blossom. Since it blooms in late summer

with petals so deep blue that they are nearly black, some people refer to it as the flower of mourning because it is said to be mourning the passing of summer. Though it is tempting, do not touch or pick flowers to protect their health and species longevity.

Another subalpine wildflower, broadleaf lupine grows as a single stem with tiered blossoms featuring small purplish-blue flowers. Above elevations of 5000 feet in Mount Rainier, this flower usually gives way to its smaller cousin the dwarf lupine. Fun fact: it's pronounced *LOU-pin* (not *LOU-pine*).

There are plenty of trees and shrubs to find in the park too! Shrubs like blue and red elderberry, mountain heather, kinnikinnick, salal, Cascade mountain-ash, and rosy spiraea

TREES WITH GOATEES

The first time my sister-in-law from the East Coast visited the park, she exclaimed, "Your trees have hair!" Growing up in the Northwest, I had never thought of it that way and smiled at her observation. The conifers and deciduous trees in the wet Pacific Northwest climate *do* have hair—otherwise known as algae, lichen, and moss.

Many of the trees are dotted with what is known as "beard lichen," which grows on the trees without harming them; in fact, they have a symbiotic relationship. Rain draws nitrogen and nutrients from the lichen and distributes it in the soil, where trees can use it for better health, and the plant photosynthesizes by itself, without harming the tree. It uses the tree bark as a roost to gather sunlight, sustaining its independent nutritional needs and using fog moisture to help keep the tree moist. Nature is a masterpiece.

In places along the Wonderland, especially near river or creek valleys, you may notice long, stringy strands of hairlike lichen, commonly known as witch's-hair lichen. It's occasionally also classified as a fungus. When it falls to the ground, it's fun to make yourself a new hairdo in the form of a wig under your hat.

Lichen, moss, and algae grow with reckless abandon in areas of the park; in some places, they've almost taken over every surface, including the trees themselves. You're likely to see many varieties of moss growing side by side, such as stairstep, rock, cat-tail, Lyell's bristle, lanky, and sphagnum. One of their main benefits is acting as an anchor for rocks, soil, and tree matter, helping to prevent erosion. They are tough, adaptable plants and have been known to survive high heat, low temperatures, and overly dry conditions. And since they don't have roots, they can grow just about anywhere, including steep hillsides, slick and rocky outcroppings, on trees, or even in water. Instead of roots, they have tiny, hairlike structures with which they draw nutrients for photosynthesis. Because they are so adaptable, they live on every continent, capable of surviving in damp, dark caves and arid deserts. They've been around a long time, dating back five hundred million years. Talk about longevity!

Nature spins around you all along the trail—even on the hairy trees.

Wildflowers surround the park's oldest backcountry patrol cabin in Indian Henrys Hunting Ground.

Ripe berries are a delectable treat as you hike.

are sprinkled around the park, but the most popular by far is the huckleberry. Huckleberry plants produce an abundance of antioxidant-rich, vitamin-laden berries that have filled peoples' bellies since the beginning of recorded history. Cascade huckleberries have bright blue berries resembling a smaller version of the classic blueberry you'd see in the grocery store. Mountain huckleberries, my personal favorite, feature a deep purple, almost black coloration and have a sweeter, more robust flavor. I bet you'd never believe that the oval-leafed variety have—wait for it—oval leaves. The berries of that variety share a mild to bright blue similar to the hue of the Cascade huckleberries, but the oval-leafed variety has a more symmetrical leaf pattern. But wait there's more! Originating from the same Vaccinium (genus) are the low bilberry, Alaska blueberry, red huckleberry, and evergreen huckleberry, all of which grow in the park—so much to digest, so little time.

Common conifers such as Douglas-fir, mountain hemlock, and western redcedar are all prevalent in the park, but the occasional lodgepole pine and Englemann spruce are also dotted around the landscape. Keep an eye out as well for deciduous trees, such as vine and Douglas maples with their stunning fall leaves, as well as a smattering of bigleaf maple, which grows primarily on the park's southwest side.

Plant nerds, unite! To study the heck out of them, visit the Learn about the Park section of the park's website and/or read *Alpine Flowers of Mount Rainier* by Donovan Tracy and David Giblin, available at park gift shops and visitor centers. You might also enjoy perusing a copy of the laminated *Mac's Field Guide to Mount Rainier National Park Flowers & Trees*, also published by Mountaineers Books.

LIONS AND MICE AND BEARS, OH MY!

It seems that almost every Wonderland trip is marked by some sort of memorable animal encounter. With a little know-how, such experiences can be a joyful highlight of your adventure.

The Bear Essentials

The odds of seeing a bear in Mount Rainier National Park are perhaps slightly higher than in other wilderness areas, as hunting is prohibited and bears are protected. The most common bear in Washington State is the black bear (*Ursus americanus*), whose population is estimated at twenty thousand to thirty thousand statewide. As far as biologists know, Mount Rainier has no grizzly bears (*Ursus arctos horribilis*). Black bears are solitary creatures and prefer to be left alone to forage, feed, and raise their young. More often than not, you'll be lucky if you see their hind end as they run away from you.

During the early and midsummer months, bear sightings are more common in the morning or early evening. Daytime sightings pick up as fall approaches because bears are working hard to fatten themselves for their long period of winter hibernation. Open meadows, hillsides, and berry patches are common places to find bears. Few experiences are more rewarding than quietly sitting and watching a bear graze on an adjacent hillside.

There is something magical and enchanting about seeing a bear in the wild. It can be a treasured memory and a safe experience, as long as you apply a little bit of common sense and bear etiquette:

Make noise when hiking through bear areas by singing or clapping your hands occasionally, especially around blind corners. For the love of all things wild, do not bring

Black bears, like this one spotted near Summerland, are often seen grazing near the trail's edges. Always practice good bear etiquette when viewing—this photo was taken from a safe distance with a long lens.

bear bells. Studies have shown that they are extremely ineffective at frightening bears, but they drive your fellow hikers crazy. Use your voice instead since bears are used to people and will recognize that sound. Plus, it's free—a win-win!

Watch for signs of bears. Tracks, piles of scat laden with berries and energy-bar wrappers (OK, maybe not the second one), small trees that have been scratched to bits by hungry bears looking for grubs—all of these are signs of bears. They also overturn logs looking for tasty bugs and in the process occasionally shred the logs. Look for broken berry bushes too. When feeding on berries, bears often use their dexterous paws to pull the branches downward, breaking the branches and sending berry bits and leaves to the ground.

Use caution with food and scents. If you happen across an animal carcass of any kind, leave the area immediately. Avoid wearing scented perfumes, lotions, lip balms, or sunscreens. At camp, it's a good idea to cook and eat away from where you are sleeping, especially if your trail name is "The Backcountry Gourmet." No matter how bad the bugs are, eating in your tent is not a great plan; ingesting a couple of mosquitoes in the name of safety will help with calories and protein anyway. Double-check your pack pockets for snack wrappers or bits of half-eaten energy bars (obviously, you've eaten all the chocolate).

Know how to behave if you encounter an aggressive bear. Although aggressive behavior is rare, a bear will defend its young or food source if it feels threatened. Startling a bear can also lead to distress and agitation. They wear their emotions on their big, black sleeves: if they're upset, you may witness jaw-popping and head-turning, huffing and vocalizing, or aggressive slamming of their paws to the ground.

If a bear behaves this way, it's trying to tell you that you've crossed the line. In this case, **do not look the bear in the eye.** Eye contact is perceived as a challenge and a sign of dominance. **Never turn your back to the bear**, but if safe to do so, slowly walk backward and give the bear as much space as possible. **Talk calmly and quietly so the bear can identify you as a human**, and do your best to defuse the situation. Occasionally a bear will bluff charge as its way of trying to resolve the situation: it will charge but then stop short of you before veering off and running away. If you practice good bear etiquette, this should never happen to you—but if it ever does, your body language could save your life. **Stand your ground**, holding as still as possible without making eye contact. Don't even take half a step backward. When it's over, find a tree to hide behind and change your soiled drawers.

A word (or two) about bear spray. Bear spray is simply pepper spray on steroids. It is not bear repellant; you should never put it on your skin to keep bears from charging you. Doing so would make you eligible for a Darwin award and possibly a trip to the ER. Designed to stop charging bears, the canisters are large and somewhat heavy, but the spray can reach a distance of up to about 30 feet. The wind direction must be perfect; otherwise the orange, burning spray can disable you instead of the bear, leaving you temporally blind and in excruciating pain. Bear behavior is somewhat predictable; if you follow bear etiquette, you'll have little need for spray. However, if the spray helps you sleep better, it may be worth the extra weight and cost. If you decide to carry it, invest in a holster and keep it on your waist so you can access it quickly, instead of in an inaccessible pocket.

High-decibel whistles will also help you avoid conflict should Yogi give you the ol' stink eye. Plus, they are lighter and depend less on wind direction than bear spray. You should have one for emergencies anyway. Get your mitts on one with at least 120 decibels and you could perhaps break windows on passing airplanes. With one of these loud puppies attached to your shoulder strap by a retractable lanyard, you'll be good to go.

Mount Rainier has come a long way from the days when trash from Paradise Inn was carelessly dumped in outdoor ditches and the bears "having at it" were a roadside attraction for tourists. People paid a dollar each to gawk at them rooting through yesterday's garbage, even occasionally touching or feeding them. Today, bear management in the park is a priority and problematic bears are rare.

Wilderness camps have bear poles where you can hang your food and trash, and front-country campgrounds have food-storage lockers. Trash cans around the park are all bear-proof, and the public today is better educated about bear etiquette, including how to keep these great beasts from associating humans with food. Report any aggressive bear behavior to backcountry rangers immediately, and use word of mouth—otherwise known as the trail telegraph—to inform other hikers.

The Elusive Cougar

Cougar, mountain lion, puma, and catamount are just a few names for one of the most feared beasts in the forest. While cougars (*Puma concolor*) do walk among us, they are shy, wary creatures. Brian Kertson, a leading cougar biologist in Washington State, spent years researching and collecting data on radio-collared cougars. During his research, Kertson and his colleagues came face-to-face with dozens of cougars in the wild and never once felt threatened. Most times when researchers moved in on a den or a cougar kill, the cougar moved off quietly. Occasionally, when the big cat did double back, it was curious about the researchers, not stalking them. Even when researchers came upon cougars with kittens, the animals were often timid and showed no signs of aggression.

The odds of seeing a cougar in the wild are very small and, for the most part, no greater in Mount Rainier National Park than in other backcountry landscapes in Washington. However, in late spring and throughout summer, you may be slightly more likely to see one due to the increased presence of elk in the park.

If you do see a cougar, grab your camera and cherish the rare and wonderful opportunity you've been given. You may also encounter cougar prints, which are easy to distinguish not only by their sheer size but also because they lack claws and have a unique heel pad—look for three distinct ridges at the bottom and two on top.

While cougars are predators and our psyches have been hardwired to fear them, Kertson enjoys the reminder that more people die in the United States from vending machines falling on them than from cougar attacks. Think of that the next time you're working to coax down that Snickers bar stuck in the machine.

In the rare event that you do encounter a curious cougar, keep these tips in mind:

Maintain eye contact. Tell the cougar you see it by making and retaining eye contact.

Don't run! No matter what.

Get big and crazy. Do your best to appear as large and formidable as possible by shouting and yelling, waving your arms over your head, or holding a jacket up high. The cat will assess the situation and may decide you are too intimidating to challenge.

Keep children close. Pick up children and hold them or place them on a stump where they appear larger. This is key, as cougars usually pick on the easiest prey.

Back away slowly. Back away only if it's safe to do so, taking care not to trip. Whatever you do, don't turn your back.

Lastly, if a cougar does attack, fight back and channel your inner Muhammad Ali. Use every bit of gumption you've got to fight off the cat. Do not play dead! Those who have survived cougar attacks did so by throwing punches, right hooks, eye jabs, and uppercuts.

Whistling Marmots

If you see a large summer sausage with stubby legs and yellow buck teeth swiftly waddling across a subalpine slope or meadow, odds are it's a hoary marmot (*Marmota caligata*). Several spots along the Wonderland Trail are teeming with them, and they're captivating to watch.

An adult hoary marmot is little larger than a house cat, weighing seventeen to twenty-two pounds, with males occasionally reaching twenty-five pounds before hibernation. The marmot looks similar to a beaver, only without the paddle tail. Occasionally, marmots stand on their hind legs and seem to wrestle, pushing each other around with their front paws for hours. This behavior is very entertaining. Once, my hiking partner and I came upon two large males near Moraine Park that were so tall we had to do a double take to make sure we weren't looking at bear cubs. They pushed and shoved almost as if the game was to knock each other over. Either that or they were in a competitive round of patty-cake.

Marmots are true hibernators and spend seven to eight months of the year underground in excavated burrow colonies. Mating takes place in the spring, and by summer the babies can often be seen close by their burrows, slightly smaller and lighter in color than the adults. A litter size averages three pups.

Marmots enjoy a diet of wildflower salads and seeds, and they spend the summer fattening up for hibernation. Fairly territorial about their feeding areas, they will chase away other marmots that get too close to their garden. Nicknamed whistle pigs or whistlers for their high-pitched alarm calls, marmots trill warnings if they feel threatened. If you hear a loud, ear-piercing whistle, it's likely a marmot. A couple years ago, a group of day-hiking teenagers from the East Coast were frantically searching for a hiker who they were sure was blowing his whistle in distress. Concerned the victim had lost his footing and was over the side of a steep embankment in a talus field, they were scrambling the slopes and nearly getting themselves into trouble when I came along and physically pointed out their furry "victim." They were in awe that such a small critter could produce such a resonant reverberation.

If startled, marmots will quickly lumber toward the safety of their burrows or stand on their hind legs and whistle loudly. I once accidentally startled a marmot, and it whistled

One of the great joys of the Wonderland is encountering the area's darling hoary marmots, who seem to enjoy posing as hikers walk past.

so loudly and for so long, I could still hear it a half mile down the trail. With so many marmots blasting their trills, if you actually need help, you should blow your whistle for three loud blasts, with each blast lasting about three seconds. Tail flicking is another means of communication that may indicate a marmot is irritated or trying to coordinate group efforts.

Like the Hollywood elite, marmots sun themselves every chance they get. It's common to see one lazily crashed out on a big boulder, paws and hind legs dangling in ultimate relaxation. Some are shy, but others tend to go about their business as usual as you hike nearby, making for some fun photo opportunities. Frolicking and relaxing marmots bring a cheerfulness to the trail; seeing them is one of the many joys you can expect on the Wonderland.

Salt-Loving Creatures with Antlers and Horns

Mountain goats, deer, elk, and one moose cruise through the park—yes, you read that correctly! In December 2002, the first ever recorded moose in Mount Rainier National Park was spotted via remote trail cams near the seasonally closed Sunrise Road. The sighting was thrilling for everyone, including biologists, who were elated to have captured such a rare sight. While you likely won't be lucky enough to spot that lone moose, you'll likely get

Nanny goats with kids are often visible in summer near Sunrise and Panhandle Gap.

WHERE THERE IS SALT, THERE ARE HORNS AND STINKY MOUTHS

Goats and deer crave salt of any kind. Both human urine and human sweat contain large amounts of salt, a mineral that is manna to the horned ones. In high country, where there are goats or evidence of them, urinating on rocks prevents goats from destroying fragile vegetation or ripping up soil. So, piddle or puddle on pebble!

Avoid creating salt licks for deer or goats in camp, too, by placing sweaty clothes such as socks or wet shirts in your tent or your pack. Backpack and trekking-pole straps also make great salt licks, so tuck them inside your tent before you head to bed.

One year, after deer made mincemeat out of my gear, I spent the rest of the trip in ripped tatters, sporting the stench of decaying deer mouth. Despite my best efforts to clean everything with limited backcountry methods, I reeked atrociously like a smelly cow. Everyone I passed swung wide away from me and must have thought I'd spent the last month as a ranch hand shoveling manure inside a barn.

to see at least one of these species during your Wonderland Trail adventure. Mountain goats (*Oreamnos americanus*) are plentiful and seen frequently near Sunrise, Panhandle Gap, and the high meadows near Indian Bar. At high elevations, goats feed on greens such as moss, lichen, and grasses and are safer from forest predators. They are most active in early morning and early evening, and their white coats stand out well against gray rocks. If you can find "snow," you can often find goats!

Mountain goats are large animals weighing one hundred to three hundred pounds. Males (billies) are generally larger than females (nannies) and have longer horns and beards. While seeing them in pairs is not uncommon, large herds roam the park. On a recent Wonderland journey, I counted thirty-two goats in one herd and twenty-eight in another.

Occasionally, several goats will take over the trail, standing shoulder to shoulder, grazing directly in your path of travel. Don't let them get your goat. Instead, find a seat on a nearby rock and enjoy the view. Though it's uncommon, goats can behave aggressively, especially if their young are present. Do not attempt to shoo them off the trail; wait patiently until it's safe to proceed—in recent history, a person was killed by a mountain goat in Washington State. As with all wildlife, use caution to avoid disturbing their activity, and enjoy them from a distance.

The most common variety of deer in the park is the black-tailed deer (*Odocoileus hemionus columbianus*), a subspecies of mule deer. By Wonderland season, mating and birthing is

During the fall rut, big bull elk can often be heard bugling, especially in park meadows.

complete and most of the fawns are one to two months old. As with most ungulates, deer tend to be more active at dawn and dusk and eat a varied amount of grasses and vegetation.

On the Wonderland, it's common for deer to visit your camp in the evening or early morning. Be sure to share the cheesy stories of the "big bucks" you found on the trail when you get home. Deer are rarely aggressive, but they are more likely to be in fall during mating season. Even though most of the deer in the park are accustomed to seeing people, do not approach them; observe them quietly from a distance.

Twice as heavy as deer, elk (*Cervus canadensis*) are kind of like deer on steroids—they're the largest of the lot found in the park—well, aside from that one moose, if he's still in the park. Also called *wapiti*, a Native American word meaning "white rump," elk have brownish-red and tan coats with distinctive, light-colored hind sides and long, slender legs. Females (cows) weigh an average of 500 pounds, while males (bulls) weigh an average of 710 pounds. Males have antlers that grow throughout the summer and shed in the fall.

During the fall rut, a bull elk will follow groups of females and compete with other males to breed with them (not too different from the singles scene at your local pub). During this time, aggressive behavior toward other elk and humans is more likely to occur. The mating season starts as early as August, runs through football season, and continues into early winter.

One crisp morning, I set out to enjoy the fall colors along the Wonderland on the east side of the park. The quietness of the morning was accompanied by heavy dew on the orange and yellow vegetation at my feet. In the distance, I heard a noise I couldn't identify, and it stopped me dead in my tracks. It almost sounded like the whistle of a marmot, but I had not seen any of the critters, and it was getting pretty late in the season for marmot activity. I continued on and rounded the trail, only to hear the noise again, this time coming out of the throat of a very large bull elk. I was not the type of female he expected, and he was not pleased. He was in midbugle when our eyes met. Unfortunately, the blind corner I had rounded put me very close to the creature. I slowly backed away as he let out a grunt, lowered his head, and then forcefully stomped the ground with one hoof. Thankfully he did not charge, but the encounter is not one I would care to repeat.

In fall, listen for bugling, which sounds like a high-pitched squeal followed by guttural grunts. If you hear it, proceed with caution, and observe elk activity remotely so you won't have to deal with any bull.

A "Whomping" in the Woods

At some point during your Wonderland adventure, it's likely you'll hear a deep, repeating "whomping" in the woods. If you're perplexed, rest assured you're not alone in wondering what in the world is making that noise. The answer is simple: male upland ground birds such as the blue grouse (*Dendragapus obscurus*) are the culprits.

Remember when you were in elementary school and kids used to make obscene noises by putting their hands under their armpits and rapidly flapping their elbows? Those were good times, right? The grouse makes his whomping noise in a similar fashion. Called drumming, the noise occurs when the grouse beats his wings and the wind gets compressed in a vacuum-like air pocket in his wing pits. Only he doesn't do it for the laughs (or does he?).

Male grouse are very protective of their little parcel of forest real estate and will shamelessly and aggressively defend it from other grouse and predators throughout their adult lives. They also use the drumming to find and attract a mate—because nothing says sexy like flapping wings. Found in moderately dense brush and conifer forests, the males usually stand on a log and advertise their location to a potential mate. If you're walking close to his turf, he might also let you know that this spot is taken so you don't decide to flirt with one of his hens.

Grouse are not aggressive to people and will often run or fly off if you encounter them. If you happen to catch sight of one drumming for a mate, you'll often see what looks like a sunflower on either side of the bird's chest, orange markings by its eyes, and ruffled tail feathers. It's a beautiful display, but it's rarely seen because of the dense forest underbrush.

Spooning in the Tent with Mice

Summer means warm, wonderful nights with bright full moons. To a mouse, or other small critters, it also means the return of the backpackers, with their crumbs and warm bodies.

When my hiking partner and I arrived at Eagles Roost Camp one evening near dusk, we found that almost all the campsites were taken. Quickly selecting the best of the remaining two spots, we made dinner and hit the hay, exhausted from our long trail day. At some point in the night, nature called and I left the tent door open while I took care of business. Approximately an hour later, I felt something gently tickling my hands, almost as if someone were running a feather across my fingers. I woke up, wondering what in the world had just done that. *Was I dreaming? Perhaps it was a spider?* Delirium won over phobia and somehow I fell back to sleep.

Two hours later there was no mistaking the tangling and wiggling in my hair. I sat up shrieking, likely alarming every sleeping backpacker in camp. Faster than wildfire to a dry meadow, I unzipped the tent and leapt to my feet outside in the dark, high-stepping and flailing. The culprit was nearly as frightened as I was. Peering out from under my sleeping bag, a small field mouse with long whiskers and shiny eyes appeared to be stunned.

I spent the next ten minutes trying to coax him toward the tent door, which he seemed reluctant to use. Once the intruder was on his way, I had to clean up scattered piles of small, fresh mouse droppings—a mess fit for a Lysol bomb.

At some point, you will likely hear a pika, which sounds like a dog's squeak toy.

The moral of my story is keep your tent door closed at all times, even on a bug-free day. Little did I know when I closed my eyes that night that I would be spooning with a field mouse. Another backpacker once told me that he had a similar encounter with a bat while camping near a lake just south of Mount Rainier.

A creature far less likely to spoon with you in your tent is a pika (*Ochonta princeps*). Relatives of rabbits and hares, pikas are generally found in rocky talus slopes and look similar to a guinea pig, only with larger, round ears. If you hear a loud, high-pitched *eeeeeeep* from a hillside, see if you can spot it. I like to call this game "pick a pika on the pumice," which is a little like finding Waldo, as they are amazingly camouflaged. Pikas are active during daylight hours and eat fresh greens, often laying them in piles to dry. This small, shy mammal is only six to nine inches long, and its high-pitched warning is often triggered by a backpacker walking by on an adjacent trail.

Quit Bugging Me

It's probably no big surprise to hear that warm summer days on the Wonderland produce bugs in copious quantities. They bite, buzz, bump, and burrow. Sometimes it feels like bathing in a kiddie pool of bug spray is the only answer. The most common nuisance biters are mosquitoes, black flies, and horseflies (a.k.a. deerflies).

Come prepared to prevent bites and diseases. Studies have shown that mosquitoes are drawn to the carbon dioxide humans exhale as well as to certain fragrances and dark colors.

Stay away from scented lotions, deodorants, hair products, and soaps that may smell delicious to bothersome bugs. Wear lighter-colored clothing and cover up as much skin as possible. Also avoid floral prints, as bees are drawn to bright, colorful patterns and may mistake you for posies.

FLIES IN DISGUISE

You might have a visit from a hoverfly or two during your Wonderland trip. These flies look like bees but are actually flies in disguise and don't sting or bite. They seem to hold completely still in the air, even though their wings are beating rapidly. You'll see them hovering (hence the name) above your skin with their large fly-like eyes, seeking permission to land on you. If you hold still, they'll land and stick out a tiny black tongue with an odd disc at the end and proceed to tickle and lick your skin. They are completely harmless, and the experience is entertaining if (like me) you are amused by the simple things in life.

Small creatures like hoverflies are some of the simple joys of the Wonderland.

There are plenty of bug-repellent products on the market, but the most effective is the chemical N,N-diethyl-meta-toluamide, or DEET. A common active ingredient found in bug spray, the amount of DEET can vary from 10 percent to 100 percent—100 percent DEET is often nicknamed "Jungle Juice." I know exactly what you are thinking about DEET right now, and I'm right there with you. It's sticky, greasy, feels awful on sweaty skin, and, considering it can melt plastic (true story, it once swallowed part of my watch band), has questionable effects on human health. The Environmental Protection Agency has given DEET a green light for safety, and complications from it are rare, but it's powerful and so best used in moderation. I've found that if I decide to use DEET, the 30 percent range works well for me—it's a nice compromise between concern and peace of mind, and it seems to do a decent job of keeping the bitty biters away.

Heralded as a DEET alternative, Picaridin is a fairly new chemical on the market. Less greasy and sticky, it seems to irritate skin less than DEET—a nice perk, but the jury is still out on its effectiveness. Every time I hear the name, I imagine a perfume commercial with a beautiful spokesmodel flitting through the trees in a flowing white gown and whispering, "Picaridin. For bugs."

Another option is permethrin, a chemical used to treat clothing, lightweight sleeping shelters, and mosquito netting before you plan to use them. Outdoor retailers generally carry the wash-in or spray, which can last up to six washings or six weeks before items need to be treated again. Apply the chemical before your trip and allow treated fabrics to dry thoroughly. Some outdoor garments pre-treated with permethrin can be bought off the shelf, and at least one online manufacturer allows you to send clothing to them for treatment so you don't have to mess with it.

Repellents made with natural ingredients, such as eucalyptus and other botanical extracts, are also available. I much prefer natural products to chemicals, but I've found the Wonderland bug battalions to be very tough opponents, and natural products are not completely effective in slap-to-slap combat. Sometimes I still use a natural repellent, reapplying often and taking a few bites for the team. As a bonus, it helps me smell better.

It's up to you to weigh the pros and cons of pesticide use versus itchy bug bites and frustrated grumbles. Then again, you could dress in clothing made from tightly woven fabric from head to toe and avoid the issue altogether. Either way, be sure to tell those bugs to buzz off.

CHAPTER 2

PREPARING FOR YOUR ADVENTURE

When the Wonderland Trail guides you through flowered meadows, past stunning vistas, and around high subalpine lakes, you'll understand why the trail is so popular. To manage wilderness campers, avoid conflicts, monitor the disposal of human waste, and, most importantly, protect fragile alpine areas, the park has a permit system for all overnight wilderness camping.

The iconic arch and sign at the Nisqually Entrance in the park's southwest corner

Unlike backpacking trips in many national forests, where you simply grab your pack, gather supplies, and hit the trail, you must have a preassigned wilderness permit in order to camp in the backcountry of Mount Rainier National Park. On the Wonderland Trail, there are eighteen designated wilderness camps and three nonwilderness (frontcountry) camps. Each wilderness camp has between one and eight campsites, a rustic privy, a food-storage pole, and a creek or lake for water within a short walking distance.

As you plan to hike the Wonderland Trail (or other park trails), you'll need to determine how many days your trip will be and how many miles per day you'll be able and willing to travel. Consider what the trail has in store and be honest with yourself.

Plan for more time than you think you'll need. The average Wonderland Trail trip takes experienced backpackers seven to twelve days. No matter how much time you've logged on other trails, the Wonderland is a challenging beast. On average, you'll be climbing up and going down roughly 2500 feet each day, with a loaded pack. Think of the Wonderland like a roller coaster, going up and down nearly the whole time, with very little flat hiking. On almost every trip, I've passed worn-out backpackers with glazed-over eyes asking how far it is to the next camp.

With careful planning, including allowing yourself plenty of time to complete the trail, you'll have a spring in your step, a song in your heart, and the advantage of marinating in the backcountry beauty with more energy, drive, and vigor. If you plan for too much time, the worst-case scenario is that you end up at camp early with more time to explore, read, or write about your day's adventures. The trail itself is more beautiful than most of the camps, so enjoy the journey—and since you have a reservation for a campsite, don't sweat your speed.

This is also a good time to mention that the only pack animal allowed on the trail is the human variety. Horses, mules, burros, llamas, dogs, and any other pack, saddle, or domestic animals are prohibited, with the exception of service dogs.

With some helpful information, navigating the permit system isn't too bad. First, decide on a direction. The Wonderland can be hiked clockwise or counterclockwise (see Which Direction Should I Go? in chapter 3). Next, study your maps and elevation profiles and calculate how far you think you can go with a heavy pack day after day. Keep in mind that as you approach your food caches, your pack will be a bit lighter. Appendixes A and B list clockwise and counterclockwise itineraries of seven to thirteen days, starting from the most popular Wonderland trailheads. Use these sample itineraries to help plan your trip and choose your camps.

Once you have your optimal itinerary and camp choices, make a plan B. If your top choices are not available when you go to secure your permit, you may need to wiggle your

SWINGING IN THE TREES

Over the years, several folks have asked me if people can successfully hike the Wonderland using a hammock instead of a tent. The answer is yes, although it's challenging. The Park Service prefers that backpackers stay in the official tent-designated areas, which means that hammocks must be erected near the camps on suitable, stable trees. Campers must stay within the wilderness camp boundaries and be prepared to use a tent or cowboy camp (camp in a bivy sack and/or without a tent) if trees, such as those in Dick Creek Camp, are too vulnerable to support a hammock.

The park also requests that hammockers hang in areas without fragile alpine vegetation and use care getting in and out of their hammock to avoid damaging vegetation. To protect trees, hammock straps should be at least one inch wide. If you insist on feeding your inner sloth, have at it!

selections around a bit. Other options might include alternative start dates with the same itinerary. Come up with a plan C, too, for good luck.

Individual campsites at the wilderness camps are limited to five people. Most sites have room for two tents, so if you think you'll need more than two tents, or if your party size is between six and twelve backpackers (twelve is the max allowed), you must use a designated group site. Some, but not all, wilderness camps have group sites, so being extra organized is key. I've seen extended families hike the trail in two separate groups, going in opposite directions and sharing stories and a high five when they meet in the middle.

GETTING YOUR PERMIT

You can use two possible methods to secure your wilderness permit: the wilderness camping reservation system or the walk-up permit system. Up to 70 percent of the wilderness camps are available through the reservation system. The other 30 percent are available for spontaneous walk-up adventurers or permit challenges. With these permit systems in place, you can enjoy your day on the trail without feeling rushed or hurried to get to a flat camp spot with a reliable water source. While this system takes the worry out of where to stay, it also requires planning and forethought.

Reservation System Permits

When this book was first published, hikers had to apply for reservation system permits via a fax machine. Ask the average high school student about fax machines, and you will likely get a blank stare. Thankfully, the park's reservation system has caught up to its overwhelming need. But the fluidity of the reservation system with respect to this guidebook has me knocking my head on my desk. I'm thrilled that hardworking park employees are getting a break thanks to algorithms and software, but it is challenging to document the rapidly changing methods in a printed guidebook.

Permits for all wilderness camps are required year-round, but reservations are accepted only during the peak, snow-free timeframes: from June to September or early October. While not required, reservations are highly recommended (see Walk-Up Permits below).

Since the year 2022, the early access lottery system offers you the best chance at getting a full Wonderland reservation—but

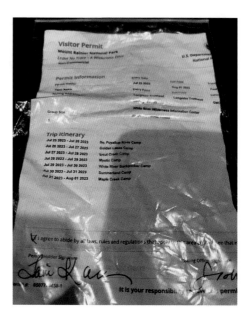

A printed permit is required for trips.

even with this system, there are no guarantees. Applications for the lottery start in late February and extend through early March. Lottery winners are granted a time frame between late March and mid- to late April to log on to a special website and attempt to create a Wonderland itinerary and secure a reservation. The rest of us get whatever is left when it opens to the public in late April. At that point, a full-loop reservation is very difficult to obtain, but section hikes, or a night here or there, are possible. It costs $6 (at the time of publication) just to apply for the chance to get a reservation via the early access lottery system, but it's money well spent if karma flips a win your way. All the reservation fees are handled online. The best advice I can give you is to visit the park's website the winter before you're planning to hike so that you can research key dates and the current application process. You may also want to start scanning the sidewalks for lucky pennies.

Should you get a chance at a reservation, have your entry trailhead, exit trailhead, travel dates, and full itinerary at the ready when you hop on the computer. Being flexible about the exact time frame and being willing to accept alternative sites, dates, trailheads, or loop directions (clockwise or counterclockwise) will increase your odds of getting a full itinerary. If your group size is between six and twelve people, however, you will be limited to group campsites, which are unavailable at Deer Creek, Dick Creek, Eagles Roost,

Klapatche Park, and Pyramid Creek. A $26 fee (at the time of publication) is required for your confirmed reservations.

Important Note: The letter you receive from the Park Service about your reservation is not your permit—it's simply a placeholder. You'll need to pick up your permit at a ranger station before you start your trip. Let the Park Service know if you'll be unable to pick up the permit before noon on the day of your trip, or your reservation will be canceled. Have the following information ready when you visit the ranger station to obtain your permit: an emergency contact phone number, the license plate number of any vehicle(s) being left in the park overnight, and the make, model, and color of the vehicle(s).

After your permit has been issued, triple-check that the dates and wilderness camps are correct. Unfortunately, I learned this lesson the hard way. On one trip, I ended up having to stay at a campsite for an additional unplanned night due to a simple permit mistake. While I enjoyed the extra day of rest and sightseeing, it caused some long and difficult trail days as the trip progressed.

The heavy-duty paper permit must be secured to your backpack when you're traveling along the trail, and it should be attached to your tent when you're at camp. Displaying your permit allows the backcountry rangers to ensure that you've gone through the proper permit channels; you'll also feel better knowing you won't have to arm wrestle someone for a camp spot after a long day of communing with marmots and mosquitoes. When "backpacker brain" sets in with the airy freedom of life in the high country, the permit will also remind you of the camp choices and goals you set for yourself.

If your plans change and you cannot use your permit or itinerary spots, be sure to call a wilderness information center or log on to recreation.gov to cancel. The same goes if you have to leave the trail and have wilderness camp reservations you cannot use. Nearly every day, reserved campsites on the Wonderland go unused when someone else could have enjoyed them. I believe we'd have a more cheerful society if more folks got the chance to spend the night out here; it's pure dopamine gasoline. Do your part to share the joy.

TOSS IT

Not only do you have the fantastic ability to resupply yourself en route on the Wonderland Trail but you will also find trash cans in various spots to throw away last night's funky tuna packets and the rest of the rubbish. Look for trash cans at the following locations: Longmire, Mowich Lake, Sunrise, White River, and Box Canyon.

Wilderness camps, like this one along the Spray Park alternative, are well-marked and easy to find.

Walk-Up Permits

Many years ago, the Park Service called these "first-come, first-served permits," but now the easier-to-remember term "walk-up permits" is used. Up to 30 percent of the wilderness camps in Mount Rainier National Park are slated for this system. Walk-up permits cost $6 (at the time of publication) and are available at any park wilderness information center (WIC), no earlier than one day before the start of your trip. Just as if you were applying for a reservation permit, have at least three itinerary options ready. With three possible camping plans, sound research, good vibes, and a good-luck dance move or two, you'll usually get a favorable permit outcome.

In the last few years, it has become easier to craft your plan for acquiring walk-up permits thanks to recreation.gov. Simply log on to the website the day of (or the day prior to) your desired trip start date, and camp availability for your selected timeframe will be listed. This way, you can show up at an issuing WIC with the best odds of getting your desired itinerary. If a camp is full, the website will list an availability of zero; however, if walk-ups are still available, it will say "w" under the date. Even better, if a number appears under the date, you can reserve it online to ensure you get that camp. Keep in mind that there are fees for reservations if you book online. At the time of publication, a reservation was $20 with a $6 service fee.

On my last full Wonderland hike, I was able to book several camps in advance of my walk-up attempts, so I had a few already confirmed before I went to the WIC, which increased my odds of getting a full-loop permit. Be flexible about trailheads, route direction, and distances—and be willing to accept any open camps, provided the itinerary is within your abilities. Klapatche is gorgeous, but don't dig your heels in about having to stay there. When it comes to walk-up permits, beggars can't be choosers.

Don't expect the rangers to plan your Wonderland itinerary. Come to the WIC armed and ready with several possible selections. Since you won't know your schedule, it's best not to send your food cache ahead of time if you intend to try for a walk-up permit. If you are able to schedule your hike for the day after you secure your walk-up permit, spend the afternoon driving your food caches around the mountain—it's a beautiful trip.

The most popular wilderness camps in the park are Summerland and Indian Bar, on the east side. When you arrive at them, you'll know why, as they are incredibly beautiful. If you're planning on trying for a walk-up permit and would like to stay at Summerland and/or Indian Bar, I strongly suggest that you calculate your itinerary so these camps fall later in your trip, an approach with a higher success rate. For example, you might consider starting at the White River Campground, backpacking counterclockwise, and spending your last trail night wrapped in starry skies at Summerland. Or start at the Box Canyon trailhead and hike clockwise, in hopes of enjoying Summerland or Indian Bar near the end of your trip.

Visit the park website at nps.gov/mora for the most up-to-date regulations, instructions, and fees for the permit system.

"I Didn't Get the Sites I Wanted"

If you didn't get exactly what you wanted via the reservation system, consider using the walk-up system to make changes either the day before your trip or on your first day. Usually, this first-come, first-served system can straighten out any challenges and send you off with an acceptable plan. The rangers don't want to see anyone get into a situation that pushes the limits of their abilities and are generally eager to help you. Remember to be flexible when crafting your itinerary. For instance, you could accept some of the camps on your original reservation but change a night or two if it helps you accomplish your trail goals.

While some camps are unquestionably more picturesque than others, you might find that after a bellyful of backcountry goulash and gorp, you're more likely to fall asleep on your camp pad than sightsee or stargaze. You'll be enjoying incredible scenery during the day, so spend time on the trail soaking it in. Think of your camp as a great place to catch some well-earned Z's, and be open-minded about where you say goodnight.

Occasionally, you may arrive at camp after a long, wonderful day on the trail and discover that all the sites are full. This predicament used to be rare but is becoming more common. The first thing to do is to look at your permit to see if you've been assigned the group site. If so, proceed to the group site, stretch out, and rejoice in the extra room for cooking, sleeping, and organizing. If you've been assigned a regular site, double-check your permit for the date and camp. If everything looks legitimate, you will have the unfortunate job of deciphering the confusing permit tangle.

Hikers sort through resupply packages while rangers visit the Mowich Patrol Cabin.

RANGERS: A JOB OF ENVY AND CHALLENGE

Outdoorsy folks may think that working at a national park, surrounded by wild nature and happy vacationing families, is glamorous. While the job is certainly a fun one, it has plenty of challenges. Do one simple thing to avoid contributing to Grumpy Ranger Syndrome: follow directions.

- Follow park rules and obey posted signs.
- Remember that the Wonderland Trail is more difficult than most trails; plan your trip wisely to boost your chances of success.
- Once you have your permit in hand, stick to your commitments.

- Be sure to put the correct information on your food cache.
- Pack it out. Pack out all backcountry trash, including toilet paper, and do not put anything except human waste in backcountry toilets.

Their pay is seldom worthy of all the hullabaloo park rangers have to tolerate, so express your gratitude for all they do. Part of their job is to manage the human waste in the backcountry. Think of that when you have your next bad day at work!

Before putting on your Sherlock Holmes hat, check to see if a ranger is in camp. During busy summer months, the Park Service often stations rangers at various wilderness camps to ensure that everyone at that camp for the night has the correct permit and to help with backcountry challenges. If you're fortunate enough to find a ranger, dance a little jig and thank your good fortune. The ranger will sort things out and get everyone and everything back on track.

If there's not a ranger in camp, bust out your supersleuth skills and put on a friendly smile as you make the rounds to each campsite. Use courteous words, think kind thoughts, and approach the situation with ample understanding that everyone makes mistakes. Give people the benefit of the doubt and try to be sympathetic. Occasionally, the mistake is the fault of the Park Service and hikers are doing as they've been told, or a party may not have realized that they were assigned the group site. Sometimes, backpackers get overeager about the distance they can travel, or an injury occurs, and they find that they can't make it to their scheduled camp. Whatever the case, be neighborly and lenient. Share a campsite if you must, listen to your fellow backpackers' tales of adventure, and employ the Golden Rule.

What Is a Cross-Country Zone Permit?

First and foremost, if you plan to hike the Wonderland Trail, this permit does not apply to you. You will be limited to only the designated trailside camps. You are not allowed to use the cross-country permit in conjunction with or in exchange for camping along the Wonderland Trail.

I mention the cross-country permit simply for clarification—I think it's interesting and important for you to know that this permit exists. The Park Service offers this permit to travelers who wish to channel their inner Lewis and Clark and head off into the great unknown, where there are no trails, campsites, nor amenities. Folks who choose this permit must be excellent navigators, skilled with a map and compass, and have a lot of backcountry experience and strong survival skills. Camps must be at least a quarter mile from any designated trail or roadway. Cross-country zones are limited to certain areas of the park and the maximum party size is five people.

If the idea of a cross-country permit interests you, contact the wilderness information center at Longmire to find out if it might be a good fit for you as an alternative to a Wonderland Trail adventure.

Park Entrance Fees and Fee-Free Days

At the time of publication, the fees for unlimited entry to Mount Rainier National Park for seven consecutive days were as follows: A private, noncommercial vehicle with seating for fifteen people or fewer costs $30, a walk-up or single bicycle rider costs $15 per person, and a motorcycle (including a driver and passenger) costs $25. An annual pass granting unlimited entry for one year to the pass holder and their passengers is $55.

Should you choose to visit multiple national parks or federally operated recreation sites in a particular year, you may be interested in an Interagency Annual Pass, also known as the America the Beautiful Pass, which allows pass owners and three adult passengers (kids under age fifteen are free) in a single, private, noncommercial vehicle to enter all federal sites for a one-time fee of $80. Fees are subject to change, so check ahead to confirm the current rates.

Keep in mind that these fees are simply what you pay to enter the park (starting from the southwest corner and going clockwise, the park entrance stations are Nisqually, Mowich Lake, Carbon River, White River, and Stevens Canyon). Fees for the wilderness reservation system and frontcountry camping are separate.

To make recreation in national parks even more affordable, there are several fee-free days (say that fast five times in a row). These special days range from mid-April, during National Park Week, to mid-September for National Public Lands Day. Unfortunately, many of these dates aren't optimal for hiking the Wonderland due to weather and early season snow, but if nothing else, they're a tasty appetizer for the main course.

The mountain looms large over tiny hikers far below its massive slopes.

Navigating Timed-Entry Reservations

You can't blame people for wanting to experience the eye-candy that is Mount Rainier National Park! Because of the large amount of visitors the park has been experiencing during peak visitation the past several years, the Park Service kicked off a timed-entry reservation pilot program in 2024 for the park's most popular entrances. At the time of publication, this program was in a pilot phase, but it will likely become permanent; other national parks that have done similar test runs have subsequently implemented such systems long term during peak season.

A timed entry reservation means that you have to plan ahead to enter the park via the most popular entrances during the busiest times of the year. To make a reservation for a timed-entry permit, you'll have to log on to recreation.gov. Such permits are usually available in two-hour windows, so you'll need to pick a time frame on a given day that you'd like to enter the park.

First, the good news about how this permit applies to Wonderland Trail hikers! If you already have a permit to stay at a backcountry camp along the Wonderland, you do not need a separate timed-entry permit. Simply show your backcountry permit at the park entrance on your trip start date. If you've followed my guidance for getting a permit using the Early Access Lottery, or through recreation.gov after the wilderness reservation period opens to the public, you will be all set. Hikers seeking a first-come, first-served permit will first need to have a timed-entry reservation to enter the park if they plan to arrive within the regulated timeframe each day. As noted in the reservation section, I highly recommend that you arrive at a ranger station before 7 a.m., when the timed-reservation system kicks in. If you take my advice, you shouldn't need to get a separate timed-entry permit, as long as you plan to stay in the park after you've visited the ranger station. More good news: The Carbon River or Mowich Lake Entrance do not require timed-entry permits. Tipsoo Lake and other hikes along State Route 410 or 123 east of the park are also exempt.

If you have a reservation to stay at the National Park Inn at Longmire, Paradise Inn, or Cougar Rock Campground the day before your hike (or a buddy is planning on syncing up with you), proof of that lodging or camping reservation will allow you (and/or your friend) access through the Paradise Corridor after 1 p.m. the day of your reservation. In other words, you don't need a separate timed-entry permit.

Hikers who want to stay at the first-come, first-served White River Campground will still need to follow the timed-entry reservation system until they secure their camping permit. After that, their campground receipt will allow them to come and go from the park for the duration of their campsite.

Now for the nitty-gritty. As of 2024, you'll need a timed-entry permit to enter the Paradise Corridor between 7 a.m. and 3 p.m. from late May through early September and from early July to early September along the Sunrise Corridor. The Paradise Corridor includes both the Nisqually and Stevens Canyon Entrances, while the Sunrise Corridor includes the White River Entrance. Timed-entry permits are offered on recreation.gov during release windows, approximately three months in advance, with some next-day permits available at 7 a.m. the day before your visit. At the time of publication, the timed-entry permit fee cost $2 and is a separate fee from the usual park entrance fees (see Park Entrance Fees earlier in this chapter). Permit and reservation systems sometimes change rapidly; I strongly recommend that you review the park website so that you are aware of any policy and/or permit system changes.

GETTING TO THE MOUNTAIN

When it comes to getting to the mountain, there is no easy means of public transportation. Mount Rainier is in the beautiful, remote boonies, which offers you serenity when you finally arrive. But you have to get there first. A few outfitters offer customized tours, but most are strictly for sightseeing and don't allow hiking or backpacking equipment on board.

Taxis. Taxis run about $4 per mile, plus tip, and it's approximately 75 miles from SeaTac International Airport to Ashford. If you have the taxi driver take you all the way into the park, the mileage and cost increase.

Buses. There is no public bus service to Ashford or Mount Rainier National Park. The only public transit option is a Pierce County Transit bus to the public library in the town of Graham. From there, you'll have to call a taxi and pay for the 40 miles to Ashford.

Rental cars. There are plenty of rental car agencies around SeaTac Airport and the Seattle vicinity. Depending on car type, a week's rental can run you $400 to $675.

Car-sharing, online resources, and parking. Over the last couple of years, car-sharing websites like turo.com have worked out for some folks looking to get to the mountain. Others have had great success ride-sharing through notices posted on Facebook groups. Getting creative with your resources is key!

Parking is allowed at all major and side trailheads, provided that when you pick up your wilderness permit, you give the rangers the make, model, and color of the vehicle. Keep other hikers in mind and execute a courteous parking job that would make your grandmother proud.

See chapter 3 for descriptions of and driving directions to the Wonderland trailheads. Parking throughout the park is included in the entrance fees and does not require a separate permit or parking pass.

LODGING AT THE MOUNTAIN

If your first or last day on the Wonderland requires a drive of some distance, it's not a bad idea to grab a room for the night at one of the two historical hotels within the park. The National Park Inn and Paradise Inn, both run by Mount Rainier Guest Services, are located near the park's southwest corner. Since the pandemic unfolded, the park has been struggling to keep staff employed and food services open. Be sure to check food and service availability before you go to avoid having to drive the long, winding road back out of the park to try to scare up your meals (see Resources for contact information).

The National Park Inn

The National Park Inn, located at Longmire, is open year-round and has twenty-five guest rooms. It also boasts a full-service restaurant, a general store full of snacks and sundries, and a post office. While clean and comfortable, the rooms are somewhat primitive and lack telephones and televisions; some lack private bathrooms, with shared bathrooms and showers located down the hallway from the guest rooms. Other rooms have only bathtubs and no showers, while others have only showers and no bathtubs. Confused? Be sure to get clarification on your room type when booking.

Before you decide that your tent is sounding better and better, here's a fun idea: if you plan your Wonderland Trail trip so that you start at Sunrise or Mowich Lake, you could schedule a night "on the trail" as a stay at the National Park Inn halfway through your journey. I know, I know, it's kind of cheating. But you'd be eating a "real meal," sleeping in a "real bed," and temporarily cleaning the trail funk off your bones. If you ask politely, they might even let you use the laundry facility. Plus, the gift shop has ice cream bars, candy bars, beef jerky, chips, fruit, and fizzy beverages.

The idea of staying at the National Park Inn while circumnavigating the mountain is not a new one; many folks do it every year. It is, however, a costly proposition, as it will run you up to several hundred dollars per night—if you can get a room. Rooms in national parks fill up quickly, especially in summer. If you do stay in the inn, you will need to remind your

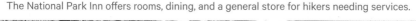

The National Park Inn offers rooms, dining, and a general store for hikers needing services.

body and your brain that this is simply a stop along the way. Creature comforts have a way of making people want to slow down.

Even if you don't stay the night at the inn, you may want to opt for a well-deserved break at Longmire. Many folks cache food at the Longmire Wilderness Information Center and find a place to sprawl out, enjoy the views, and refresh their supplies. The wilderness information center is also a great place to check in with the rangers about weather, bridge outages, wildlife issues, and other challenges you may encounter as you continue your journey. Should you have permit issues or find you have bitten off more than you can chew, the rangers can look into the possibility of reassigning you a less aggressive schedule. You can scope out a few neat things here, including the Longmire Museum and the transportation exhibit, which take visitors back to the early days of the park.

You may also want to swing in for a real meal at the National Park Inn's restaurant—don't worry, they're used to grubby hikers. Seasonally, they serve a warm blackberry cobbler that's to die for. Check the restaurant hours on the inn website in advance, and pace yourself at the trough. One year we came upon a group of hikers heading up the hill from Longmire who looked a little woozy. When we stopped to chat, we heard all about their meal of eggs, bacon, and trimmings; they would not stop talking about how good it tasted. But they were paying for their overeating with indi-trail-gestion, a wicked combo of the waist strap on your pack hitting you squarely on your very full muffin top.

Paradise Inn

Paradise Inn is not nearly as close to the Wonderland Trail as the National Park Inn. To reach Paradise Inn, you must detour more than 2 steep miles from the Wonderland. The trail to Paradise diverts from Reflection Lakes or Narada Falls and heads north.

Built in 1916, Paradise Inn is a gorgeous historical building with 121 guest rooms. While it has charm, it does not offer in-room telephones or televisions, and the rooms are small by today's standards. The guest rooms in the main building have shared bathrooms and showers, located in the common areas. The annex added in 1920 offers private bathrooms and even suites, with sitting areas and amazing vistas.

The large dining area at Paradise Inn is known for its unique bourbon buffalo meatloaf and delicious Sunday brunch. The coffee shop, called the Tatoosh Café, is a good spot for ice cream, snacks, beverages, and fresh pastries, while the gift shop has your souvenirs covered with sweatshirts, mugs, and key chains.

The Paradise Inn is open seasonally from late May to early October. Room rates range up to several hundred dollars, depending on dates and type of room. There are no laundry facilities available to backpackers at Paradise.

Stop by the Wilderness Information Center at Longmire for details related to backcountry travel, such as weather, challenging bridges or washouts, permit issues, and other data.

Outside the Park

In addition to the lodging options within Mount Rainier National Park, a few quaint cabins and inns are located not far outside the park. If your travel plans include arriving or departing from the Nisqually Entrance in the southwest corner of the park, look into lodging in the towns of Ashford or Elbe. If you plan to enter or exit the park at the White River Entrance in the park's northeast corner, Greenwater and Enumclaw are your best options for a warm bed and shower. Wherever you choose to stay, be sure to get your reservations early, as lodging is limited and tends to fill quickly. You won't be the only one seeking out warm drywall instead of chilly nylon.

CACHING FOOD

The ease of caching food is one of the fantastic things about the Wonderland Trail. No matter how many days you take to complete the trail, carrying less food and storing more makes for a much lighter pack and therefore a more pleasant experience overall. Since backpackers should count on needing about one and a half pounds of food per day, that weight can add up quickly.

The Park Service has made food caching so accommodating that you won't be taking many needless steps off the trail to pick up what you've stored. There are three food-caching locations in the park: the Longmire Wilderness Information Center, the Mowich Lake Patrol Cabin (via the Carbon River Ranger Station), and the White River Campground behind the ranger station. The locations are logically spaced a useful distance apart. Each caching location is accessible by vehicle for ease of delivery, except for the Mowich Lake Patrol Cabin—if you want to cache food there, the park kindly requests you deliver or mail it to the Carbon River Ranger Station, which will forward it on to Mowich Lake. The park recently closed the Sunrise food cache location, though it may still be listed on some park information sources. Hikers wishing to cache near here will need to use the White River Campground location. If you aren't mailing your food cache to White River, the Park Service requests that you drop it off at the wilderness information center (look for the patrol cabin) just inside the White River Entrance. Or you can mail your food caches to the various locations (see Resources for details). Note that some locations accept only UPS or FedEx and not USPS. Either way, your back and knees will thank you later.

Where you cache your food will depend on where you start the Wonderland and the direction you are hiking. For example, if you are starting clockwise from Longmire, you'd likely want to cache food at Mowich and White River. Starting at Box Canyon and going either direction allows you to make use of three food caches.

The availability of the Mowich Lake Patrol Cabin food cache depends on the snowpack: the earliest it opens is late May; the latest is mid-July. Check with the park if you plan to cache during the shoulder seasons.

How Do I Cache My Food?

It's easier than you might think! Once you have pinned down the specifics of your permit, you can figure out how many days of food you'll need to cache. Always think light and small. Dehydrated noodles, freeze-dried food, oatmeal, and trail bars generally work great. If you hand-deliver your cache and your pick-up date is within a few days, adding a couple of small, perishable or fragile treats, such as an apple or chips, will make for a tasty trail

NOTHING IS "IN TENTS" AT LONGMIRE

There is no tent camping at Longmire—the closest wilderness camps are Paradise River and Pyramid Creek. If neither of these wilderness camps works for your schedule, you can also try Cougar Rock Campground, a car campground 1.8 miles east of Longmire. Car camping is available seasonally via reservations and on a first-come, first-served basis. Prices range from $20 to $60 depending on your site and, like most amenities in the park, the campground fills up quickly. See Resources for a list of the park's car (frontcountry) campgrounds.

delight. If weight isn't an issue, you may even want to add a can of stew or some fruit cups to slurp up when you arrive at your cache. Just make sure they have a pull-top. Also, remember that the park rangers have to move your caches around, so don't make them too heavy.

After you've calculated how much food you'll need, get yourself a few five-gallon plastic buckets or other hard-sided containers with tight-fitting lids, such as small food-storage bins. Rodents have been known to surf for food, so hard-sided containers are required to limit problems. Seal the container with a few strips of duct tape once you've packed. To help the park fit all the caches into the self-serve containers, use a bucket or container that best suits the size of your cache. In other words, if a five-gallon bucket is overkill, opt for a smaller plastic tote or container. All food buckets and containers must be clearly marked with the name of the permit holder, the permit number, the intended pick-up cache location, and the intended pick-up date.

You can either mail your food caches or drive them to the cache locations before the start of your trip. If you choose to hand-deliver your food, keep in mind that getting from one cache location in the park to the next can mean a full day of driving around the mountain.

A chipmunk enjoys a natural snack.

Unfortunately, the park does not have an alternative way to transport food from cache to cache, so be sure to leave plenty of time for the drive. Thankfully, the Mowich Lake Patrol Cabin cache requires you to leave your bucket at the Carbon River Ranger Station, which saves tons of time; the road to Mowich Lake is atrociously long and bumpy. The park will ensure your supplies arrive at Mowich Lake before you do. Additionally, the park requests that you leave your White River cache at the White River Wilderness Information Center, just inside the park's northeast entrance.

If you want to mail your caches, see the addresses listed in Resources. Note that Mowich food caches should be mailed to the Carbon River Ranger Station; park rangers will deliver them to the Mowich Lake Patrol Cabin before your pick-up date.

FOOD ETIQUETTE IN BEAR
AND RODENT COUNTRY

Always store your food immediately after you arrive at camp—a lesson I learned the hard way. I had just finished setting up my tent and was feeling tuckered and blissful from a full day of huffing and puffing. Distracted by the warm glow of accomplishment entering my mind, I didn't notice the well-fed, golden-mantled ground squirrel entering my food bag. I didn't hear the rustling until I was on my way out of camp to grab some photos in the fading daylight. By that time, the famished hooligan had already enjoyed a satisfying feast. Thankfully, the only casualty was my busted bag of salty-sweet trail mix, which was scattered among a ghastly array of tawny pellets.

Keeping food away from wildlife is a priority in the park. **Never leave food unattended**, as any number of furry or feathered beggars might accidentally get fed and conditioned. Go through your pack pockets at night for any food or wrappers you may have forgotten about and leave your pack pockets unzipped. It seems counterintuitive, but if a rodent is curious about a crumb or scent, it may chew a hole in your fancy-dancy backpack just to get at it.

Most camps have tall metal poles (bear poles) or bear lockers where you can keep your **food bag**. Hanging food on these poles protects fragile subalpine trees and vegetation from damage caused when we all try to hang our food with ropes. In the future, the park may require bear-proof canisters, so check the park's website before you go. At the time of publication, the bear poles were still in use.

Along with your food, **hang anything with a scent**, including lip balm, sunscreens, toiletries, and your trash. Bears have an incredible sense of smell.

Never eat in your tent, no matter how bad the bugs are! If you accidentally spill food, try to wipe it up with a tissue and toss it in your trash bag.

Lastly, **keep a cleaner campsite than the backpackers around you**. It's kind of like being able to swim faster than others when snorkeling in shark-infested waters.

Most park wilderness camps have bear poles to keep food secure from bears, along with other critters like squirrels and mice.

Tips and Tricks for Caching Food

So, you've calculated your tummy's rumblings and figured out your food requirements. You've got your trusty containers or buckets clearly marked and ready to drop in the mail. What's left? Several important things as described below.

When you arrive at your cache of food and fuel during your hike, you'll either be greeted by a ranger at the Longmire Wilderness Information Center and asked to sign for your cache, or your cache will be in a self-serve metal storage bin, usually brown and made by the company Knaack. They look a little like small dumpsters (only thankfully cleaner). Once you've located your food and emptied your bucket, you can either leave the bucket with the intention of picking it up later, or you can donate it to the national park. They have plenty of great uses for buckets and containers, and donating one is a nice way to thank them for giving you the opportunity to lighten the food weight in your pack.

At Longmire, since you'll need to pick up your food cache at the wilderness information center, you'll need to get there when they are open, which most years is from 7:30 AM to 5 PM. Getting there before they close may require a hustle and some careful planning if you intend to hike big miles from a far-off camp. Double-check the hours before you go so you don't end up hungry and sad.

There is a container of freebie food, usually labeled a hiker box, at most food cache locations, usually the result of either overpacking or repetitive snacking exhaustion (I'm looking at you dry, crumbly oat bar). In a pinch, you could grab something from the freebies, but it may not be exactly what you want or need. One year there were several small packets of dried fiber supplements; I'm assuming it hadn't occurred to that backpacker that

Look for your food caches in these self-serve bins in designated spots along the trail.

Take an oatmeal packet or leave one. The hiker box is a great place to pick up a few goodies and leave behind the food that sounds less delicious than it did when you packed it.

blueberries, eaten in large quantities and accompanied by miles of walking, would yield the same results.

In early to mid-September, the park starts preparing for the end of the season. Sunrise and the Mowich Lake Road often close shortly after Labor Day. Backpackers should have their caches delivered no later than mid-September. Any caches left unclaimed when the park closes for the season are donated to local food banks.

CACHING FUEL

In addition to caching your food, you can also cache fuel for your camp stove. But the question of whether to cache fuel is a little trickier than the question of caching food. The answer depends on how much you plan to cook and how long you expect to be on the trail. Since campfires are prohibited in the park, you should plan to have your stove available for each hot meal or hot beverage. The efficiency of your stove also has a bearing on how much fuel you'll need, as does whether you are simply boiling water to rehydrate food or cooking Thanksgiving-style feasts in the backcountry.

Follow some straightforward rules about caching fuel to help keep things safe and accident-free. First, keep in mind that *fuel cannot be mailed*. The only option is to hand-deliver your fuel containers. As with food, backpackers tend to overpack fuel and sometimes have a surplus when they reach their cache. In mid- to late season, rangers occasionally end up with a supply of leftover fuel and may be willing to share some with you if you are running low.

Fuel for Thought

When using a backcountry stove, the most common question hikers have is, How much fuel do I need? The answer depends on many factors, including whether you cook fancy meals or simply boil water. Outside temperature, wind, elevation, and type of fuel mix all affect stove performance, as does the type of stove.

WATERPROOF FOOD BAG

When backpackers start poring over their gear list, one important but often overlooked item is the bag you'll store your food in. The bag should be tough enough to handle being stuffed inside a pack and tossed about at camp day after day. But most importantly, it should be lightweight and waterproof. There is nothing worse after a rain-soaked night than discovering your tortillas doing the backstroke in a baggie of rainwater and your oatmeal looking like bad papier-mâché. Check out bags made with Dyneema Composite Fabric (DCF)—they are tough and light! While you're at it, order one for your sleeping bag, too.

Because there are so many unknowns, you can either be scientific or venture a guess. If you're feeling scientific, weigh the canister or fuel bottle on a small scale, and then cook your intended backcountry meal at home on your patio. This is a great way to test out trail recipes. Once you're done, weigh your fuel canister again to see how much fuel it took to cook your meal. Calculate how many meals you'll need to prepare and then multiply that by the weight of fuel you'll need for each meal. This method will give you a somewhat scientific estimate of how much fuel to pack.

If you want to just guess, I can tell you that it takes me about two and a half hours to boil down an 8-ounce (227-gram) isobutane/propane mixture. My stove boils somewhat efficiently and I use it for about fifteen minutes a day, so my canister lasts roughly ten days.

LEARNING TO LOVE YOUR CAMP STOVE

Your memories of camping as a kid probably involve glowing faces over the warm glimmer of a campfire and maybe even a s'more or two. Car camping offers the luxury of fire-containment rings or fire pits, plus plenty of easily accessible water to take care of things should a spark hit the picnic table. As you know, camping miles away from any vehicle or emergency equipment comes with an added level of responsibility.

Forest tinder in the backcountry is very fragile: a single spark can not only put lives in danger but also take out acres of ancient forest. Therefore, **campfires are prohibited in the Mount Rainier backcountry**. Instead of cooking over an open flame, you'll learn to love using your trusty backpacking stove to make tasty, outdoor cuisine.

And what will you do instead of watching the campfire? When the evening gets dark and chilly, throw on your jacket and entertain yourself by reading or playing cards. Or throw down your camp pad and relax, looking up at the changing sky as the sun passes the torch to the moon. One time when I did this very thing at Granite Creek Camp, I was treated to the sight of a northern flying squirrel gliding back and forth across the overhead trees. It was the one and only time I've seen a flying squirrel in Washington. Clichéd though it may be, by embracing the dark you may be able to find your inner fire.

When cooking moderately elaborate meals, my loose calculation is to plan on needing 15 grams of fuel per person per day. These are just my measurements and not an exact science by any means. You'll want to do your own math and adjust accordingly. Carry a touch more fuel than you think you'll need, as running out is a bummer—ever tried cold-soaked, freeze-dried lasagna? It will haunt you. Occasionally, the food caching locations have extra fuel you can use, but Murphy's Law says it probably won't be compatible with your stove. It's best to be prepared rather than battle the beast of the belly.

ESSENTIAL GEAR

The key to a happy body and a happy hike is to keep your pack as light as possible without compromising too much comfort or safety—easier said than done. If you are new to backpacking, social media is a good place to start your research—but it's also a good place to get overwhelmed. Folks are absolutely set on *their* gear and will gladly tell you what works best for them. But as with almost all products, what works best for one person may not be a perfect fit for another. Gear is always changing, and even after over thirty years of backpacking, I'm still testing new items and playing with different options on every trip.

What if the latest and greatest is better than what's in my gear garage? Good gracious, I could be carrying an extra two ounces and not even know it! I'm being sarcastic (sort of), but you get my point. You'll dial into what gear works best for you by getting a bucketful of opinions and then comparing those suggestions to your bank account balance before purchasing anything. After some smaller trips, you'll ditch some of it, keep some of it, and become a master at knowing what is perfect for *you*. The following year, you'll probably go through the same process, only on a smaller scale—keeping some of the tried and true but upgrading items that might be lighter, stronger, better, or tastier. Hey, nobody said a romp in the wilderness was cheap!

I See the Light (Weight)!

A light pack weight is one of the hardest Wonderland goals to achieve; it requires experience in figuring out exactly what you *need* to bring versus what you *want* to bring. On one Wonderland trip, I actually saw a guy carrying a bag of potatoes around the mountain. Nothing says breakfast, lunch, and dinner like a starchy, dense tuber. Then again, he was dining on nutrient-rich vegetables while we ate bags of processed slop (#winner).

Focus on getting your base weight as low as possible. Your base weight consists of the items in your pack that never change in weight, like your pack itself, your sleeping bag, tent,

THE TEN ESSENTIALS

On any hike, whether you intend to be gone a few hours or a few days, you should bring several key items. You will likely already have most of this stuff with you anyway, but it's not a bad idea to give your packing checklist a once-over to be sure.

The point of the **Ten Essentials**, originated by The Mountaineers, has always been to answer two basic questions: Can you prevent emergencies and respond positively should one occur (items 1–5)? And can you safely spend a night—or more—outside (items 6–10)? **Use this list as a guide and tailor it to the needs of your Wonderland adventure.**

1. **Navigation** (map and compass—or at very minimum, mapping software and an external battery pack for your phone)
2. **Headlamp** (or flashlight, including spare batteries)
3. **Sun protection** (sunglasses and sunscreen)
4. **First aid** (bandages, painkillers, etc.)
5. **Knife**
6. **Fire** (firestarter and matches and/or a lighter, for emergency use only)
7. **Shelter** (likely the tent you are carrying)
8. **Extra food**
9. **Extra water**
10. **Extra clothing**

TRAIL LUXURIES YOU CAN'T LIVE WITHOUT

When I hiked the Appalachian Trail recently, I met a man carrying an electric fly-zapper tennis racket. He thought it might come in handy. I asked him for a picture, and he obliged with a grin.

Luxury items are those that you want, but don't really need. On the trail, sometimes your desire to bask in the comforts of home far exceeds any added pain to your knees caused by carrying the extra weight. We all have our luxury items and, if you are new to backpacking, you'll soon figure out yours.

Once, I saw a man carrying a collapsible lawn chair around the Wonderland Trail. It wasn't one of those tiny, lightweight ones that fit nicely along the edges of your pack; it was one that folds in half, like you'd carry to the beach. He had it strapped with bungee cords to the outside of his backpack, and he was the envy of the trail when he stopped for breaks. All he needed was a sunshade umbrella and a fresh piña colada to complete the look.

An AT hiker poses with his trail luxuries.

A friend of mine won't hike without a razor. According to her, parts of her anatomy get prickly and itchy when she doesn't shave, so she periodically scurries off into the forest and hides behind trees to take care of her stubble. To me, this sounds like a prescription for chafe and rash, but it's her signature move, and we love her for her quirks.

Yours might be something a little subtler, like a camp pillow instead of clothes jammed into a stuff sack, wet wipes, earbuds, or an external battery pack. You do you—carry what you like. Your fellow hikers might laugh if your trail luxury is unusual, but underneath the giggles, they'll likely be envious of your creature comforts.

camp pad, stove, filter, and so on. This calculation doesn't include things like food and fuel weight, which change daily with use. Invest in a small scale and weigh your items individually, then see if you need to upgrade them with new, lighter items. Optimally, your base weight should be under twenty pounds—go even lighter if you can.

The Right Pack

Finding the right pack can be a daunting task. You know those jeans you bought years ago on a whim that fit you perfectly? You can't find any other ones just like them, right? Packs are similar because instead of carrying a pack, you're wearing it. Find a pack that fits you perfectly and you'll be happy as a pig in a puddle, while the wrong fit can mean trailside trauma. Most packs have internal frames, unlike the old-school external frames you see in old-timey photos. Internal frames are awesome for balancing the load when you have to navigate tricky water crossings or execute fancy footwork over slippery logs.

Your pack's physical weight is almost as important as what's inside it, so manufacturers have been trying to one-up each other for decades in a kind of lightweight craze. Before you settle for an outdoor-shop special, be sure to look online; some manufacturers conduct all their sales through their website. And research which packs long-distance hikers, like those doing the Pacific Crest Trail, are using—those folks are lightweight gear experts. As a side note, you sometimes have to compromise on durability when you choose lightweight fabrics, so these packs are usually designed for lighter loads. They are also expensive and may not last as long as other packs, but your body will be happier. Only you can decide what's right for you.

Stuffing Your Stuff Sacks

I like to use water-resistant, lightweight stuff sacks to organize my pack's innards. Most of mine are made from Dyneema Composite Fabric (DCF), primarily available online, but you can also choose some made from more readily available materials, such as silnylon (silicone-treated nylon). I bring along a variety of sizes, using separate stuff sacks for food, clothes, sleeping bag, toiletries, and first-aid supplies. The added weight is nominal, and you'll appreciate the water resistance when you have to fish something out of your pack in misty weather.

Fancy Tents

Most two-person backpacking tents weigh three and a half to five pounds, with non-freestanding, fancy-dancy ones weighing half that. Non-freestanding tents work fine on the Wonderland Trail, as most camp spots have penetrable soil that can support stakes. Do your homework and choose the lightest one possible for your needs. You'll need to consider size, special features, and durability when making your decision. If you're committed to the idea, you can use a hammock instead of a tent in some places (see "Swinging in the Trees" sidebar earlier in this chapter).

Figuring out what gear works best for you is often a matter of trial and error over many years of hiking and backpacking.

Modern Sleeping Bags

The latest and greatest sleeping bags aren't really sleeping bags at all! Most lightweight hikers are trading their mummy-bag designs for specialty backpacking quilts, which can lay open like a blanket or be cinched at the top and bottom for more warmth when you need it. Most don't have zippers (which makes them lighter), and they generally also don't have built-in hoods, so users compensate by wearing a hat to bed on cold nights. I tend to be cold even when standing by a woodstove, so I refuse to give up my ability to snuggle into a tight mummy with a cozy hood. Figure out what's best for you and then decide whether to purchase down or synthetic. Down, often lighter and more compressible than synthetic, is comfortable in a wider variety of temperatures—but it does not retain its warming properties when wet, so you'll also most likely want a waterproof stuff sack for your down bag.

No matter what gear you're seeking, it's easy to get sucked into the "what the heck, it's only a few ounces more" mindset when comparing prices and features. But you'll be cursing that extra weight when you are on the Wonderland, schlepping all that stuff up big, seemingly endless hills. As clichéd as it sounds, the "every ounce counts" mantra is absolutely correct.

To Bring My Fishing Rod or Not

If you're someone who loves to not only "fish" but also actually "catch," there are better places to do so than Mount Rainier. The Wonderland Trail is anything but blue-ribbon fishing—the fish are small and the creeks, lakes, and streams aren't stocked. But if you must bring your rod and reel, there are several things you need to know.

The Park Service pulled the plug on stocking fish in the early 1970s. Several species of native fish still live in the park's waterways, but many of them are listed as endangered. Barbless hooks and artificial lures are encouraged, as is practicing catch and release. Using bait or lead tackle is prohibited. Although no fishing license is required inside the park, Washington State fishing regulations still apply. Fishing is allowed from one hour before sunrise until one hour after sunset. Fishing off a car bridge is prohibited, and the following areas in the park are also closed to fishing: Klickitat Creek above Sunrise Road, Ipsut Creek above the Ipsut Creek Campground water-supply intake, Laughingwater Creek above the Ohanapecosh water-supply intake, Edith Creek basin above the Paradise water-supply intake, Frozen Lake, Ghost Lake, Reflection Lakes, Shadow Lake, and Tipsoo Lake. Many other restrictions apply, including specific rules for reporting and retention of native and nonnative species. If you choose to wet a line, please see Mount Rainier's fishing web page for the specifics.

WONDERLAND TRAIL
BACKPACKING CHECKLIST

Modify these suggestions to fit your needs:

Backpack
Sleeping bag or quilt
Tent or other shelter
Sleeping pad
2 moisture-wicking shirts (either 2 short-sleeve, or 1 short-sleeve and 1 long-sleeve)
1 pair of long pants (comfortable enough for hiking, sleeping, and wearing under rain pants)
Waterproof jacket
Waterproof pants
Insulating fleece, down, or synthetic jacket

Hat (sun hat and/or beanie)
2–3 pairs of socks
2 sports bras (not cotton)
2 pairs of underwear (not cotton)
Toothbrush and toothpaste
Personal toiletries (small comb, lip balm, lotion, etc.)
Sunscreen (small amount)
Sunglasses
Bug repellent
Small first-aid kit (including prescription medication)
Water filter or water treatment
Water bottles (I prefer plastic water bottles from the grocery store instead of heavier, outdoor-retailer brands)

Spoon (I designate a baggie for my spoon and it lives in there the whole time)
Knife or multitool
Stove
Pot
Fuel
Waterproof matches or waterproof lighter
Toilet paper, trowel, and baggies to pack out used TP if nature calls when you aren't in camp
Headlamp or flashlight
Pack rain cover (or waterproof interior liner)
Garbage bags
Waterproof stuff sack for your food
Whistle (for emergencies)

OPTIONAL

Camp pillow
Gloves or mittens (required for many hikers, especially in off-season or uncertain weather forecast)
Lightweight camp shoes
Gaiters
Bandanna
1 pair of hiking shorts
1 pair of sleeping pants
Change of clothes to leave in the car
Mosquito head net
Ice axe and shoe-traction devices (in early or late season)
Stuff sacks for clothing, toiletries, etc.
Pack towel

Sit pad
Trekking poles
Hydration bladder (instead of water bottles)
Camera or phone
Personal locator beacon or satellite communication device
Map in waterproof case (optional if you bring a smartphone with map app and a power bank)
Extra power bank with charging cables (for headlamp, phone, etc.)
Fishing rod and flies and/ or lures
Bear pepper spray
Monocular or binoculars

Guidebook or field ID information
Collapsible basin or large bowl for bathing
Bowl (or just eat out of a baggie or cookpot)
Mug (or just drink out of a baggie or cookpot)
Antibacterial hand gel (small container)
Biodegradable soap (small container)
Journal and pen (or just use your phone's notes app)
Book and/or cards (for entertainment)
Duct tape (wrapped on a trekking or tent pole)

FIRST AID AND OTHER SAFETY CONCERNS

Most people have a first-aid kit sitting on a shelf at home that hardly ever gets used (thankfully). Multiday backpacking trips are the perfect excuse to make sure it's ready to roll. Scaling down your first-aid supplies to a reasonable level will help you achieve your goal pack weight. Of course, there's always a risk you might leave something at home that you end up needing. Since you can't bring a medical clinic with you, you'll have to do your best to anticipate what you'll need.

For example, are you prone to blisters? If so, stock your kit with a lot of blister-specific bandaging. Do you have a chronic grouchy ankle? Throw in a small compression bandage. Does sun in your eyes or shoulder strain give you a headache? If so, bring plenty of pain relievers. (If you grab them from your home first-aid kit, double-check the expiration date.) Don't forget to also bring any prescription medication you may be taking. If you generally don't eat a lot of starches but are introducing them to your system to simplify your backpacking cuisine, you may want some antacids.

Apply the multipurpose rule to your first-aid kit: A small multitool with tiny scissors is a good substitute for larger first-aid-style scissors, and the multitool has more uses, such as fixing a broken tent pole or repairing a pack rivet. Duct tape wrapped around one of your trekking poles can double as medical tape in an emergency. Bandannas or shirts can serve as tourniquets, sticks can serve as splints, and plastic baggies can help with giant wounds. Countless backcountry accidents have been treated successfully with what people happened to have on hand.

A NOTE ABOUT SAFETY

Safety is an important concern in all outdoor activities. No guidebook can alert you to every hazard or anticipate the limitations of every reader. Therefore, the descriptions of roads, trails, routes, and natural features in this book are not representations that a particular place or excursion will be safe for your party. When you follow any of the routes described in this book, you assume responsibility for your own safety. Under normal conditions, such excursions require the usual attention to traffic, road and trail conditions, weather, terrain, the capabilities of your party, and other factors. Keeping informed on current conditions and exercising common sense are the keys to a safe, enjoyable outing.

—*Mountaineers Books*

In addition to anticipating what you will need, think logically about what you probably won't need. Since ticks are rare in the park, you may not need those tweezers. Do you need the whole roll of antacids or just a few tablets? Bug repellent should do a reasonable job preventing bug bites, so you may not want the extra weight of anti-itch bug wipes or hydrocortisone cream. Finally, if your first-aid bag is thick nylon, save yourself a few ounces and put your supplies in a plastic baggie or small lightweight stuff sack. While you're at it, grab another one to use as a wallet.

THE DREADED BLISTER

Three simple things in combination cause blisters: friction, moisture, and heat. If you eliminate any one of these three things, you won't get blisters.

Friction. Blisters are one of the biggest challenges for hikers of all experience levels, with all types of footwear. Whether due to a seam on your sock or an ill-fitting boot, rubbing of any kind on your feet spells trouble. If you feel any rubbing—also known as a "hot spot"—stop immediately and apply a covering or bandage to the affected area. Be sure your feet are dry first, or you can make a bad thing worse. Getting a good buffer between your skin and the irritant will usually stop the blister in its tracks. Some people like to wear thin liner socks inside their hiking socks, perhaps even toesocks that separate toes, to reduce friction against their skin.

Moisture. To control moisture, try stopping once every couple of hours to take off your socks and shoes. Letting air circulate around your feet helps repair delicate skin and allows your feet to dry. Changing socks throughout the day can also help with moisture control.

Heat. To combat feet heat, use air-conditioned socks. (Oh, how I wish these existed!) Instead, try the moisture-control strategies above. You may also find it refreshing to take a break at creeks, cooling your feet with some chilly water. If you indulge in this water therapy, be sure to let your feet dry completely before putting your socks back on.

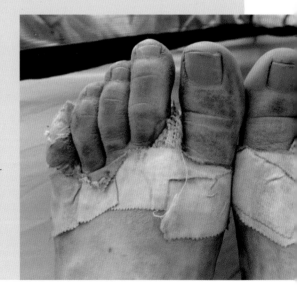

Friction, moisture, and heat cause blisters. Tape and bandages, especially hydrocolloid blister-specific bandages, can help prevent blisters and cover them up once they form.

Using Satellites for Safety

Mount Rainier recently contracted to bring a couple of cellular phone towers into the park to help with backcountry connectivity. At the time of printing, cellular coverage is still very limited and will likely continue to be so in deep river valleys, even after the technology is installed. The odds are good that you'll have a great trip and will want to unplug from screens, but in case an unfortunate situation presents itself and your phone does not have a signal, a satellite device offers peace of mind.

Satellite messaging devices. These days, many hikers carry small, lightweight devices that can signal satellites to transmit messages in places where cellular phone service is limited or unavailable. Most of these devices run via a subscription-based service, through which you can send predetermined messages or use two-way texting to contact emergency personnel as well as friends and family. These devices are great for arranging transport to or from a trailhead, notifying family and friends if you are running late on your trip, or for someone at home to reach you in case of an emergency. Individual units cost anywhere from $250 to $600, and subscription fees run between $12 and $65 per month. I have used mine on day hikes and backpacking trips for various reasons, including checking the weather and communicating with my husband.

Satellite phones. If you need to have a two-way spoken conversation in the backcountry, your cell phone may not work, and a satellite phone may be your only option. Satellite phones are still quite a bit larger than most cell phones, but they're getting smaller. They're also the most expensive option for backcountry communication, draining $500 to $1200 from your wallet for the unit, plus $0.15 to $2 a minute for a call, as well as a service contract. Renting a satellite phone for occasional use is more affordable; a handful of online providers offer this service. Realistically, a satellite phone is overkill for most people on the Wonderland Trail.

If you are dying to post on your social channels because that marmot whistling video is just too cute to not share immediately, the Longmire Wilderness Information Center has Wi-Fi that is accessible 24/7. Just find the network called NPS Visitor—no password required! You might have spotty cell service near Sunrise and on the way to Summerland. Where you have cellular service along the route will depend in part on your service provider.

Tips for Staying Safe at the Trailhead and on the Trail

As far as trails go, the Wonderland is fairly safe. Crime rates in the park are low, and the odds of anything happening while you are enjoying your adventure are slim. However, we all know that crime can happen anywhere, and protecting yourself with a few safety tips can't hurt.

Strip your car of valuables. Leaving a parked car anywhere for a few days is an invitation for someone to break in. Leave valuables at home or carry them with you. I deliberately spread trash around in my car to make it unappealing, and I also leave a laminated sign on my driver's seat that reads, "No valuables in vehicle. No money, medication, jewelry, purses, or even car or personal paperwork—not even a candy bar. Don't waste your time." Does it work? Impossible to say—I haven't interviewed any would-be thieves lately. But I hope that they won't see my car as a worthy target.

According to the King County Sheriff's Office, it's perfectly legal to have a clear photo of your car's registration on your phone instead of in your glove box. Be sure to save it to your "favorites" or to a specific album, so you can find it quickly if you need to. In fact, it's a good idea to keep any paperwork with personal information, including car repair records or receipts, saved in photo form instead of on printouts in your car. If you drive your own vehicle (instead of a rental), be sure to remove any physical garage-door openers. And if you're tempted to hide your keys under a bumper or behind a bush instead of carrying the extra weight, suck it up, Buttercup—it's a far better idea to take them with you.

Never tell anyone where you're spending the night. This is a hard rule to follow on the Wonderland because your campsites are predetermined and folks you meet are often interested in how far you're going. But keeping your itinerary private may deter creeps from knowing where to find you if they have bad intentions. When asked, keep things vague with responses like, "We're taking things easy today." Or flip the question on them and move the conversation in a different direction.

Pay attention to red-flag feelings. Instincts are rarely wrong, so if the creep factor is sliding upward, allow yourself to be guarded and firm—even rude if necessary.

Never mention your party size, especially if you're hiking alone. If you come across someone who gives you the heebie-jeebies, pretend to be waiting for someone by shouting off into the woods. Saying things like, "Would you hurry up?" or "Are you done yet?" and using "we" instead of "I" when talking to a stranger may create confusion about the number of people in your group and thwart a crime.

Avoid hiking with headphones or speakers. Although rocking out as you climb some of the Wonderland's big hills may be tempting, keeping your wits and awareness about you is key in bear and volcano country. If you must have that podcast or smooth groove to distract you on the hills, consider getting earbuds with transparency mode or bone-conduction technology so you can still hear the outside world. Or if nothing else works, put in only one earbud. And, as always, leave the Bluetooth speaker at home. You'll be passing by and camping with other people, and obviously it's discourteous to have your jams blaring when others are trying to enjoy birdsong and quiet time.

Leave your itinerary with someone at home. In a world of cellular and satellite connectivity, this may seem excessive, but because cell service is somewhat unreliable in the park, it's not a bad idea to buy (or print) two maps—one to bring with you and one to leave at home with a trusted individual. On the home map, mark where you'll be each night and write down phone numbers for the park and wilderness information centers. Specify the date you expect to be back in cellular range (i.e., a nearby town) and also a firm date for your friend or family member to contact rangers if they don't hear from you. You may want to give yourself a small buffer of time in case something unforeseen, but non-life-threatening, happens.

THE CHALLENGES OF WATER, A NECESSITY

You've likely seen the commercials for bottled water that show a stream flowing out of a pure mountain lake, bubbling down a hillside on a sunny day. On the Wonderland, you'll see your fair share of creeks playfully tumbling over stones. Some park waters are pristine, inspiring, and clear; others are silted, dangerous, and murky. Knowing where to get water and carrying just enough, but not too much, is key.

Staying hydrated is critical to your backpacking efficiency. Drink four to six ounces of fluid every twenty minutes to keep you running on full steam and to avoid that sluggish feeling of mild dehydration. Set a goal of never carrying less than sixteen ounces of water. Start drinking in the morning before you hit the trail to give your body a jump-start.

When I first wrote this book over a decade ago, hydration reservoirs were all the rage. Some people still really like them, and as a bonus, they are compatible with some inline water filters. No doubt, they are convenient, and it's helpful to have a hose near your face as a reminder to drink, but they also come with some challenges. Since the bag is hidden in your pack, it's tough to tell exactly how much you are drinking. Becoming dehydrated on a hot day is a real possibility if you aren't sipping as much as you think. Hydration reservoirs also tend to encourage you to carry more water than necessary because refilling them is a bit of a floppy pain. What's more, they are hard to clean should you decide to drop in some electrolyte-replacement mix; hoses can become moldy and sugary residue hides in the tiniest of valve crevices.

Most long-distance thru-hikers carry long, skinny, sixteen-ounce plastic water bottles purchased from the grocery store. They are inexpensive, lightweight, durable, and tall, which means they are easy to grab out of your side pockets. It's easy to keep a close eye on how much water you are drinking, and you can take a big drink without having to bite a valve. Consider designating one bottle for your drink and hydration mixes and keep the others for unflavored water so you don't inadvertently add a fruity taste to your meals. Sawyer filters fit onto the threaded top, though because the bottles are somewhat rigid, having a squeeze bag is usually a better option—plus the extra water vessel is helpful on hot days. Technically, these types of plastic water bottles are designed for single use; however, I reuse mine several times, cleaning them thoroughly between trips and using them over and over again as my primary backpacking bottles.

Water on the Trail and in Camp

Lucky for you, Mother Nature has made water on the Wonderland Trail very accessible. Water is scarce in only a couple of spots, and those locations are noted in the trail descriptions. You'll need to plan accordingly, especially from about mid-August through October.

Looking at a map, you'd think that every creek and river contains palatable water—not so. Glaciers are the main culprit: many waterways in the park are glaciated or milky in color and contain fine sand, silt, and pulverized stone that can clog a water filter faster than you can blink. Avoid glaciated water; stick to clear water for drinking and cooking. Your taste buds and your water filter will thank you.

Most Wonderland camps have a water source within 200 feet, although occasionally the source isn't optimal. For example, good water treatment is a must at Golden Lakes Camp late in the season, as the lake there can be brackish and stagnant. At Klapatche Park, Aurora Lake can have a large algal bloom with thousands of tadpoles wiggling around in the mud, or it may be dried up altogether. On the other hand, some camp water sources will set off a hallelujah chorus in your head. The creek at Mystic Camp sings to you as it bounces down clean rocks into small pools. Granite Creek runs crystal-clear and seems to giggle while promenading around large boulders.

Purifying Water

While water that bounces and giggles may appear clear and pure on the surface, it's impossible to tell if it contains contaminants with names straight out of biology class: cryptosporidium, giardia, salmonella, and others. Consider all water sources suspect: treat it chemically (with iodine or chlorine), filter it (using one of the many portable water-treatment devices on the market), or boil it.

Personal water filters are compact, lightweight, and effective at treating waterborne bacteria. Tablets and drops are also good options, though some require a substantial wait time before the water is fully "cooked." Larger groups may find gravity-based systems to be the most efficient way to collect filtered water for the whole crew. Whatever you choose, remember that the Wonderland has plenty of water. Don't carry more than you need—that stuff is heavy!

No matter how pure and crystal-clear water looks, it can still harbor contaminants. Treat water you gather in the backcountry to prevent illness.

Boiling water is an incredibly effective way to treat water—in fact, it's the only way to 100 percent eliminate protozoa, bacteria, and viruses. Should you choose to boil your water, the safety standard requires a rolling boil for one minute. If you're higher than 6500 feet, increase that rolling boil to three minutes. While boiling is effective, it's a bit of a hassle. You must allow the water to cool before you can drink it, and the extra fuel required adds up to extra pounds on your back.

On the Wonderland, try to collect and treat the clearest water possible. This practice sounds like common sense, but you'll be surprised at the number of stagnant ponds and glaciated water sources in the park. Instead of filtering water from them, opt to wait until you happen upon clear creek crossings or flowing springs.

Lastly, always have a backup plan when it comes to water purification. Iodine tablets stowed in your first-aid kit are an easy and lightweight plan B should your filter give up the ghost.

Swimming Responsibly

Nothing is more refreshing than a cool dip on a hot afternoon, and alongside the Wonderland you'll come across several tempting places to do just that. But before you take the plunge, keep a couple of things in mind.

First, you could be swimming in someone's drinking water, so before you dive in, consider whether alternative water sources are nearby. If not, please respect the water source and don't pollute it with your sweat, bug spray, sunscreen, and other trail scum.

Second, there has been an increase in salamander and amphibian deaths in park waters, and the Park Service suspects it could be due to pollutants introduced to water sources. Take a quick trailside bath with a water bottle or hydration reservoir at least 200 feet from

HORSEFLIES AND A WET BODY

Horseflies, deerflies—whatever you call them, their bite is excruciating. You'll know someone has been nailed when you hear a loud "ouch, owwwwww," followed by profanity, swatting, and thrashing about. Be sympathetic—you'll get your turn soon enough. Once a horsefly has found you, it often follows you around like stink on a pig, sometimes for a mile. And for whatever reason, when your wet, naked body comes out from under the layers, beware. Horseflies have a knack for landing on your back, conveniently (for them) out of reach.

It's the females who bite, using their mandible-like serrated jaws, slicing off the top layer of skin and feeding on the blood beneath. The bites can be more painful than a bee sting and can cause welts and swelling just as severe.

Horseflies don't like DEET, but that won't help you when you're bathing, as you'll be washing off any bug spray. If you get hit, clean the bite and apply a topical hydrocortisone or antihistamine cream, followed by a loose bandage. The pain should subside in about a half hour, and the bite should heal in a couple of days. Keep an eye out for rare allergic reactions, such as weakness, dizziness, hives and/or a rash, and, very rarely, anaphylactic symptoms. If these symptoms occur, seek medical help immediately. Otherwise, consider your bite a trail tattoo and wear it proudly.

No matter how annoying horseflies are, they do serve a purpose. We have these mischief makers to thank for pollinating the flora we enjoy on the Wonderland and for producing larvae and nice plump flies that feed the birds we hear in the trees.

natural water sources if you decide to freshen up. The pollywogs will be grateful and will go on to live a long, "hoppy" life.

HYGIENE IN THE GREAT OUTDOORS

I'm convinced that inside every single one of us is the need to cultivate our instincts for survival and adventure. Whether we're curious about what life is like without modern conveniences or simply want to see how we fare spending a week or more outside, the explorer and adventurer in all of us deserves a chance to get out on the trail and give primitiveness a high five.

The Privilege of Backcountry Privies

Part of that primitiveness means leaving flush toilets behind. But don't despair! The Park Service has outfitted every wilderness camp with some form of toilet or privy. Along the Wonderland, you'll encounter hybrid composting toilets, actual outhouses, and the most primitive of all, the wooden box with a toilet seat.

Like long-lost friends, these backcountry "think and stinks" are welcome sights and comfortable alternatives to a trowel and cat hole. Keeping them clean and maintained is a group effort. Never dispose of any garbage in these privies—the poor park rangers have the terrible job of fishing it out and disposing of it properly! A broom usually lives in each outhouse, used for sweeping debris off the floors and cobwebs off the walls. It's everyone's job to keep things tidy, as the maid took off with the milkman years ago in these parts. Grab the broom, whistle while you work, and do your part.

Since the wooden-box-style privies do not have doors, you may follow the toilet trail only to surprise the potty squatter who made it there before you. Approach toilets slowly and with discretion. When your turn arrives, you may want to leave a sign letting other trail travelers know the privy is occupied. One of my favorite signals is to crisscross my trekking poles in an X on the trail,

Box-style pit toilets like this one at South Puyallup River Camp are common along the Wonderland Trail.

just before the throne comes in to view. I've also seen folks hang hats or coats on neighboring tree limbs as a warning. Otherwise, you might try singing. A rousing rendition of your favorite song from *The Dark Side of the Moon* is sure to scare away potential intruders.

Should duty call when you are out on the trail and not near a privy, dig a cat hole at least 6 inches deep and at least 200 feet from water and pop a squat. Cover the waste with as much dirt and organic matter as you can to help speed up composition. Unlike the backcountry toilets, where you can leave used toilet paper, in cat hole situations, the park requests you pack out (instead of burying) your toilet paper. I know what you are thinking—gross, right? If you pack a few biodegradable dog waste bags, you can use a bag to make a glove over your hand, pick up the TP, then pull the bag over your hand and tie it in a knot. That lets you stay clean and avoid touching the soiled paper. Put the bag in with your garbage and dispose with everything else. Poo-paper problem solved.

Splish-Splash, I'm Gonna Take My Bath

Going days without a shower is not very common in modern society, even though for thousands of years humankind walked the earth unbothered by thoughts of personal cleanliness. If you aren't fond of smelling like a goat, a couple of simple tricks will help you stay clean while on the trail, reducing your likelihood of being hit on by a creature with antlers.

A tiny container of biodegradable soap is your friend, but don't wash directly in creeks or streams. Instead, fill a collapsible basin or zip-top baggie with water, add a drop of soap, and find a private spot at least 200 feet from lakes and streams. Using a bandanna for a washcloth, take your bath. Focus on the critical areas—a little leftover bug spray on your arms might not be such a bad thing. Using wet wipes is also a great way to execute a quick clean; just remember to pack out the dirty ones.

TRAINING FOR THE WONDERLAND TRAIL

The Wonderland Trail is tough—tougher than most trails in Washington State and even most in the country. One of the park rangers I spoke with said that most people have no idea what they're getting themselves into, especially with respect to elevation gain and loss. That said, you'll be able to walk comfortably at the end of your trip if you follow a good training program before you set your boots on Wonderland dirt.

Train by doing the same activity you'll be doing on your journey—in other words, grab your pack and hit the trails. Hike up and down hills carrying your trail-weight backpack. Do it day after day to replicate multiple trail days, eating snacks similar to those you plan to eat on the trail. Use the same boots or trail shoes you plan on hiking in. If you plan to get new boots or shoes, buy them during your training phase and properly break them in. All these things will get your body conditioned and familiar with what you'll experience on your trip.

Even if you're in decent shape, never expect to be ready to roll "off the couch." Start by taking a short day hike with only lightweight essentials in your pack. On your next hike, add five to ten pounds to your pack and increase your distance and elevation gain. Keep building your endurance over several months until you can hike a "mock trail day" with your anticipated pack weight, elevation gain and loss, and mileage. When you can complete at least two back-to-back mock trail days with only a few aches and pains, you're ready to tackle the Wonderland.

If you live in flat country and are unable to train on hills, get yourself to a gym with a good treadmill and work out on a high incline. Bring your pack and your boots or shoes; ignore the stares from people who don't venture outdoors. Don't forget that the downhills on the Wonderland are almost as tough as the uphills, so it's a good idea to train for downhills

The quiet shore of Mystic Lake is a calm place to relax and reflect.

too. If you don't have hills in your area to train on, try walking up and down stadium steps to simulate elevation gain and loss.

If you aren't in great shape, you might want to pick up a book on training and fitness to help you get started. I recommend *Fit by Nature*, by John Colver and M. Nicole Nazzaro, which walks you through a twelve-week fitness program using nature as your gym. The book also explores stretching, nutrition, and injury prevention in detail—all helpful information to have as you dust off your hamstrings and find your heart rate again.

LEARNING TO LOVE TREKKING POLES

Trekking poles literally go hand in hand with backpacking and are becoming increasingly popular on long trails. When you're dancing on loose pebbles or navigating precariously steep hillsides on the Wonderland, trekking poles can act as an extension of your arms, reaching down to help you stabilize each step. Streams and patches of snow become safer and easier to cross. Poles also take pressure off your knees and ankles by redirecting energy to your arms and, as a bonus, give you an awesome upper-body workout.

Another benefit is their ability to set you on a metronome-like stride, helping you keep your cadence when you're tired. And they're great for whacking brushy hillside vegetation growing over the trail or for knocking water off wet brush as you pass.

When purchasing a pair, consider weight, materials, and features. Adjustable-length poles are the most versatile, allowing you to lengthen them when walking downhill and shorten them when walking uphill. Poles can weigh ten to twenty-two ounces per pair, with carbon fiber being much lighter than aluminum. Flip-lock adjustments are becoming more popular than twist locks, primarily because they tend to be a bit more reliable. Before you invest in a pair, check that they are compatible with snow baskets (if you want to use them for future snowshoe romps) and also check on the availability of replacement parts. With gear coming and going off the market so quickly, it's not a bad idea to purchase replacement parts now and store them for future use—a lesson I've learned the hard way.

During your training hikes, don't forget to nibble and drink frequently, even though you may not feel you need it. When hiking, you need twice the caloric intake that you do just sitting at home, and training is a good time to try out new trail food ideas, like new energy bars or chews. Go for something with a balance of protein and complex carbs to keep you from bonking as you power up big hills. If you like to eat, this is a green light to give food guilt the boot and have at it. Eating is the silver lining to this tough training, and the pot of gold at the end is your Wonderland trip.

Take the time to stop and soak in the scenery as you move from camp to camp.

GETTING PASSED BY SUPERHEROES

Some folks are just crazy and superhuman enough to attempt to run the entire Wonderland Trail. The sport of trail running has become extremely popular over recent years, and many publications have listed the Wonderland as one of the best places in the United States to do so. Some organized running clubs even sponsor events along this glorious track.

Here you are, puffing up a big hill, cheeks red as raspberries, rivers of sweat pouring off you, when all of a sudden you hear someone say, "Excuse me." You step aside, too tired to look back, and someone in a hydration vest and nylon shorts whizzes past you. You do a double take as this winged wonder runs off like helium into the clouds. *Did you just see the cover of a Wheaties box in real life?*

The fastest known time to complete the Wonderland Trail (at the time of publication) is 16 hours, 40 minutes, and 55 seconds, which was accomplished with the help of support crew—in other words, a cheering squad that carried food and supplies to access points. The fastest time for an unsupported run—meaning the runner carries everything they need for the trip themselves—is 18 hours, 49 minutes, and 11 seconds. At the end of the journey, these runners gallop into a waiting camp complete with a prepared meal, luxurious camping accommodations, and a hardy pat on the back from those they love. You'll hear them before you see them, because in order to talk to each other, they have to yell through the wind passing by their ears.

Another group of superheroes are the "fast packers," who often finish the trail in about three days. Since they are moving so quickly, they don't need much food, and they are minimalist packers, using the smallest and lightest gear possible.

Resist the urge to trip these speedsters; instead, applaud their incredible fitness finesse as they pass. Give them a smile and bat your eyelashes in hopes they might share their veal scaloppine if you happen to be at the same camp near the end of the day. Go, winged wonders, go!

TRAIL ETIQUETTE AND LEAVE NO TRACE

With you, me, and half the sea out enjoying the fresh air and beautiful backcountry, following Leave No Trace (LNT) principles is more important than ever. Much of this might seem obvious and make you say, "no kidding," but let's review.

- **Plan ahead and be prepared.** A good friend of mine who works for search and rescue describes how minor situations become major ones when something as simple as a headlamp gets left at home. Getting turned around is one thing; add darkness and things can go downhill quickly. Make a checklist and use it to double-check you have packed everything. Also, keep your eyes on the weather forecast for the day you leave and be well prepared for whatever the sky decides to do.

Marmots welcome hikers in the alpine country near Panhandle Gap.

- **Travel and camp on durable surfaces.** Walk on surfaces that can tolerate footsteps, such as established trails (please don't cut switchbacks), campsites, stone, snow, and gravel. Avoid walking in meadows or fragile alpine areas where trails are not established. Assess the surroundings when you stop for a break and select a durable surface to set your pack and your rear end, such as a rock or log.
- **Dispose of waste and trash properly.** Use the privy in camp, even for late-night relief if at all possible. If not, step as far away from the campsite as you can. This may seem like a no-brainer, but a tired body that has to tinkle is looking for *any* bush, *any* place. There's nothing worse than the smell of aged urine wafting by as you sit down to enjoy dinner. Remember, every single Wonderland campsite is used nearly every night for over three consecutive months, and dry summers offer little rain—'nuff said. Also be sure to pack out all your trash, even those itty-bitty wrappers.
- **Leave what you find.** If you happen to find Ben Longmire's alleged Noah's Ark, please don't chop it into pieces and carry it out in your pack; leave it where you found it. Same goes with Indian Henry's mysterious gold mine. But if you find that, be sure to let me know. I promise, it will be our secret.
- **Minimize fire hazards.** Campfires are prohibited in the Mount Rainier backcountry, so carry a small stove and call it "kitchen."
- **Respect wildlife.** Don't kidnap the marmots—their families can't read ransom notes.
- **Be considerate to other visitors.** On the trail, stay to the right in areas where the path is wide and others may want to pass you. If you decide to pass someone, be sure to announce yourself to avoid startling them, giving them a courtesy "On your left." If you're with a group, hike single file to allow others to pass. When you stop for a break, be sure to move yourself and your pack off the trail so you're not in the way. Hikers huffing up big hills are working hard, so be sure to give ascending hikers the right-of-way.

IN CAMP AND ON TRAIL, use a normal talking voice, allowing others to enjoy the sounds of nature. Campsites are fairly close together, so respect the quietness at camp, especially in the evenings. While howling laughter is a sign of happy campers, it can be like a fly in the ear to an exhausted backpacker trying to catch some Z's. Share or barter supplies if you have extra. I once traded a bag of cookies for some fresh crackers and smoked salmon, which was a divine bargain. Use the Golden Rule as you travel, realizing that in some situations you may need to share a campsite or offer first aid.

CHAPTER 3

BACKPACKING THE WONDERLAND TRAIL

Being on the Wonderland Trail fills up your soul's internal cookie jar. Like an oven-fresh, home-baked cookie, the trail is worth savoring and enjoying to the fullest. Take your time, eat it up, and pace yourself. Daylight is your only constraint on time. Wake up when your body says it's time, smell the fresh clean air, and enjoy the challenging uphills by taking plenty of breaks and soaking in the views. While the trail can be tough to tackle, your memories of this place are sure to be treasures, so get in touch with the present and revel in it.

The mossy landscape showcases the often damp
hillside between Mowich Lake and South Mowich River.

Since the Wonderland Trail is a loop, you'll need to make two big decisions as you plan your adventure: where to start and which direction to go. There's also the question of overall distance: how long is the trail really, given alternative routes and year-to-year detours? Should you go through Spray Park or around? Read this chapter to explore your various options before moving on to actual trail descriptions in the following chapters. Appendixes at the back of the book suggest possible itineraries, including the number of campsites available and elevation gain and loss along the trail. Happy planning!

WHERE SHOULD I START?

First, let's look at starting locations and their pros and cons. From Longmire to Box Canyon, the following trailhead descriptions are in order by their popularity.

Longmire

> **DRIVING DIRECTIONS.** From Tacoma, drive State Route 7 eastbound for 46 miles to the town of Elbe. From Elbe, continue east on SR 706 for 13 miles to the park's Nisqually Entrance. Once you enter the park, stay on the park's main roadway (Nisqually–Longmire Road) for 6.5 miles. The Longmire facilities are on the south side of the road.

Most Wonderland Trail hikers start at Longmire, in the southwest corner of the park, because it offers a host of services, including overnight lodging at the National Park Inn, a wilderness information center, and a restaurant. A bed, shower, and warm meal before or after your trip can be a great way kick off your adventure or reward yourself for trail time. Given the popularity of national parks, if you get a Wonderland reservation and are able to align your visit to coincide with a night at the inn, buy a lottery ticket immediately—luck is on your side.

Starting at Longmire also gives you a nice flow to wilderness camps in either direction. Going clockwise, Devils Dream is 5.5 miles from the trailhead, although it's a decent climb with around 2500 feet of elevation gain. Going counterclockwise to Paradise River Camp, 3.8 miles from Longmire, re-

Don't forget to check out the transportation exhibit and the museum at Longmire.

WHO WAS THIS LONGMIRE DUDE, ANYWAY?

Close your eyes for a second and pretend you're in the 1850s. OK, I know that sounds crazy because we can't possibly imagine what it was like to live back then, but stay with me. It's late summer or early fall and you're part of a group of thirty oxen-pulled wagons, coming across the rugged Cascade Mountains from your home in Indiana. The landscape is very different from home, and the travel is difficult as you navigate deep rivers, thick forests, and steep slopes. In places, you even have to lower your wagons several hundred feet with ropes as you blaze a brand-new route known as Naches Pass. You endure armed confrontations with Native peoples and fellow settlers and hunt buffalo for survival as you watch your livestock weaken. Your young children are with you, including one who learns to walk as you journey. Your goal is to find a better life out West.

It took plenty of grit and determination, but James Longmire eventually completed this arduous journey and set up a homestead near Yelm, about 40 miles west of today's Mount Rainier National Park. Becoming familiar with the landscape and foothills near Mount Rainier, he developed a reputation as a good guide and was eventually hired to prep pack animals and arrange expeditions. In 1883, he climbed Mount Rainier for the third time and stumbled upon a business opportunity—the discovery of hot springs near today's Longmire visitor area. This prompted the construction of a wagon road, and shortly after, the Longmire Springs Hotel and several subsequent cabins opened to the public. Visitors who flocked to the mineral baths after hearing stories of their therapeutic powers could also enjoy backcountry guiding services, led primarily by Longmire's sons. The famous Sierra Club co-founder John Muir stayed here on his way to the park in 1888.

In 1897, James Longmire passed away at the age of seventy-seven, two years prior to Mount Rainier becoming a national park. The Park Service was eager to build a newer hotel in the area, with modern conveniences like plumbing, lighting, and even entertainment, which caused conflict with the Longmire family. The old hotel, now run by Longmire's son Elcaine, was starting to become disheveled and the relationship with the park continued to be troublesome until his death in 1915. By the 1920s, the Longmire family's buildings had been removed, save for one of Elcaine's rugged cabins, which can be visited by taking the Trail of the Shadows Loop (0.7 mile roundtrip, 20 feet elevation gain) across the street from the National Park Inn. This little cabin is the oldest structure in Mount Rainier National Park. Today, the Longmire name is synonymous with the development of Mount Rainier National Park, paying homage to the entrepreneurial efforts of bygone days.

quires only a little more than 1000 feet of elevation gain. Either way gives you a decent shot at making camp before sundown even if you choose to drive to the mountain and start your trip all in one day.

Starting at Longmire also means you'll have two nicely spaced food-caching locations: one at Mowich Lake and another at White River. Starting elsewhere, however, may allow you to take advantage of all the food-caching locations, including Longmire.

Since most folks hike clockwise, and so many people start at Longmire, getting a permit for the optimal schedule may be tough, even if you apply for a reservation in the spring. Most folks want to stay at Devils Dream Camp the first night, so it fills quickly, as do any other camps that are logical stopping points after a full day on the trail from Longmire.

Sunrise

DRIVING DIRECTIONS. From Enumclaw, drive State Route 410 southbound for 43 miles to the park's northeast corner. Turn right (west) onto the Sunrise Road and find the White River Entrance in just over 1 mile. Continue on the Sunrise Road for another 16 miles to its end.

In the northeast corner of the park, Sunrise is the highest-elevation Wonderland trailhead at 6400 feet. Starting here grants you front-and-center views of Mount Rainier in all her glory before you even set foot on the trail. The drive up to Sunrise on a clear day also

The Sunrise area, with its winding, high-elevation road, offers stunning mountain vistas.

Near Mystic Lake, the trail winds through a debris field from the receding Winthrop Glacier.

affords you an amazing view of neighboring Mount Adams, the second-highest volcano in Washington State. Sunrise has a visitor center with exhibits and interpretive programs, a day lodge with snacks and hot meals, a gift shop, and civilized restrooms with running water. There are no hotels or overnight lodging options.

At Sunrise, many trails meander with gentle elevation gain and loss through subalpine meadows, with plenty of day hikers out enjoying the impressive views and pathways. It's a beautiful place to kick off your journey.

Going clockwise, your first true wilderness camp is 10 miles away at Summerland Camp, and you'll start with a steep, knee-quivering downhill, losing nearly 2000 feet of elevation in roughly 3 miles. After reaching the White River Campground, you'll kiss the smell of breakfast sausage and fire pits goodbye as you duck back into the trees. The trail parallels the road for another 1.5 miles before heading up 2000 feet to Summerland. (Summerland is popular, so you might not be able to get a campsite if you're using the walk-up permit system.)

If counterclockwise is your choice, your first night can be either 5.6 miles away at Granite Creek Camp or roughly 10.2 miles away at Mystic Camp. Granite Creek Camp is tucked into a forested hillside near the babbling creek. Most of the trek to Granite Creek Camp is through the Sunrise "tundra" hillsides, where vistas, wildflowers, hoary marmots, and ground squirrels abound. Like the gentle up-and-down of horses on a merry-go-round, the trail ascends 400 feet, then drops 300 feet, ascends 300 feet, and finally drops almost 900 feet to reach the somewhat unexpected Granite Creek Camp and its few flat camping spots on the hillside. Pushing farther on toward Mystic Lake, you'll continue downhill, losing another 1200 feet of elevation, to an interesting crossing of Winthrop Creek. From there, you'll follow rock cairns and travel over glacial deposits until your 1000-foot ascent to forested Mystic Camp.

Because Sunrise is the second-highest elevation you'll encounter on the Wonderland Trail, the weather can be challenging. Fog can move in quickly and the wind can be merciless and frigid, even in summer. Hiking here in mid-August one year, I was head-to-toe in hats, mittens, and waterproof clothing in an attempt to stay warm. The following night, the folks staying at Sunrise and Granite Creek Camps received half an inch of snow.

You have a couple of other camping options if you start at Sunrise. One is actually at Sunrise, a wilderness camp off in the woods, 1.3 miles from the Sunrise Visitor Center. This camp is helpful if you're passing through on the trail or need a place to camp when you first arrive at Sunrise. Because of its location, it's managed as a wilderness camp; you should not camp there unless it is part of your permit plan. Your second alternative camping option is on your way up to Sunrise at the White River Campground, which is first-come, first-served and does not accept reservations. At the time of publication, this frontcountry campground was $20 per night. Campsites are set amid old-growth trees, and the White River purrs along right next to your fire pit. If you choose to spend your first night at the White River Campground, you may want to consider leaving your car in the overnight parking area and starting your Wonderland trip from there.

If you start at Sunrise, your logical choices for caching food are Longmire and Mowich Lake. These two caches provide a nice reprieve from food weight, as they are a perfect distance apart.

Mowich Lake

DRIVING DIRECTIONS. From Puyallup, drive State Route 410 to the town of Buckley. From Buckley, head south on SR 165 through the towns of Carbonado and Wilkeson. Continue on SR 165 and cross the Fairfax Bridge. At the junction of Mowich Lake and Carbon River, bear right (southeast) onto Mowich Lake Road, which quickly shifts from pavement to gravel. Follow the road approximately 11 miles to a self-serve pay station at the park entrance. After you have obtained your park entrance pass, proceed another 7 miles on the gravel road to its end at Mowich Lake Campground (first-come, first-served, walk-in only, or wilderness permit required if this site is part of your itinerary).

Mowich Lake is key for access in the park's northwest corner.

The Mowich Lake trailhead is accessed by a gravel road on the northwest side of the park. While the trailhead is accessible by car, it has a remote feel, and there are no services except pit toilets and an often unstaffed patrol cabin. The camping is walk-in and primitive, and only tents are allowed. Fires are prohibited. Interestingly, Mowich Lake is the deepest and largest lake in the park, but it's relatively small in comparison to many northwest lakes.

If possible, stay somewhere other than Mowich Lake your first night. The camping area at Mowich is an abandoned parking lot, now closed to car traffic and covered in gravel for sustainable tent camping. It's less than desirable for serenity and offers very little privacy between sites.

Going clockwise from Mowich, you'll want to decide whether to go through Spray Park or stay on the Wonderland Trail via Ipsut Pass (a choice discussed later in this chapter). Ipsut Pass follows the official Wonderland Trail route, but Spray Park is a tempting deviation that meets up with the Wonderland near Carbon River Camp.

If you choose the Spray Park option, your first night could be at Eagles Roost Camp, only 2.1 miles from the Mowich Lake trailhead. This is a good option if you have a long

TAMI'S WONDERLAND TRAIL CAMP SUPERLATIVES

Do you agree? Hike it and see! When you post your opinion, tag me (@tamiasars)!

Best alpine view: Indian Bar Camp (runners-up: Klapatche Park and Summerland)

Best deep-forest camp: Pyramid Creek (runners-up: Paradise River and Devils Dream)

Best toilet cleanliness: Summerland

Best place to see Sasquatch, a.k.a. most remote feeling: North Puyallup River Camp

Best view from a toilet: Indian Bar Group Camp

Best overall camp: Klapatche Park (due to remoteness, beauty, and views)

Best base camp for day-hiking adventures: Sunrise

Best camp for water in late season: Granite Creek

Best camp to kiss and/or propose marriage: Summerland (runners-up: Indian Bar and Klapatche Park)

Best group campsite: Mystic Camp

Most likely to wash out: South Mowich River Camp

Most creative camp placement: Dick Creek (runner-up: Eagles Roost, a Spray Park alternative)

Worst overall ambiance: Mowich Lake (runner-up: Carbon River Camp, a Spray Park alternative)

Worst toilet for privacy: Nickel Creek Camp (runner-up: Mystic Camp)

Worst overall camp: Mowich Lake (due to commotion and lack of privacy)

Worst camp for water in late season: Devils Dream (runner-up: Klapatche Park)

travel time to reach the park, and it sets you up nicely for an early morning hike through the glorious meadows of Spray Park. Eagles Roost is a forested little camp set on a hillside deep in the woods. If you choose to press on past Eagles Roost, your next opportunity is Cataract Valley Camp, which is 6.8 miles beyond Mowich Lake and near the end of the long descent from Spray Park. Either way, Spray Park offers another opportunity to cherish the views and smell the wildflowers. Be sure to plan enough time to soak it all in while daylight is upon you.

If you are a traditionalist and choose to stick with the official Wonderland Trail, your first camp in the clockwise direction is Ipsut Creek Camp, 5.4 miles and roughly 2700 feet below Mowich Lake. Not long ago, Ipsut Creek Campground was a car campground buzzing with families and vehicles. Then, in fall 2006, flooding in the park changed the lay of the land forever, washing out the Carbon River Road and making vehicle access impossible. Exhausted and broke from repairing roads year after year, the Park Service finally waved the white flag to Mother Nature and a new wilderness camp was born. Ipsut

Gorgeous Ipsut Falls and the turquoise waters below it are great places to visit and gather water when camping at Ipsut Creek.

is a spectacular, peaceful camp that has all the wonderful things you imagine when you think of remote places: solitude, owls, squirrels and other critters, water for white noise, and plenty of giant, old-growth trees for friends. Various structures and picnic tables hint of bygone days, but as with all wilderness camps, fires are prohibited.

Going counterclockwise from Mowich Lake on the Wonderland puts your first camp at the South Mowich River Camp, 4.2 miles from the lake. It's a true river camp with plenty of silty water, brushy bushes, mossy trees, and an old lean-to (which provides very little shelter from the wet weather that often hangs over this camp). Going beyond the South Mowich River Camp on your first day is a big commitment, as the climb to Golden Lakes is a doozie. But, if you have the gumption, you will find Golden Lakes 9.5 miles from Mowich Lake. In mid-August, this area has a lot of bear activity because blueberries abound near the top of the climb. 🐾 If possible, make sure daylight is in your favor and berries are in your mouth.

Starting at Mowich Lake, you are in a prime position for food caches at Longmire and White River.

White River Campground

> **DRIVING DIRECTIONS.** From Enumclaw, drive State Route 410 southbound for 43 miles to the park's northeast corner. Turn right (west) onto the Sunrise Road and find the White River Entrance in just over 1 mile. Continue on the Sunrise Road for approximately 4.5 miles to the White River Campground, located to the left (west).

The White River Campground, in the northeast corner of the park, is no stranger to adventure seekers. It has a decent-sized parking area where hikers and climbers can leave their vehicles as they set out into the hinterlands. The campground parking area serves as the starting point for those climbing Rainier's Emmons Glacier route to the summit, and it's also a start for the Wonderland Trail or various day-hiking adventures.

Going clockwise, your first camping opportunity is Summerland, 6.9 miles away. Summerland Camp is a respectable but reasonable 2000-plus-foot climb from the

A curious, young hoary marmot pops up to contemplate hikers.

White River Campground; the way starts out gradually and then kicks in harder as you approach camp. From Summerland, you'll travel across the highest part of the Wonderland Trail—Panhandle Gap—and back down the other side to Indian Bar Camp, 11.3 miles from the White River Campground.

If you choose to make the full day's push to Indian Bar for your first camp, be forewarned: it's a very long day with a full pack. While 11.3 miles may not sound like much, hiking Panhandle Gap involves permanent, occasionally hazardous snow crossings, small snow bridges, routefinding via rock cairns, and rocky terrain. Once you reach the gap, you've only passed a small portion of the difficult terrain, with at least another mile to come. Eventually the trail descends 1800 feet on a steep, seemingly endless trail staircase to Indian Bar Camp in the valley below. If you do choose to make the push, make sure you have enough daylight to cross Panhandle Gap and the terrain after it. There are a lot of cliffs and hazards in this area, and losing the trail in darkness or fog could prove deadly. Also, remember my advice to pace yourself? Panhandle Gap is one of the most scenic and memorable areas on the entire Wonderland Trail. Take your time and savor every turn.

Because of the popularity of Summerland and Indian Bar Camps, they are almost always full when you try for a walk-up permit. If you are using the walk-up permit system to change your itinerary or to get your permit in the first place, you'll have more luck putting these camps near the middle or end of your trip.

Going counterclockwise from White River Campground, you'll take the roughly 3-mile, 2000-foot climb to Sunrise, getting it out of the way. It's a great warm-up and a good way to remind your legs that you've just gained some pack weight. If you go this direction, your closest wilderness camp is at Sunrise Camp, 3.4 miles away. If you want to push on a bit farther, you could try for Granite Creek Camp at 7.7 miles—or for a really big day, Mystic Camp at 12.3 miles.

Starting at White River affords you the chance to take advantage of two nicely spaced food cache locations: Longmire and Mowich Lake.

Fryingpan Creek

DRIVING DIRECTIONS. From Enumclaw, drive State Route 410 southbound for 43 miles to the park's northeast corner. Turn right (west) onto the Sunrise Road and find the White River Entrance in just over 1 mile. Continue on the Sunrise Road for approximately 3 miles to the Fryingpan Creek trailhead parking lot, located to the right (north) on a hairpin turn.

The Fryingpan Creek trailhead is about 2 miles by road from the White River Camp-ground, in the northeast corner of the park. Starting at Fryingpan Creek gives you great opportunities to cache food at Longmire and Mowich Lake. If you hike clockwise and make Summerland your first camp, starting at Fryingpan Creek (instead of White River) shaves 2.6 miles off your first day's trek. Summerland is 4.4 miles from Fryingpan Creek, with 2000 feet of elevation gain. Starting at Fryingpan Creek is a good idea if you have a long drive to the mountain but you also want to enjoy a little trail time on your first day. One note of caution: the Fryingpan Creek trailhead is a very popular parking area for day hikers. On weekends, parking spots are at a premium, so arrive early for the best chance at snagging one.

If you travel counterclockwise to a first night at Sunrise Camp, you'll start out with a gentle elevation gain of 500 feet in 2.6 miles and then proceed to get the big hill climb up to Sunrise out of the way at the start of your trip. Sunrise Camp is 6.1 miles away with roughly 2500 feet of elevation gain.

Box Canyon

DRIVING DIRECTIONS. From Enumclaw, drive State Route 410 southbound for 47 miles. Stay right (southbound) toward Cayuse Pass and merge onto SR 123. Continue on SR 123 for approximately 11.5 miles, and then turn right (northwest) at the Stevens Canyon Entrance. From the entrance, follow Stevens Canyon Road approximately 10 miles to the Box Canyon exhibit parking area, located on the left (south) side of the road.

The meadows at Cowlitz Divide invite you to pull out your camera.

Starting at Box Canyon is ideal if you don't mind driving a bit to start your trip, as this trailhead is located deep within the park and has no easy or quick driving options. But if time is not a big issue, the proximity to camps and caches makes Box Canyon a good place to start your Wonderland adventure.

Heading clockwise out of Box Canyon, you'll cover the least scenic part of the trip first, although there are plenty of waterfalls to keep you company and marshy foliage to identify on your way to Longmire. Your first camp in this direction is Maple Creek at 2.3 miles, after a very gentle grade of hardly noticeable ups and downs. This decent little camp is set among deciduous trees, evergreens, and wetland plants and has a great water source—Maple Creek is swift and clear year-round. Pushing on to the next camp at Paradise River, 8.7 miles from the Box Canyon trailhead, makes for a long but doable day, as the elevation gain and loss is manageable and spread out across the miles.

Going counterclockwise, you'll hit your first camp almost before you get a feel for your backpack: Nickel Creek Camp at 0.8 mile. This nicely forested camp was moved a couple of years ago to this location, which has a bit more privacy. The sites are fairly private and nicely levelled.

Should you choose to hike farther, you're in for a tough day along arguably one of the best vistas in the park, the Cowlitz Divide. The next camp is a huff-n-puff up from Nickel Creek, gaining 2530 feet to reach the Cowlitz Divide ridgeline. This area will take your breath away, literally—because it's a long climb—and figuratively—its sheer beauty cannot be depicted by words. From the ridge, you'll drop to the headwaters of the Ohanapecosh River and an area called Indian Bar. Indian Bar Camp is 6.7 miles beyond Nickel Creek Camp and 7.5 miles from the Box Canyon trailhead. Because of all the picture-taking, log-sitting, bear-watching, and lollygagging you'll want to do en route and at Indian Bar, you may want to just crash at Nickel Creek, saving this section for a day when you're not rushed and have plenty of daylight at your disposal.

Starting at Box Canyon sets you up nicely for caching food in three locations: White River, Mowich Lake, and Longmire. Storing food at all three places is the perfect prescription for a lighter pack.

WHICH DIRECTION SHOULD I GO?

The trail descriptions in this book are written in the clockwise direction, as that's how most hikers travel. However, I've added occasional notes for counterclockwise hikers, should you choose the direction less traveled.

As you ponder which direction to backpack the trail, be comforted by the knowledge that both routes offer fantastic mountain views and great vistas. No matter which direction

you go, you'll also find challenges and tough sections that balance wild beauty and gentle grades. The Wonderland Trail makes you earn your bragging rights, and neither direction is a cinch. Either way, you will experience roughly 22,000 feet of elevation gain and loss over hills and valleys.

Many Wonderland Trail travelers will tell you that clockwise is the easiest way to go, but "easy" is not a word I ever use to describe this trail. So perhaps the clockwise direction is best described as the lesser of two evils. Why? Because going clockwise, most hills you'll en-counter will be a gentler grade going up and a steeper grade going down. Steeper descents tend to make your ankles and knees wobble and creak a bit more, but steeper ascents get the ol' ticker talking. When someone asks whether you prefer uphills or downhills, what is your answer? If it's downhills, as most hikers reply, then clockwise should probably be your direction of choice. But if going downhill wreaks havoc on your knees or ankles, you may want to elect for the counterclockwise direction.

The most popular camps in either direction are Summerland, Indian Bar, Klapatche Park, Golden Lakes, and Mystic, partially because of their locations along the trail but also because they have vistas and/or a special feature, such as a lake or backcountry patrol cabin. If your goal is to stay at the most desired camps, an itinerary of eleven or twelve days allows for enough time, given the proximity of trailheads and distance between camps.

MILEAGE, MAPS, AND THE SPRAY PARK ALTERNATE

What map to use, how far to travel, and which route to follow are all things to consider as you plan your trip. No matter what you decide, expect to encounter beauty and adventure at every turn!

How Long Is the Wonderland Trail, Anyway?

The exact distance of the Wonderland Trail has been debated to exhaustion. The park web-site lists it at 93 miles, most maps calculate trail distance at between 90 and 92.5 miles, and a bevy of folks tout their own special accuracy online, with similar numbers down to the decimal. The mileage varies for several reasons.

- Staying at the Carbon River Camp adds 0.4 mile if you choose the Ipsut Pass route as opposed to the Spray Park route.
- If you go through Spray Park counterclockwise and need to pick up cached food at Mowich Lake, you'll add 0.6 mile.

The mountain peeks out along the trail, heading counterclockwise toward Summerland. When the skies are clear, the trail offers superb views in all directions.

MOUNT RAINIER WORD SALAD

Many of the namesakes around Mount Rainier originate from languages of tribes in the region and can be tongue-twisters for visitors. You can often tell who is a local by the way someone pronounces them. Here's how to say the most challenging names, with phonetic spellings by yours truly.

Ipsut: This name is choppy and short but can be a stumbling block. Pronounced "Ip-soot," as in black carbon soot residue. Avoid saying "Is-put" or "Ip-suit" if you want to be in the know. A Chinook Jargon word meaning "hidden" or "to keep secret," it is often spelled as Ipsoot along the coastline. You'll see why it's hidden after you walk through this mossy, deep valley in the northwest corner of the park.

Mowich: "Ma-ow-itch." The first part looks like "mow," but it's pronounced like Mao, as in Mao Tse-tung or the sound a kitten makes. Avoid saying "mow-ish" if you wish to fit in with the cool kids. Meaning deer, venison, game, or even game meats, it's commonly used by coastal tribes. It can vary in spelling, sometimes appearing as "mowitch." The park simply spells it Mowich, a reference to the deer head that many people see in the silhouette of the mountain's upper slopes, easiest to spot from Spray Park and the South Mowich River valley. (see Golden Lakes to Mowich Lake in chapter 4).

Ohanapecosh: You'll see this name near Indian Bar, the source of the headwaters for the Ohanapecosh River in the valley below. It's also a campground in the park near the Stevens Canyon Entrance. There are two correct pronunciations: "Oh-hannah-peh-cosh" and "Oh-ha-na-peh-cosh." The exact meaning is up for debate but is likely: "standing on the lip of a rock," "standing at the edge," "looking down on something wonderful," or "clear stream, deep blue, and/or deep blue holes," all of which make sense for the area. Pick one and impress your friends.

Olallie: This name isn't hard to pronounce, but it's a good one to know as you travel through the Pacific Northwest. Pronounced "Oh-law-lee," the word is Chinook Jargon for "berry" or "huckleberry/blueberry." Olallie Creek Camp is off the Cowlitz Divide Trail not far from the Wonderland, and hikers often use it as an alternative when other camps are full. It's set in a forest full of seasonal huckleberries. You may look like you have a medical condition after you eat them in large quantities, turning your hands and mouth cyanotic, but truth be told, Pacific Northwest huckleberries have some of the highest amounts of antioxidants and anti-aging properties of any berry in the world—and they're free! Eat away, Blue Boo.

Puyallup: "Pew-AL-up," "Pew-OWL-up," or even "Pew-ALL-up" are all fair game. Even longtime residents vary in their pronunciation, and all are considered correct. Avoid looking like a rookie by saying "Poo-yeah-lup." Puyallup is the Lushootseed (tribal language) name of a Coast Salish tribe in Washington State. It's also a city southeast of Tacoma, best known for the Washington State Fair, one of the top-ten largest annual fairs in the US.

Summerland: "Sum-er-land." Just kidding. You got this.

Wauhaukaupauken Falls: You'll get serious bonus points if you can say this fast. "Wow-how-cow-pow-ken." This is the waterfall that shoots out underneath the bridge near Indian Bar Camp. Its name means "spouting water," which aptly describes the powerful water that muscles through the canyon.

Park signs along the trail are helpful markers, but often list inaccurate distances.

- Side trips—such as the one you'll be making to the gift shop at Longmire to buy ice cream bars and the extra steps needed to peer inside the park's oldest patrol cabin at Indian Henrys Hunting Ground—add miles.
- Ipsut Creek Campground is 0.6 mile out and back from the main Wonderland Trail.
- Detours from trail washouts add roughly 0.3 mile near the Carbon River Suspension Bridge.
- If you start at the Sunrise trailhead or visit the snack bar there, you'll take an uncounted detour that technically isn't part of the Wonderland.

To complicate distance even more, the park has placed signs with mileages at nearly every turn and trail intersection. These signs are nice reminders of direction, but the distance can vary by nearly a mile. Get a reliable topographical map and stick with those mileages instead. So much changes on the trail from year to year that it's hard for even the most up-to-date and precise measurements to be exact. Mother Nature is a master at redecorating and rearranging.

Maps

Honestly, the Wonderland Trail is very easy to navigate. Park-sanctioned signs posted at intersections point you to various destinations along the route, and it's pretty hard to get lost. That said, you could still have issues if you aren't paying attention and take a side trail by mistake. Carrying a paper map in a waterproof case (or a waterproof map) is highly recommended as part of your Ten Essentials. Your choices for topographic maps that cover Mount Rainier National Park and the Wonderland Trail are USGS quadrangles, the National Geographic park map, and the Green Trails map. The park also has its own maps listed on its website, but they aren't detailed enough for navigation. Depending on which map you choose, your total Wonderland mileage can vary by 3 to 5 miles.

Mileages and elevations in this book are based on the Green Trails Mount Rainier Wonderland Map No. 269SX. Green Trails gives a full-circle mileage of 90.5 miles—or 91.1

THE APP TAP

These days, smartphones run apps that do everything from help you navigate a gnarly bush-whack to order your caramel macchiato post-hike. I'm a sucker for a great trail app, and I believe that mine, Wonderland Trail hosted by FarOut (formerly known as Guthook Guides in trail circles), is one of the best tools out there for circumnavigating the big, beastly volcano. You can find it at faroutguides.com/wonderland-trail-map. The app works offline and can tell you exactly how far you are from the next water source, camp, bridge, or whatever waypoint you need. It provides real-time elevation profiles and maps, and even contains photos so you can see what the waypoints look like. Crowd-sourced comments from other hikers also help you, with last-minute updates on everything from water-source issues to bridge outages.

Even though this trail is easy to navigate, it's best to never rely solely on technology—batteries die, and phones get broken or lost. A paper map and compass will help you find your way in case you find yourself up confused creek without a smartphone.

miles via Ipsut Creek Camp—which seems accurate, give or take small reroutes of the trail from year to year. The maps printed in this book are for overview purposes—make sure to get a bona fide topographic map to bring on your hike.

Camps and features are often above or below the Wonderland Trail proper. These areas can vary by 100 feet or more from the Green Trails map intersections, such as the camp at Golden Lakes, which is perched on a hillside. Occasionally, the Park Service changes a camp or trail location slightly due to hazards or usage issues. Other maps may include features that Green Trails leaves out and vice versa.

Regardless of which map you follow, or which direction you go, overall distance will not be the largest feather in your bandanna when you're done. That feather will be the memories of all your eyes have seen while lapping the circumference of Mount Rainier, powered only by your gumption and your own two feet. Wear that feather proudly!

The Spray Park Debate

Along the upper northwest corner of the Wonderland Trail, you'll have to decide between frolicking through Spray Park or rambling over Ipsut Pass. Either way, you won't be disappointed.

Ipsut Pass is the traditional path along the Wonderland Trail. If you yearn to crow triumphantly about your feet hitting every step of the actual Wonderland Trail, choose this route for peak bragging rights. As you meander through old-growth behemoths, let your imagination take you back to a time when these monsters were prolific in most of our Northwest forests. The woodlands here feel alive; these trees are forceful and commanding, and there is something calming about their companionship as they keep a vigilant eye on you from above. Closer to Ipsut Pass, get your camera ready for the giant, hollowed-out cores of departed trees, a captivating trailside exhibit. A photo of you standing inside makes for a fine Wonderland souvenir. What's more, Ipsut Creek has more solitude and fewer day hikers once you pass the turnoff to Tolmie Peak.

The Ipsut Pass area starts out with great views and then drops down into some of the park's largest trees.

The Spray Park trail offers full-on Mount Rainier views, wildflowers, and marmots and puts you nicely back on the Wonderland near the Carbon River Suspension Bridge. As you amble through wildflower meadows, flirting with creeks and misty-eyed views of Rainier, don't forget to greet the creatures along the way. Hoary marmots take their afternoon naps along boulders near the trail, and pikas sound alarms as they play peekaboo through talus fields. Spray Park is a photographer's dream, and if you get the chance to stay at either Cataract Valley or Eagles Roost Camp, treat yourself to alpenglow as the sun sets on the volcano high above the camps. Day hikers flock here in abundant droves because it's easily accessible from Mowich Lake. Prepare for speedy company (day hikers don't usually have big packs), and give a nod when they pass.

Snowfields are common in Spray Park and linger late into the season, if not throughout the year. Use caution if visibility is limited due to fog, rain, or snow. Bears are frequently seen in this area, especially in mid- to late August through September, thanks to healthy

Alpenglow sets in on a gorgeous summer evening in Spray Park.

huckleberry populations. 🐾 Be aware and on the lookout for bears, and make noise as you wish to make them aware of your presence, especially on blind corners (see The Bear Essentials in chapter 1).

STAY A DAY! TOP SPOTS FOR EXTRA ADVENTURE

Isn't it enough just to hike the whole Wonderland? Well, yeah, of course! But what if I told you that you could see some more amazing backcountry destinations just off the Wonderland Trail by booking an extra night in camps here and there? The Mount Rainier backcountry will blow your mind—both along the Wonderland and on its outskirts. I've listed my favorite bonus "stay a day" hikes below so you can see more if you wish. To fold them into your itinerary, note the "originates" location for these hikes and schedule your overnight stays accordingly. The roundtrip distances, high point, and elevation gain are the total calculations to and from the camp of origin, so you can be prepared for your extra day's mileage.

This is also a good time to mention one of my other guidebooks, *Day Hiking: Mount Rainier*, 2nd edition. It's full of day-hiking suggestions that you could tag on should you have extra time. For example, if you stay at Granite Creek Camp, you could hike up to Skyscraper Mountain (Hike 15 in *Day Hiking: Mount Rainier*) to view the sunset. If you head clockwise from Sunrise Camp, you could take an extended detour to Glacier Basin, also exploring Burroughs Mountain before making your way to White River and beyond. Or head up to Mount Fremont Lookout on your way to Sunrise. The options are plentiful!

Hike 1

South Puyallup Trail to Lake George and Gobblers Knob

Originates: South Puyallup River Camp
Roundtrip distance: 7.7 miles
High point: 5465 feet
Elevation gain: 2460 feet

IF YOU ARE LOOKING FOR a wonderful out-and-back diversion from the South Puyallup River Camp, it doesn't get better than this. This side adventure gives you a chance to visit the rarely seen Marine Memorial off the defunct Westside Road, as well as quiet Lake George and one of the four remaining fire lookouts in the park.

From the South Puyallup River Camp, head southwest, passing andesite columns to your left (south), across from the camp toilet. The path you are following isn't just used for the camp, it's also a maintained park trail called the South Puyallup Trail. Due to its proximity to the South Puyallup River, it's been prone to washouts and can sometimes be swampy in places or a bit tough to follow—but it's generally straightforward. In roughly 1.1 miles from camp, the trail splits at a Y junction. If you bear right (west), you'll continue on the South Puyallup Trail to a random spot along the Westside Road. Instead, bear left (west/southwest) on the Round Pass Trail as it climbs in deep forest. In just over 0.5 mile, arrive at the abandoned Westside Road in what is called Round Pass.

Over two decades ago, the Westside Road was open to the public and hikers were able to reach trailheads and attractions without much effort. But because the fitful Tahoma Creek kept washing out the road, the park surrendered to Mother Nature and closed it permanently. Now, it's only accessible to those who wish to walk or ride their bikes along the old roadway. Incidentally, bicycles are only allowed on the road, not on adjacent trails. The Park Service and contractors still use the old road, so don't be alarmed if you see or hear a vehicle now and again.

Walk a few steps to the right (north) to find a sobering Marine Memorial. On December 10, 1946, bad weather was to blame for the disappearance of an aircraft carrying thirty-two US Marines, most of them eighteen- and nineteen-year-old privates. Due to snow and winter weather, the search proved difficult—until in July of 1947, a ranger spotted the wreckage on the South Tahoma Glacier. Unfortunately, efforts to reach the site and remove the bodies proved too hazardous, and as the years passed, the glacier absorbed the remains. The mountain became their final resting place. As a tribute to the fallen marines, this memorial was placed within sight of the glacier—though these days, trees have mostly obscured the view. When the road closed, the families of the marines were asked if they wanted to move the memorial, but the consensus was that the increased peacefulness of the area made it an even better place to pay their respects. Throughout the road closure, the Park Service has made exceptions for the family members, many of whom are now in their twilight years, allowing them to be transported via vehicle to this site. Pause for a quiet moment of gratitude, then pop back out to the road and jog approximately 470 feet to the left (southeast) until you see a large former parking area to the right (southwest). A sign here tells you that this is the Lake George trailhead, but if you miss it, scan the tree line around the parking area to the north, and you'll see the pathway.

Built in 1933, Gobblers Knob is one of four remaining fire lookouts in the park.

The trail climbs gently through the forest for 0.85 mile until you reach the serene north-ern shoreline of Lake George. A lean-to and a wilderness camp with a primitive toilet are on the eastern side of the lake. As with all wilderness camps in the park, this one requires a pre-planned permit to spend the night. This area doesn't get nearly as much traffic as other places in the park, so it has that wonderful, remote feeling. Take a minute to enjoy the quiet, then continue onward, following the main trail around the lake's northern tip. In just over a mile, including a bit more climbing, the trail reaches a junction with Gobblers Knob Trail coming in from the right (north). Turn right and continue for another 0.3 mile until you reach the rocky summit, where the Gobblers Knob Lookout has stood proudly since 1933. Fingers crossed: you might even have the lookout to yourself before you head back to the South Puyallup River Camp.

Hike 2

St. Andrews Creek Trail to Patrol Cabin and Denman Falls

Originates: Klapatche Park Camp
Roundtrip distance: 6 miles
High point: 5500 feet
Elevation gain: 2010 feet

IF YOUR ITINERARY ALLOWS, STAYING an extra day at Klapatche Park to take in a sunrise and sunset is a great way to soak in the true splendor of the Mount Rainier backcountry. During the day, hike down the St. Andrews Creek Trail to see a remote ranger cabin and the very rarely visited Denman Falls, a 140-plus-foot waterfall plunging off a rocky cliff.

From the Klapatche Park camp entrance, walk a few steps south on the Wonderland Trail and locate the St. Andrews Creek Trail jogging off to the west. Descend the trail through classic northwest understory, such as Cascade blueberries, queen's cup, deer fern, and bunchberry. As you drop in elevation, the evergreens thicken, and the trail throws in a few switchbacks to ease the steepness. In 2.7 miles, arrive at a signed junction for the St. Andrews Patrol Cabin, located to the trail's left (south). It hardly seems possible that a historical structure would be sitting out in this deep, mossy forest; follow the short spur trail for roughly 300 feet and see for yourself! Built in 1922, the one-room log cabin is on the National Register of Historic Places and is still in use by park officials, who access it via Westside Road (closed to public vehicles).

The St. Andrews Patrol Cabin still occasionally hosts park personnel, despite the closure of the Westside Road.

Once you've visited the cabin, take the spur trail back to the St. Andrews Creek Trail and turn left (west). After a few steps, pop out on the defunct Westside Road. This road used to be busy with car traffic, but it was closed for good in the late 1980s, thanks to the watery outbursts of Tahoma Creek. Turn left (south) on the road and walk just over 100 feet to a small sign noting the Denman Falls Trail to the right (west). Pop back into the forest and follow the trail as it meanders northwest, crossing St. Andrews Creek on a footbridge in roughly 0.1 mile. After the bridge, arrive at a T junction. Turn left (northwest) and follow the trail for just shy of 0.1 mile as it wanders down a few steep drops to arrive at a viewpoint of lovely Denman Falls. Ben Longmire named these falls after A. H. Denman, a photographer who documented the park in the early 1900s.

When you've finished viewing the falls, return to the trail on which you arrived, following it until you come to a T junction. Go straight here to make a loop, returning to Westside Road in 0.1 mile. Once at Westside Road, turn right (south), and find St. Andrews Creek Trail on your left (east) after a few steps. Use this trail to return to Klapatche Park.

Hike 3

Tolmie Peak and Eunice Lake

Originates: Mowich Lake Campground
Roundtrip distance: 6.4 miles
High point: 5940 feet
Elevation gain: 1250 feet

STAY AN EXTRA DAY AT Mowich Lake Campground and take this side trail to one of the last four remaining fire lookouts in the park. Under the watchful tower sits the tranquil shores of Eunice Lake—the perfect place to enjoy lunch and a day off from carrying your big backpack.

From Mowich Lake, follow the Wonderland northbound along the lake's southwestern shore for 1 mile. Bear left, signed for Tolmie Peak, and bob and weave through large boulders under the shoulders of an unnamed peak. The trail gets steeper as it reaches a series of switchbacks before arriving at the shoreline of Eunice Lake, 2 miles from Mowich Lake. Several small spurs reach the lake's edges—visit them now or save them for the way back.

Give your quads a rah-rah speech, then continue west along the lake's southern shoreline until the trail begins a series of three long switchbacks along open, subalpine slopes. Find the historical fire lookout 1.2 miles from Eunice Lake (3.2 miles from Mowich Lake). The weathered but still-cared-for tower was built by the Civilian Conservation Corps in 1933 and is one of less than a hundred left in Washington State. In Mount Rainier National Park, it's one of just four towers left standing (the others are at Mount Fremont, Shriner Peak, and Gobblers Knob). While small aircraft and satellites now do most of the fire-spotting, Park Service personnel still occasionally use the tower for patrols.

Enjoying sunset on the slopes of Mount Rainier from the Tolmie Peak Fire Lookout

On a clear day, the views of Mount Rainier from the tower's walkways are outstanding. Mount St. Helens, Mount Baker, and the Olympic Mountains are also visible, along with plenty of other peaks and valleys. Your camera will smile and so will you. Head back the way you came when you've had your fill.

Hike 4

Burroughs Mountain and Glacier Basin

Originates: Sunrise Camp to White River Camp
One-way distance: 12.2 miles
High point: 7775 feet
Elevation gain: 3220 feet
Notes: This trail passes through high-elevation terrain that is not usually snow-free until mid-July.

WHILE MOST OF THE STAY-A-DAY options featured in this book are out and back from a given camp, this one is instead a detour from one camp to another. Going clockwise, book a night at Sunrise and the night after at White River, and then instead of taking the Wonderland Trail 3.4 miles down to White River Camp, detour on one of the park's most breathtaking trails. You can still make this detour work if you are going counterclockwise, but you'll need to consult a map and follow along in reverse.

From Sunrise Camp, hop back on the Wonderland and follow the Burroughs Loop Trail westbound toward the first Burroughs. The path climbs to a viewpoint of the White River Basin and Mount Rainier's gorgeous glaciers in 0.3 mile. From there, it ascends into a tundralike environment where it flattens out onto a plateau known as the First Burroughs. Burroughs Mountain was named in a tribute to American naturalist and nature writer John Burroughs, whose eloquent essays include his observations of birds, fish, and landscapes. The high points along this trail are often referred to by numbers, such as "First Burroughs," though all three are collectively known as Burroughs Mountain.

At 1.4 miles from Sunrise Camp, arrive at a signed trail junction, which points back to the right toward Sunrise. Our path continues straight ahead, climbing steadily through the barren hills. This unique tundra area is similar to the earth's arctic zones. A few sparse plants grow here with strength and moxie, such as pussypaws, which produces rosette offshoots that lie flat to the ground to avoid being broken by high winds and heavy precipitation.

At 2 miles, the trail reaches the Second Burroughs where it starts to descend toward Glacier Basin, but before it does, look for a narrow, rather unofficial trail heading uphill, straight ahead toward the Third Burroughs. Keep on trucking—you'll want to get up there! Follow the game trail, and at 2.8 miles from Sunrise Camp, find yourself staring face to face with Mount Rainier with a view so close you feel as if you could almost touch the crevasses in its glaciers. Soak it in—this is what dreams are made of. Is that thing even real or a hologram? Head back 0.8 mile to return to the Burroughs Mountain Trail, and go right to start to descend to Glacier Basin on Sunrise Trail.

Switchbacks take you from the alpine areas back to the forest until you reach the Glacier Basin Trail, now 5.2 miles from Sunrise Camp. Turn right here and head up toward Glacier Basin. In 0.7 mile pass the Glacier Basin wilderness camp, a camping option (with a privy) if you can't get a spot at White River. The end of this valley, just 0.3 mile beyond the camp, is your destination, where natural history and mankind collide.

This valley leads to the technical climbing route to the second most popular path up Mount Rainier. Known as the Emmons Route, folks usually stop at high mountain base camps (Camp Curtis and/or Camp Schurman) before attempting their summit bid. If you see people with ice axes, helmets, and ropes, they are likely headed to the top. For the rest of us, Glacier Basin is a place to take a load off and enjoy watching marmots, while reflecting on its history. In the late 1800s and early 1900s, this area contained two mining tunnels, a barn, two cabins, a sawmill, a power plant, a plank flume, and a 13-room hotel. Unfortunately for claim holder Peter Storbo, who along with his uncle bough 41 claims on these 800 acres, the mine yielded more rocks than ore and eventually it closed down. Rusty relics from the day are strewn around as a reminder, but nature has taken much of the terrain back.

Wander to your heart's content in the valley, then head back on the Glacier Basin Trail, only this time, instead of ascending back up to the Burroughs on the Sunrise Trail (though I know you were dying to climb that hill), stay on the fairly gradual trail as it makes its way toward the White River Campground.

At 8.7 miles from Sunrise Camp where you started, reach a signed junction to the right with the Emmons Moraine Trail. Turn right and follow it onto the moraine above an un-named turquoise lake, whose brilliant coloration, a gift from Mother Nature, is due to light refracting off suspended glacial flour. Enjoy this weird and wonderful area, and then retrace your steps to the Glacier Basin Trail once again. Turn right and follow the former old-mining-road-turned-trail to White River Campground. Walk through the campground and find the hiker camp behind a historical cabin on the left side of the road. Smile widely at those car campers while hoping that they invite you over to share their dinner and dessert.

CHAPTER 4

THE WEST SIDE: LONGMIRE TO MOWICH LAKE

Spanning 34 miles from Longmire to Mowich Lake, the west side of the Wonderland is many backpackers' first brush with the legendary trail. Hailed as the most difficult and remote section of the Wonderland, it's a perfect showcase of the trail's elevation challenges interwoven with isolation and beauty. This section exhibits everything that hikers crave during a Mount Rainier visit—wildflowers, vistas, raging rivers, wildlife-viewing, volcanic landscapes, and opportunities to exercise both the legs and the soul.

When planning your trip, allot more time for this section to give your knees and heart a break. The trail goes up and down as much as the stock market and may have you regretting the decision to tuck that extra luxury item in your pack.

A marmot soaks in the view from
his home on Emerald Ridge.

From Longmire, the trail acts defiantly, almost mocking you as you struggle to schlep a full pack up the first of many hills right from the get-go. As you travel onward, the trail becomes more welcoming, showing you the power of nature at Kautz Creek and rewarding your ambition with a kaleidoscope of wildflowers near Indian Henrys Hunting Ground. More yo-yo trail follows, with a grand crossing of the Tahoma Creek Suspension Bridge and the wonderfully odd meadows and volcanic terrain of Emerald Ridge.

By the time you reach Mowich Lake, you'll be well on your way to experiencing the magic of the Wonderland, your mind humming with memories of scenery past and anticipation of scenery future. Your legs may have hit their own stride, your soul may be starting to feel rested, and there's a chance you will have forgotten what your cell phone ringtone sounds like. These moments are the reason we backpack.

Longmire to Devils Dream

One-way distance: 5.5 miles
High point: 5060 feet
Elevation gain/loss: +2510/–220 feet

BEFORE SETTING FOOT ON THE trail, be sure to swing by the Longmire Wilderness Information Center (WIC) to hobnob with a ranger about a few important things:

- Ensure that your physical permit is in hand and that there are no trail issues afoot.
- Ask about the condition of any bridges over troubled water on the trail, especially in early season.
- Find out about challenging snow crossings, landslides, and washouts.
- Ask about availability of water, especially in late season and particularly at Devils Dream and Klapatche Park.
- Consider asking about recent bear activity.

The rangers usually post a current weather report inside the WIC, with anticipated conditions for the next week. This is also a great time to grab any last-minute sundries from the Longmire gift shop in the National Park Inn. Once you've done your due diligence at the WIC, throw on your pack, tighten your laces, and get ready to hit the trail. This is the moment you've been anticipating for months and the start of an unforgettable adventure.

Starting out, head northeast from the WIC to locate the trail. Snap a few pictures with the Wonderland Trail sign to document your memories. In a little less than a quarter mile,

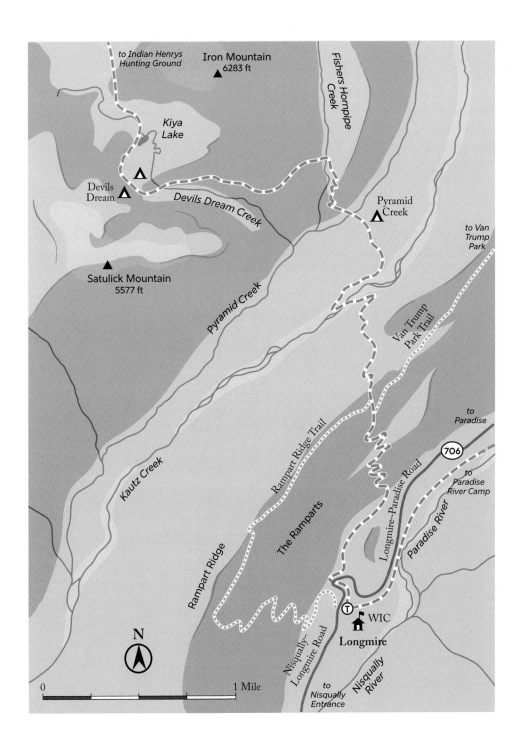

to Indian Henrys
Hunting Ground

Iron Mountain
▲ 6283 ft

Fishers Hornpipe
Creek

*Kiya
Lake*

△

Devils
Dream △

Devils Dream Creek

Pyramid
△ Creek

to Van
Trump
Park

Pyramid Creek

Satulick Mountain
5577 ft

Van Trump
Park Trail

to
Paradise

706

to
Paradise
River Camp

Rampart Ridge Trail

Kautz Creek

Longmire–Paradise Road

Paradise River

The Ramparts

Rampart Ridge

N

0   1 Mile

Nisqually–
Longmire Road

T   ♟ WIC
Longmire

Nisqually
River

to
Nisqually
Entrance

you'll cross over the Nisqually–Longmire Road to its north side, where the trail continues. The Wonderland starts off deceptively gradual and then gains elevation at a decent clip, which may leave you huffing. You'll quickly forget about civilization as you slip deeper into an ocean of green, surrounded by salal, Oregon grape, ferns, and vanilla leaf.

After about 1.8 miles, you'll approach an intersection with a side trail (heading right) to Van Trump Park. Continue straight on the Wonderland Trail, enjoying a bit of a reprieve from the climb. The gentle slope gives way in 0.2 mile at an intersection with the Rampart Ridge Trail (heading left, to the southwest).

It is common for the trail to have to be rerouted in river valleys, like the Kautz Creek area shown here.

Leaving most day hikers behind, continue straight on the Wonderland and enjoy the meanderings of the nice wide trail as you nibble on seasonal huckleberries and begin a mild descent. Standing dead trees in this area are reminders of volcanic outbursts from seventy-plus years ago, including mudflows and forest fires. In October 1947, heavy rain and snowmelt caused the lower portion of the Kautz Glacier to break loose. Due to the narrowness of the canyon, the massive flow of mud and debris backed up until its pressure surged, giving way to utter destruction. The volume of material that swept down this canyon—estimated at fifty million tons—took out forests, roadways, and bridges. Boulders the size of cars bounced with speed off the canyon walls, and trees catapulted downhill like missiles. The snags here are testimony to the strength and power of Mount Rainier.

At just shy of 3 miles, reach a crossing of Kautz Creek and stop to take it in. This area was hit heavily by mudflows in 2006, and the damage is impressive. Use your imagination to recreate the scene: a massive flow of water and mud, trees and boulders hurtling downstream, the surrounding terrain getting torn apart by debris. Kautz Creek created quite a mess during the 2006 floods, jumping its banks farther down near the Nisqually–Longmire Road and flowing more than eight inches deep over the road. The flooding river ripped the road edges apart, changing its channel and undercutting the vulnerable road. The destruction made a mess of park travel, closing off access to Longmire and Paradise and requiring park rangers to escort some unlucky overnight park guests out via an administrative access road—unquestionably, a trip they'll not soon forget.

Kautz Creek is named after German climber August V. Kautz, who in 1857 became the first person to attempt a summit bid of Mount Rainier. Unfortunately, he had to turn back 400 feet shy of the summit. He had deep roots in the Pacific Northwest and spent several years in the armed forces, tackling projects such as the major reconstruction of Fort Steilacoom in Lakewood. Kautz passed away in Seattle on September 4, 1895.

Cross the log bridges here at Kautz Creek, but use caution: they can be on the bouncy side. Follow the sandy trail (it's outlined by large rocks) as it leads you back toward the forest.

After Kautz Creek, the trail continues to the first wilderness camp you'll encounter, Pyramid Creek Camp. This forested camp is quiet and peaceful. Admire the hard work of volunteers and park officials who rebuilt this camp after the floods and mudflows of 2006. To date, no other wilderness camp has suffered as much destruction as this quiet little gem. Pyramid Creek to the north can be muddy and silty; if it is, backtrack south on the Wonderland to find a small seasonal creek for cleaner water.

Continuing north, leave Pyramid Creek and prepare to climb. A series of challenging switchbacks makes you grateful for the forested shade on hot days. About a mile from

Pyramid Creek, cross Fishers Hornpipe Creek and avoid opening your mouth: black flies and mosquitoes are prolific here in warm weather. If huckleberries are ripe, grab a few handfuls to eat as you dodge the persistent winged ones. Huff and puff uphill as the rocky walls of Satulick Mountain play peekaboo with you through the trees on your left. A series of tough switchbacks greets you, reminding you of your very full backpack.

Two miles past Pyramid Creek Camp (including 1400 feet of elevation gain), arrive at Devils Dream Camp. Nestled in deep forest, Devils Dream provides a welcome reprieve from your climb with seven flat, individual campsites; one large group site; and a deluxe outhouse, which perches on the hillside like a beacon for travelers. Check out sites 5 and 6 if they're available; they generally yield more privacy and seclusion. The water source here is a small stream below the camp, which can dry up in late season or during a hot spell. If it's dry, head 0.5 mile north up the trail for a sneak peek of the next day's adventure, and filter water from Kiya Lake or one of many tributaries.

Ben Longmire, grandson of legendary park founder James Longmire and one of the first to circumnavigate Mount Rainier, named this area Devils Dream, as he deemed the creek here to be as crooked as a devil's dream.

Devils Dream to Klapatche Park

One-way distance: 11.2 miles
High point: 6000 feet
Elevation gain/loss: +3420/−2980 feet

THIS SECTION IS A TREAT for the senses and a true test for the knees, back, and feet. Like a yo-yo, you'll go up and down repeatedly, until you feel that flat ground is a thing of the past. You'll pass fields of flowers in Indian Henrys Hunting Ground, as well as the park's oldest, still functional ranger patrol cabin. Farther along the trail, you'll cross the mighty wonder that is the Tahoma Creek Suspension Bridge and head up to the volcanic vista of Emerald Ridge, where more rainbows of flowers abound. You'll pass the raging South Puyallup River and head back up to the brilliant blue waters of subalpine Saint Andrews Lake. Finally, you'll arrive at Aurora Lake and Klapatche Park, the closest thing to flat ground since you left Indian Henrys. This section of trail is phenomenal, whether you cruise through it in one long day or stretch it out across a couple of shorter days. A camera is one of the Ten Essentials here.

Heading northwest from Devils Dream, your climb breaks from tree line into the wetlands of Kiya Lake. Note that the name of this lake was changed in 2022, to remove the

The climb up to Devils Dream from Longmire passes through a large, healthy forest.

derogatory former name, which may still appear on some maps. *Kiya* means "grandmother" in the Whulshootseed dialect, native to the Puyallup Tribe. This beautiful little lake was a frequent campsite and hangout of Indian Henry's wives as they waited for him to hunt in the fields above. They spent their days picking berries and enjoying the beautiful views and peacefulness of this area. Continue the stair-step routine as you gain more elevation, hiking into the heart of Indian Henrys Hunting Ground, which affords views of Mount Ararat (to the west), Copper and Iron Mountains (to the east), and Mount Rainier (do I need to tell you where to look?).

This area has a rich history, and your imagination can go a little wild with stories of yesteryear. Mount Ararat, for instance, was named by Ben Longmire, who wrote, "I named it because I found there some long slabs of wood that had turned to stone and I thought they might have been part of old Noah's boat. I also found a stump with a ring around it as if his rope might have been tied there. It was all stone" (as recounted in Dee Molenaar's *The Challenge of Rainier*). Ararat, of course, is the mountain where Noah's Ark is said to have come to rest. The mystery of what Longmire actually found is still up for debate.

THE BUGS OF DEVILS DREAM

Year after year, a few spots on the Wonderland are so buggy that they send backpackers into a frenzy of uncontrollable swatting, disrupting thoughts and creating bad dreams. After suffering through one of these areas, you'll keep randomly spraying yourself with anything smelling of citronella or eucalyptus long after arriving home. Devils Dream is such an area. One minute, you're a happy hiker lightheartedly schlepping your pack, and the next, you're ambushed by hemoglobin hunters looking to dine on the cheapest piece of real estate around—namely, the backs of your knees and arms. This gang of bellicose biters won't take no for an answer, which forces you to initiate the beleaguered hiker's trademark "Whack, Smack, and then Whack-with-Your-Pack" ritual as you whirl around trying to see what kind of creatures could be capable of such hullabaloo.

The lakes, creeks, and stagnant pools around Devils Dream are the perfect place for insects to propagate and raise their young. It wouldn't be a bad idea to start a petition to change the name of Devils Dream to Insect Infestation—but I'm fairly certain that wouldn't go over well for tourism. Regardless, if you happen to be staying at Devils Dream on a hot summer day, prepare to spend a lot of time inside the insect-free walls of your tent, or wear your head net around camp and introduce yourself as a space traveler. Either way, you'll be more comfortable than amid the buzzing hordes.

The trail narrows through meadows of wildflowers as you get closer to Indian Henrys Hunting Ground.

The trail runs by newly renamed Kiya Lake, a quiet area near Indian Henrys Hunting Ground.

Indian Henrys Hunting Ground comes with its own stories. In 1862, two pioneer explorers are said to have encountered a friendly Native American man near Mount Rainier. When the pioneers, James Packwood and Henry Windsor, asked the man his name, they recall it sounding like "Sotolick." Since that name was too difficult to articulate, they decided to rename him Indian Henry, and from there, legend was born. The jury is out on whether Sotolick was in fact his real name, though Satulick Mountain is a phonetic variation of it. History has it that Indian Henry had recent contact with Jesuit missionaries, and he may have misunderstood the pioneers when they asked his name. Instead, he may have been trying to say the word "Catholic," imparting a religion.

Indian Henry became fast friends with many explorers, including James Longmire, and offered to guide Longmire's climbing party up to Paradise in 1883 for a fee of $2 a day. Ten years later, he headed up the labor efforts to help Longmire clear the first wagon road into

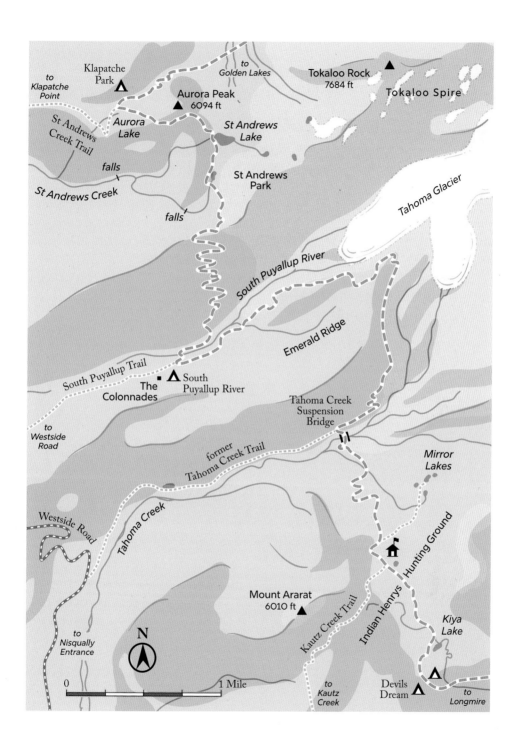

to
Klapatche
Point

Klapatche
Park

to
Golden Lakes

Tokaloo Rock
7684 ft

Tokaloo Spire

Aurora Peak
6094 ft

St Andrews
Creek Trail

Aurora
Lake

St Andrews
Lake

St Andrews
Park

Tahoma Glacier

falls

St Andrews Creek

falls

South Puyallup River

Emerald Ridge

South Puyallup Trail

The
Colonnades

South
Puyallup River

Tahoma Creek
Suspension
Bridge

to
Westside
Road

former
Tahoma Creek Trail

Mirror
Lakes

Westside Road

Tahoma Creek

Indian Henrys Hunting Ground

Mount Ararat
6010 ft

Kautz Creek Trail

Kiya
Lake

to
Nisqually
Entrance

N

to
Kautz
Creek

Devils
Dream

to
Longmire

0   1 Mile

the park. Indian Henry had three wives, a successful farm, and a log home. In addition to broken English, he spoke three Native American dialects.

Pioneers speculated about how Indian Henry made his wealth. One theory was that he had found gold in the hills around Mount Rainier; another was that he had slyly changed the route to the mountain, diverting travelers to his farm and collecting money for much-needed supplies and accommodations. Eventually the pioneers' curiosity got the best of them and one day they followed Indian Henry as he headed into the hills. To their surprise, they found a meadow with wildflowers as far as the eye could see, amazing vistas, and a rich supply of wildlife. Speculation still swirls about whether Indian Henry had a secret gold mine, but we do know that he used this area for hunting, grazing his horses and cattle, and picking berries. As you pass through Indian Henrys Hunting Ground, imagine this area as it was many years ago, teeming with mountain goats, deer, and bears.

This special place is featured in twentieth-century park lore too. In the early 1900s, the park was still establishing rules, boundaries, and important regulations, such as how au-

There is plenty to explore in Indian Henrys Hunting Ground.

Mirror Lakes is a nice bonus destination, only 1.2 miles roundtrip off the Wonderland Trail.

tomobiles and horses would interact on roadways. Things in America were changing, and the park was trying to keep up. In 1908, the US Department of the Interior began issuing annual permits to a few small businesses in the park in an attempt to corral tourists into specific camping areas, which officials hoped would prevent forest fires. Already established at Paradise was the so-called Camp in the Clouds, where folks could pay $2.50 per night to do just that. The popularity of Paradise spurred the creation of a smaller camp concession near Indian Henrys Hunting Ground called the Wigwam Hotel. It wasn't a hotel at all but

rather a campground—and an awful one at that. It had fifteen tent sites and poor sanitiza-
tion for human-waste disposal and camp cooking. It was only partially successful because
it was difficult to compete with the Camp in the Clouds—the trail to Paradise was much
more aesthetically appealing, passing by the Nisqually Glacier as opposed to through a deep
forest. The Wigwam Hotel closed in 1916, and there is no evidence of it today.

Smack-dab in the middle of Indian Henrys Hunting Ground, you'll come to a junction
with the Kautz Creek Trail on your left (west). A bit farther along, pass a trail junction on
your right (east) to the park's oldest still-operating patrol cabin. Built in 1915, this park
treasure is a stellar example of primitive architecture and was listed on the National Register of Historic Places in 1991. Take some time to sit on the porch and enjoy the gorgeous
scenery in front of you. This is also a great place to find shelter from sun, rain, or sleet. Just
beware of panhandling gray jays, who like to look at you with sad eyes as if they are famished and undernourished. There are plenty of bugs and seeds around, so resist their sweet
faces.

Farther on, a junction with the Mirror Lakes spur trail pops up to the right (east). If
time allows, head up to the appropriately named lakes (more like small ponds) for a view
of Rainier reflected in their waters. The 1.2-mile round-trip affords some wonderful photo
opportunities. Catching the sunset here is also a treat if you are camping at Devils Dream,
but make sure your headlamp has enough battery power for the trip back down to camp.

Back on the main trail, begin your descent from Indian Henrys, leaving the meadows and
wildflowers behind and heading back into forest. Approximately 0.3 mile from the Mirror
Lakes trail junction, the Wonderland comes to a rocky crossing of a tributary creek flowing
down from Indian Henrys above. This fast-flowing freshwater creek is the perfect place to
stop and get water. A couple of other water sources flow seasonally here, but they can be
spotty. From this point to the South Puyallup River Camp, 4.8 miles away, water is tough
to come by—so fill 'er up when you can and remember to stay hydrated.

In 1.4 miles beyond the Mirror Lakes junction, the scenery changes dramatically as you
come to the mighty Tahoma Creek Suspension Bridge. Approximately 150 feet long and
more than 200 feet high, this massive bridge spans the moody Tahoma Creek far below.
The bridge is not for the faint of heart—it creaks and swings slightly as you walk across the
planks. If you're using trekking poles, tuck them in your pack for the crossing to free up your
hands and to avoid dropping them into the valley below. Secure the contents of your pack
and give yourself a pep talk, if necessary. Head out gently onto the bridge and heed the sign
recommending that only one person should cross at a time. Put on your bravest superhero
face and stop halfway across to look out at Tahoma Creek.

The mighty Tahoma Creek Suspension bridge is one of the trail's most fascinating features.

Be sure to check out the impressive andesite columns near the South Puyallup Camp.

The valley below has a dramatic history of lahars, glacier outbursts, and floods. Not long ago, hikers could cross this creek on a little footbridge: the deep gorge below did not exist. From 1967 to 1992, at least twenty-three lahars or glacial outbursts from the South Tahoma Glacier ripped down the great gorge below your feet. Park crews and volunteers assessed the suspension bridge after the 2006 floods and determined it was not damaged; however, the bank nearest to the south tower sustained substantial destruction from erosion. Concerns over the bridge's stability were relieved after an assessment showed the footings were solid and the bridge safe for travel.

The banks of the creek tell a story too. Logs and trees of yesteryear are stuck in the embankment like candles in a cake, and boulders are buried deep within the layers. This volatile creek throws out a mudflow every five years or so, but seldom do its waters make it up as high as the suspension bridge. An older, decrepit suspension bridge was replaced by the current Tahoma Creek Suspension Bridge in 1994, and for a time it spanned the creek next to its new larger-bridge cousin. The old bridge, removed for good in 1995 because it was a safety hazard, was slightly to the east and just below the new bridge.

Once on the other side of the bridge, ascend back into the forest. Pass a sign indicating a trail junction with the Tahoma Creek Trail to the west; follow the Wonderland as it turns slightly right and continues north. Note: the Tahoma Creek Trail is now closed due to washouts and navigation. A couple of openings through the trees to your right provide panoramic photo opportunities of the Tahoma Creek Suspension Bridge, now behind you. Head up several switchbacks and continue upward as the trail turns from dust to pebbles and the scenery moves from forest to volcanic and subalpine terrain. Success Divide, on the flank of Rainier, is visible here, as is the rocky and barren moraine of Success Cleaver above the divide. Just slightly to the northeast is rocky Glacier Island, tucked between the Tahoma and South Tahoma Glaciers like a large, crumbling stone tower.

As you approach Emerald Ridge, you'll discover the reason for its name. The wildflower meadows and grasses make this high subalpine meadow a vision in green, providing a perfect packs-off opportunity to sit and take it all in. Flowers like asters, harebells, and western pasqueflower thrive in the volcanic earth; enjoy their subtle fragrance as you pass through. From this odd angle, Rainier seems decrepit, fragile, and ancient, the top almost within arm's reach.

Watch for hoary marmots in the summer; they like to make their holes under nearby rocks. 🐾 If you haven't unpacked those trekking poles since crossing the Tahoma Creek Suspension Bridge, now is a good time to do so. The descent from Emerald Ridge has arguably the loosest footing on the whole trail, so go slow and steady to avoid skateboarding downhill or getting a case of rock burn on your rear end.

The volcanic rock gives way to forested canopy as you cautiously continue to descend. Cross an unnamed creek on a footlog. If you're camping at South Puyallup River Camp, you may want to stop and get water here. The water at camp can be a trickle during the summer, but this creek flows clear and steady year-round.

Shortly after the creek crossing, 1.5 miles beyond Emerald Ridge, come to a junction with the South Puyallup Trail (to the left/west), which leads to Westside Road. The South Puyallup River Camp is along the South Puyallup Trail; the Wonderland continues straight ahead to the north. If this is your camp for the night, head left (west) along the South Puyallup Trail and enjoy some rest and reprieve in this wooded but occasionally buggy camp. There are four individual campsites and one group site (located farther along the South Puyallup Trail to the right/north, past the individual campsite area). Not far from the group site, a small creek serves as the camp's water supply, usually yielding at least a dribble. Note that hearty day hikers use the South Puyallup Trail coming from the Westside Road. You'll know these folks when you see them, as they smell of crisp linen, carry fresh fruit, and have packs the size of lima beans.

Continue along the South Puyallup Trail past the water source to see some magnificent andesite columns, called the Colonnades, to your left (south) on a cliffside above. These unique geologic formations resulted from a volcanic eruption several thousand years back. Andesite is most commonly found in composite volcanoes, like the ones in the Pacific Northwest. During an eruption, molten andesite flows slowly and has high viscosity, forming steep and often abrupt-looking structures. Here at the Colonnades, it looks as if a giant comb was run through the andesite as it cooled, forming long strands of stone.

If you need the privy, continue down the South Puyallup Trail a few steps to find the toilet trail to your right. Be sure to give a yodel to ensure it's not in use—the pathway to get there is short and can lead to embarrassment. South Puyallup is a fairly large camp, and the privy here seems to be a celebrated and popular attraction. See Hike 1 in the Stay a Day

BLUE RIBBON AREA: EMERALD RIDGE

You'll be walking on Emerald Ridge when you are either going to or coming from the South Puyallup River Camp, so you'll want to stop and take it in—this place is a treasure! Looking at the mountain to the east, you'll see a side of Mount Rainier visitors rarely observe—it doesn't look like the classic peak most visitors expect. On the left side of the mountain is a high wall known as Sunset Amphitheater, a showcase of pyroclastic debris (rock fragments from volcanic events) and exposed layers of what was once fast-flowing lava and ash. This area formed between 40,000 and 15,000 years ago—imagine what it has witnessed! Descending from Sunset Amphitheater, the Puyallup Glacier is just around the corner, while sprawling out in front of you are the Tahoma and South Tahoma Glaciers. The last rays of sunshine hit this area and turn it a majestic pink, so if you are camping nearby and the weather is favorable, you may want to stay and watch the show.

To the right, at the top of the mountain, Point Success is one of the three classified summits of Mount Rainier; it's the second highest at 14,158 feet. The highest is Columbia Crest (14,411 or 14,410 feet, depending on the source), and the third highest is Liberty Cap (14,112 feet).

Nature is carrying out her primitive mission right before your eyes. In front of you across the valley is a large green meadow popular with mountain goats. 🐾 If they aren't hanging out in the meadow, stop and scan the neighboring hills—they are often somewhere close by, and trying to find them is a fun game. Waterfalls pour down high cliffs as the Tahoma Glacier crumbles, cracks, and dumps its melting ice and gritty sand down the valley toward the South Puyallup River. Hoary marmots sound whistles to alert their families of your presence; some pop out of their burrows to check you out, watching the world go by from their rocky perches. Others scamper about the meadow undeterred, focused on finding their meal greens.

Emerald Ridge is a true Wonderland gem: you can return to it in your memories whenever life throws you a curveball and you need to find your happy place.

Emerald Ridge is a sight to behold.

section of chapter 3 for a great day hike in this area. Planning an extra night here will grant you fantastic access to one of the most remote areas in the park.

Back on the Wonderland, cross a sturdy bridge and admire the silted pace of the turbulent South Puyallup River below. Tip your bandanna in honor of the brave folks who installed this crossing, and then head back into the forest to a series of switchbacks. Gain roughly 1400 feet of elevation to attain a ridgeline that meanders slightly up and down as you near the subalpine terrain of magnificent Saint Andrews Park. Keep a close eye out for bears, as they love hanging out in this area almost as much as you will. 🐾

Just before you reach Saint Andrews Lake, an almost unidentifiable climbers route leads east up the Puyallup Cleaver and onto the Tahoma Glacier above you. Look for climbers bivouacking high above in early summer. Stop and fill up your water at Saint Andrews Lake if you plan to camp at Klapatche Park, as water there can be iffy, especially in August and September.

A group of travelers from Saint Mark's Episcopal Church camped near this lake in the late 1880s, and they named this area for Saint Andrew. History has it that Saint Andrew was then known as the patron saint of Scotland, Russia, Sicily, Greece, Malta, and Romania. Incidentally, he was also known as the patron saint of fishermen. Perhaps the campers hoped that naming the area after Saint Andrew would provide protection for the landscape and those who used it for food.

Enjoy the meadows of the subalpine wonderland as you travel out of Saint Andrews Park. The gentle, rolling trail is a welcome relief for your feet, knees, and shoulders. In just under 1.5 miles from Saint Andrews Lake, arrive at the junction of Saint Andrews Creek Trail and Klapatche Park, on the shores of Aurora Lake. Klapatche Park reportedly got its name from an important chief of the Puyallup Tribe.

If you plan to stay here, you'll be pleased to call it home for the night. There are four individual sites but no group site. Site 1 has the best view hands down, with Rainier front and center, but it has almost no privacy. The other sites also have pleasant views. An outhouse provides a welcome bit of privacy in the limited camping area. Aurora Lake affords amazing photo opportunities, with the mountain reflected in the water and glistening above you.

The back side of Klapatche Park Camp, looking westward, is also a treat. If you're lucky enough to be here on a clear day and you have a sharp eye, you can watch the sun dip into the very distant waters of Puget Sound. Golden Lakes, to the north, shine like buttons in the landscape as they take on the sun's reflection.

If you're keen on frogs and tadpoles, you're in luck: Aurora Lake is teeming with them. Due to the lake's prolific aquatic life, frequent algae blooms, and stagnant waters, you'll want to gather water somewhere other than the lake—unless you fancy frog-poo stew with

Even in harsh, squint-worthy sunlight, the areas near St. Andrews Lake are sublime.

a side of polliwog punch. Make your way around the lakeshore to the east side, where you may find a small natural spring—be forewarned that it dries up from year to year. If you aren't too tired, or if desperate times call for desperate measures, you can also hike west 0.5 mile along the Saint Andrews Creek Trail to an unnamed creek that usually produces at least a small flow year-round.

One final note: Bears are common in the Klapatche Park area. 🐾 Several years ago, a female bear and two yearling cubs decided to camp out in one of the campsites for a few days, causing all sorts of mayhem for tired backpackers. Be sure to store food and all scented items properly.

Grasses and algae can linger in the still water near Klapatche Park's Aurora Lake.

Klapatche Park to Golden Lakes

One-way distance: 7.8 miles
High point: 5500 feet
Elevation gain/loss: +1500/−2100 feet

AS YOU LEAVE KLAPATCHE PARK, you'll be treated to a couple of amazing views of Rainier and wildflower meadows. Next up, a steep descent to the North Puyallup River. Creative trail-builders put in switchbacks at nearly every possible place to help your feet stick to the side of this hill. Use trekking poles if you brought them, and watch your footing carefully, as there is little margin for error in some places.

In a pinch, you can find a couple of small water sources on the steep descent leaving Klapatche, heading down toward the North Puyallup River valley; otherwise, wait to get water below. Plenty of brush and riparian vegetation, such as thimbleberry, bleeding heart, and devil's club, fight to take over the trail in late season. In wet or dewy weather, sporting waterproof pants or gaiters down this hill is a good idea if you don't want your socks to turn to soup.

While your quads are treated to a workout, your eyes are treated to the ever-changing look of the mountain. Stop for a minute and see if you can find Tokaloo Rock, the boldest rock near the base of the Puyallup Glacier, and its pointy companion to the south, Tokaloo Spire. Tokaloo Rock is a class 2 scramble, with a somewhat flat summit on its northwest side. If you're a skilled mountaineer or rock climber, file "scrambling up Tokaloo" somewhere under future fun and research its hazards before attempting the climb.

After a long descent on the shoulder of Aurora Peak, a beautiful, unnamed tributary creek with a log primed for sitting is a picture-perfect place to take a break before heading down to the North Puyallup River area. It's also an excellent, reliable water source. From

COUNTERCLOCKWISE TIP

After the North Puyallup River Camp, be sure to fill up on water at an unnamed tributary before you start going up the hill. Water sources can be iffy on the hill above you and at Klapatche Park. The hill you are about to climb is one of the steepest on the Wonderland, and it will tax even the strongest hiker. The good news is that it's fairly short and goes by quickly. Near the top, the views will distract you from the rapid metronome of your breathing, and some great photo opportunities await once you crest the ridge.

In season you may encounter beautiful wildflowers as you head toward the North Puyallup River from Klapatche Park.

there, the Wonderland Trail pops out onto the terminus of the decommissioned Westside Road, and this part can be a little confusing. The group site for the North Puyallup River Camp is located to the left, but the individual sites are still ahead, on the opposite side of the river. Jog right on what was the old road and then look to your left for the remains of an old-timey retaining wall. The trail continues on the other side of the wall, then comes to the North Puyallup River Bridge. The interesting rock walls and concrete pads, built almost a century ago, are skeletons of the abandoned Westside Road, which has been converted to the North Puyallup Trail. The North Puyallup Group site is located in this area, but the regular sites are straight ahead after you cross the bridge. Nature has been trying to consume the aspirations of former dreamers with moss and encroaching foliage overtaking the charming asymmetrical stone walls and roadway. This historical auto road was once originally intended to go all the way to the Carbon River, but stopped short due to rugged terrain and extravagant cost.

Find your superhero cape again, as crossing the North Puyallup River bridge can be a little unnerving—it's sturdy, wide, and strong, but the turbulent river and silted waterfall below could swallow you whole in seconds. Imagine yourself back in November 2006, when

South of the rushing North Puyallup River is a much quieter creek where water is available year-round.

ten-ton boulders full of pep and vigor were carried swiftly along in muddy water, knocking out a similar bridge. Shudder at the thought but admire the power.

After the bridge, the trail turns left (west). Straight ahead from the bridge, the North Puyallup River Camp offers three campsites and one group site. Site 3 provides the most privacy, but all are level, peaceful camps. While North Puyallup is not the most beautiful camp on the trail, the white noise from the river will help you drift off to dreamland, and the huckleberries here make a fine dessert in season.

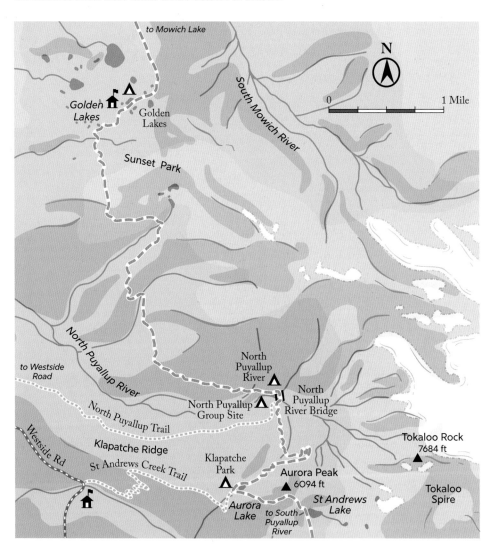

A burn zone from the 1930s greets you north of the North Puyallup River valley near Golden Lakes.

The climb up to Golden Lakes looks worse on the map than it feels. Compared to some of the climbing you've already done, this ascent is more gradual and forgiving. Cascade blueberries (*Vaccinium deliciosum*) from here all the way to the descent to South Mowich River (past Golden Lakes) will satiate that craving for fresh fruit. In season, they're plentiful, juicy, and worth a packs-off "pick" stop. For now, continue in the forest, gently gaining elevation next to salal, ferns, and vanilla leaf.

About 3 miles past the North Puyallup River Camp, the scenery dramatically changes as you enter an old fire-event area with gobs of Cascade blueberries. In the 1930s, a fire burned fast and furiously through this area, destroying nearly all the trees in its path. The impressive silver forest of standing dead trees is a testament to how stubborn nature can be. Winds of up to 120 miles per hour ripped through here during the 2006 storms, yet few trees succumbed. Today birds flutter playfully in these ghostly tree houses. Bears are also plentiful here: it seems like nearly every Wonderland traveler gets to see or hear one in this area. 🐾 Activate your bear-country wisdom and use caution on any blind corners.

The trail levels slightly as you enter Sunset Park, along the shoulder of an unnamed peak. On a clear day, stop for views west to Puget Sound and the Olympic Mountains far beyond. Sunset Park encompasses Golden Lakes and many small unnamed lakes, tarns, and ponds, several of which are obvious along the trail. Stop and tango with insect repellent if you need to, especially in the warmer season.

Start to descend slightly and be on the lookout for the Sunset Park Patrol Cabin. Almost everyone who passes this way can be heard exclaiming, "We're here already?" as the cabin magically appears around a corner. Built in 1922, this quaint patrol cabin serves as a cornerstone for the Golden Lakes Camp, located on a hillside to the north, and rangers are often stationed here.

Golden Lakes has five individual campsites, one group site, and a decent outhouse (as opposed to a wooden-box-style privy). Site 1 is quite smelly since it's within a stone's throw of the outhouse. If you end up at this site, consider yourself a hero who is taking one for the team. The group site sits closest to the main lake and is very large. Sites 4 and 5 are the most desirable, as they have water access, views, and more privacy. If you end up at a different site, be sure to wander over to visit your neighbors and enjoy the limited but pleasant view of the mountain to the east, from the other side of the knoll.

Side note: Late in the season, the Golden Lakes become a little stagnant, so respect the water source by refraining from bathing or washing in the quiet waters. And, as always, be sure to treat your water before drinking it or using it to cook.

Golden Lakes to Mowich Lake

One-way distance: 9.5 miles
High point: 4929 feet
Elevation gain/loss: +2330/−2300 feet

LEAVE GOLDEN LAKES CAMP AND wander through forest, meadows, and tarns before popping out in a meadow that was a casualty of a 1930s forest fire. The rich soil and sunlight in this area make the Cascade blueberries so fantastic, you'll wish you had packed a cheesecake—or a gallon-sized bucket to bring them all home. Skim them off the vine as you walk, or just park yourself at a bush and nosh until your lips are so blue other hikers will think you're oxygen starved. Bears also love the smorgasbord, so keep your eyes open. 🐾

Mount Rainier looks in the mirror at Golden Lakes.

Continue skirting the ridgeline, with views of clear-cuts not far off. You're very near the park boundaries and private lands. As you take in the sights, be grateful that in the late 1800s so many interest groups pushed hard for this beautiful place to be preserved as a national park.

Just after the crest of the ridge, the trail takes a turn to the northeast and starts a long, rather steep 3.1-mile descent to the Mowich River valley. The thirty-plus switchbacks seem endless, but the forested canopy is pleasant and the trail wide and welcoming.

After the big descent, discover a clear brook at the base of the hill. The water source for the South Mowich River Camp, it is one of the few water sources between here and Mowich Lake. This is a river valley, sure, but filtering the silted, milky water from the Mowich Rivers is not recommended. Not only will you need to have a memorial service for your water filter ("Brothers and sisters of the trail, we are gathered here today to share our grief over the loss of our filter friend, Trickle Ted, who is dead . . ."), you'll also have some sandy gunk in your stroganoff. Had you been on this trail prior to the floods of 2006, you would have had fresh water available only steps from camp. The river's deluge made a mess of this area, sending a former freshwater creek and the small bridge over it packing. Once again, Mount Rainier proved herself to be the ultimate remodeler, using the river as a water chisel to change this area forever. On a recent hunt, I was able to find the remnants of the creek, which gave me only a sketchy dribble, and the sad skeletal ruins of the bridge.

Years ago, there were several camp areas in this river valley, but now there is only one. Because the branches of the Mowich River are so active, there are a bunch of old trails and paths in this stretch. If you see a sign that says "camp" with an arrow, follow it! The South Mowich River Camp is on the land between the North Mowich River and South Mowich

COUNTERCLOCKWISE TIP

The climb from South Mowich River, heading toward Golden Lakes, is one of the most mentally taxing in the park. The elevation gain to the top is 2000 feet in 3.1 miles, a difficult trudge. You'll lose count of the switchbacks, but be glad they are there, as going straight up the thing might cause your heart to short-circuit. Take your time and remind yourself that at the top you'll be rewarded with berries and a fairly level grade all the way to Golden Lakes.

Near the top, the scenery changes from trees to shrubs and the grade eases a bit. The Wonderland turns slightly at the crest of the hill, wandering back to the east. Be sure to get water at the base of the hill before you begin your ascent, as the hill itself is dry.

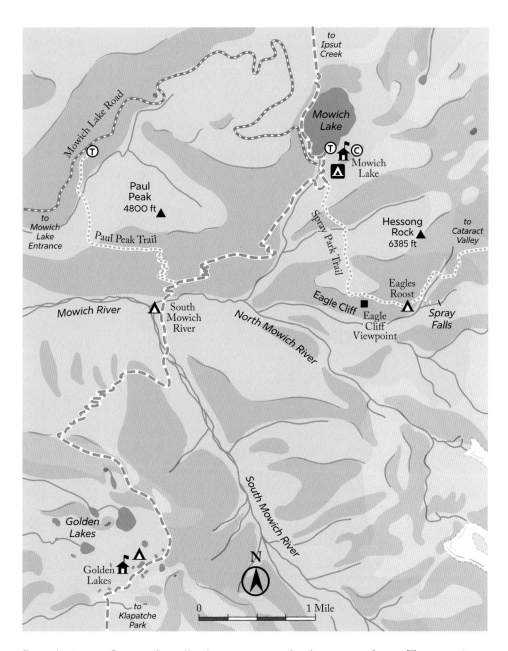

River, but water flows and small tributaries can make the area confusing. The camp has a decent outhouse, several forested campsites, and an old shelter that serves as a campsite only if you're seeking novelty. The shelter is decades old, with a leaky roof and a few fuzzy, long-tailed occupants who have staked a claim on a warm place to sleep. The graffiti in it must have been written by those who didn't know any better. A favorite says, "Will it ever stop raining?" The hiker who wrote that was clearly having serious weather woes, surely not improved by the drippy roof, which can make being inside the shelter as wet as being outside.

Some words of caution about the Mowich River valley and the bridges in this area: The level of both the South and North Mowich Rivers changes hourly with snowmelt coming from Rainier above, especially in warm rains or summer heat. Heavy, silted water can crest the top of log bridges—or worse, wash them away. The Park Service does its best to maintain the footbridge crossings, but Mount Rainier reserves the right to decide whether or not she wants to keep them in place. One year, red bandannas were tied to trees at both sides of the South Mowich River, indicating the safest crossing. A different year, a bridge was in place over the North Mowich crossing but AWOL at the South Mowich crossing. Retired park trails foreman Carl Fabiani told me that he has replaced the bridges here forty or fifty times in his career, sometimes twice in one week. If you've done your due diligence before the start of your trip, you'll know what to expect here, unless you have the misfortune of the bridge washing out after you've started your trip. If so, the "trail telegraph" among backpackers can usually keep you up-to-date. If the bridges are out, proceed with caution and attempt to cross as early in the day as possible.

John H. Williams chronicled a brief history of the Mowich River valley in his 1911 book, *The Mountain That Was God.* Williams writes that the Mowich Rivers were given their names by Native Americans after they saw the figure of a deer, or a *mowich* (as translated into Chinook Jargon), in the rock and ice on Mount Rainier's northwest flank. More than a century after his book was published, you can still see the *mowich*. Several great views exist of the deer's head on the mountainside (though perhaps the best views are from Spray Park).

Next up? You guessed it! Another big climb to get you out of the river valley. But before the climb, a 1-mile warm-up via a sandy trail through red huckleberries, thimbleberries, and moss wraps up your crossing of the valley. At 1 mile past the South Mowich River Camp, come to a junction with the Paul Peak Trail to the left. Continue right on the Wonderland, and commence the great huff and puff up the large hillside. The unrelenting trail yields a consistent pitch for just over 3 miles to Mowich Lake.

The greenery along the way is beautiful, with large trees constituting the swaying canopy above you. Oregon grape, salal, ferns, mosses, and other woodsy plants accompany your steps. Be thankful for switchbacks, which make your climb a little easier, and be sure to stay hydrated. At 2.9 miles from the Paul Peak Trail intersection, come to a junction with the

Views of the "mowich," or deer's head (see box on photo), are visible from several locations, including the South Mowich River valley and Spray Park.

the area where the
mowich can be seen

Backpackers work their way across the South Mowich River Valley.

Spray Park Trail, which heads off to the right. Stay straight and continue for 0.3 mile to the sign welcoming you to Mowich Lake.

Until now, you've likely been enjoying the quiet along the trail, away from the noise of cars and picnicking people, so try to prepare your mind for the mild commotion you'll encounter at Mowich Lake. People are plentiful in the summer but generally respectful; many of them are here for the day hikes around Spray Park or Tolmie Peak or are camped out with their families for a few nights.

Mowich Lake Campground is a gravel parking lot turned campground, with first-come, first-served car-camping areas and a section reserved for hikers who use it as part of their wilderness permit. Fires are prohibited, and there are vault toilets but no running water. As in most national park campgrounds, quiet hours are observed from 9 PM to 7 AM to show respect for other campers. The water source is Mowich Lake itself, which is the largest and deepest lake in the park and always looks clear and clean.

Cars come and go from an adjacent parking lot, with folks dragging coolers full of deliciousness into camp to cook gourmet meals over large camping stoves and portable grills. Avoid drooling on their steaks and veggies; the fresh food you'll get to enjoy at the end of your trip will be all the sweeter for all the work you've put in. If you've cached food here, visit the ranger patrol cabin on the east side of the lake to gather your goodies from the bins. With any luck, you tucked a delectable treat inside when you packed it some time ago.

CHAPTER 5

THE NORTH SIDE: MOWICH LAKE TO SUNRISE CAMP

Every section of the Wonderland Trail has a mystique of its own, and the 21.8 miles on the north side, from Mowich Lake to Sunrise Camp, are no exception. There are sights to behold around each turn—such as the Carbon Glacier, which has the lowest elevation of any glacier in the Lower 48; the magical mossy meadows near Mystic Lake; and the devastation of the Winthrop Glacier area. On top of all that, you'll get some great vistas of one of the most hazardous climbing routes on Rainier: Liberty Ridge.

Your one major decision is whether to go through Ipsut Pass or take the Spray Park Trail. It's a tough choice; see The Spray Park Debate in chapter 3, Backpacking the Wonderland Trail, for guidance.

A pathway near the quiet edge of Mowich Lake guides hikers toward the patrol cabin and resupply area.

Mowich Lake to Dick Creek via Ipsut Pass

One-way distance: 9.3 miles
High point: 5100 feet
Elevation gain/loss: +2070/–2700 feet

THE WONDERLAND TRAIL LEAVES Mowich Lake, skirting the lake on its west side. While map contours make this part seem pretty level, slight ups and downs result in a little elevation gain before you reach the top of Ipsut Pass and the trail junction to Tolmie Peak at 1.5 miles. If time permits, consider the Stay a Day option (Hike 3 on page 118) to see Tolmie Peak and Eunice Lake. Getting up there at sunset will take your breath away. A historical fire lookout adorns the top of Tolmie Peak and looks down on a stunning mountain lake with postcard views of Mount Rainier.

If time does not permit, put Tolmie Peak on your list of future "must-dos" and begin heading northeast, down from Ipsut Pass. To your right are the large cliffs of Castle Peak. Near the top of Ipsut Pass, the terrain is alternately steep and brushy, soaking your shoes and socks in wet or dewy weather. Try knocking the water off the leaves ahead of you with your poles. Or if the foliage is dry, thank your lucky stars.

Once you hit tree line, the downhill pitch seems less taxing and you are surrounded by towering giants. If you've ever wanted to feel small in nature, this is the place to put things in perspective. Many of these trees have been around for more than five hundred years or more, thanks to a lack of fires and the temperate rainforest that exists in the valley below you. As you wander through this area, enjoy the so-green-it-hurts views of the forest ecosystem beneath your feet and above your head. Water runs almost year-round on this hillside, starting about 1 mile from the Ipsut Pass intersection.

About 2 miles past the intersection, start looking to your left (northwest) for a very large tree—the largest of the bunch so far. One of the largest Alaska yellow cedars in the world stands tall and proud here, a result of perfect climate and elevation conditions and a lack of disturbance or wildfires. You may never see a tree this old and large again in your lifetime, so be sure to stop and take it in.

Continue onward, losing elevation and paralleling the flowing waters of Ipsut Creek. After a large rain, or during snowmelt, cascading water creates countless small waterfalls not far from the trail. At nearly 4 miles from the top of Ipsut Pass, stop for a must-have photo-op in the giant, hollow tree roots that sadly are no longer alive. As with everything in these ancient areas, please take only pictures and leave only memories.

At 3.6 miles from the intersection at the top of Ipsut Pass, find the trail junction that leads to Ipsut Creek Campground straight ahead. If you're spending the night at this camp,

Thick vegetation dwarfs the trail near Ipsut Pass.

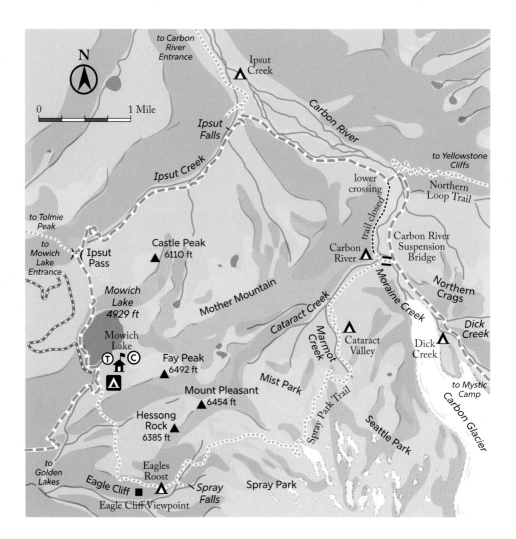

hike the 0.3 mile to the quiet but large (now wilderness) camp. In 2006, floods washed out the access road to this former car campground, which was once filled with vehicles, coolers, and families. The only access from the park's northwest corner now involves a 5-mile walk or bike ride, and the campground has been converted into a wilderness camp. Don't be surprised to see transportation devices of the two-wheeled, pedaled variety tied up to posts and trees. Bicycles are allowed on the former road to the campground, to allow day hikers and campers to approach the trail faster. They are, however, prohibited on trails. There is no potable water at Ipsut Creek Camp, but the lush and somewhat hidden Ipsut Falls is a clear and lovely place to gather water; reaching it requires a short backtrack from where you came. The toilets, picnic tables, and sheer size of the place give nods to yesteryear's busy car campground; now it's peaceful and quiet.

The Wonderland Trail jogs right at the intersection with the trail to Ipsut Creek Campground and continues southeast up the Carbon River valley. Flooding in this area has plagued the park for years. Repairs to the Wonderland Trail are seasonal necessities, as the Carbon River continues to erode its banks each fall and winter. Nearly every year, the Wonderland Trail is in a different place than the last. Whenever you are crossing big riverbeds, where routefinding is tough, look for pink or yellow flagging tape tied to trees, wooden posts, or rock cairns to help you get through the mess. During the 2006 floods, the trail in this section was annihilated, and a detour, which over all these years has sort of *become* the Wonderland, is in place.

Follow the Wonderland Trail 1.7 miles to a junction with a lower crossing of the Carbon River to your left. Cross the river here and follow a section of the Northern Loop Trail for 1.1 miles until you arrive at the Carbon River Suspension Bridge. You don't need to cross the suspension bridge

Picnic tables are a novelty near quiet Ipsut Creek Campground.

unless you're staying at the Carbon River Camp—or if you choose to do so just for fun.

Retired park trails foreman Carl Fabiani headed up the construction of the Carbon River Suspension Bridge in 1984. Before that, a wobbly, Indiana Jones–style bridge graced this crossing, and each fall it had to be partially disassembled because it could not support the snow load. Fabiani and his trail crews were tasked with building the current suspension bridge during the summer of 1984. Parts and pieces of the bridge were flown into the construction site, and Fabiani and his teams consulted the blueprint, attempting to figure out how to assemble it—a serious challenge, no doubt! A hanging seat, also known as a bosun chair, was rigged to a pulley on a high wire strung across the valley. From there, a lucky crew member was strapped into the chair and sent out to attach the suspender cables to the main cables of the bridge. I imagine there was some adrenaline involved.

On the day the 205-foot-long bridge officially opened to hikers, a champagne toast took place at the site. To this day, the bridge is quite an attraction. Before the bridge was built, day hikers would frequently ask Fabiani how far it was to the Carbon Glacier. After construction, the question morphed into, "How far is it to the suspension bridge?" Despite the massive stirring of ice and snow that makes up the Carbon Glacier, the bridge crossing is every bit as exciting and awe-inspiring for hikers.

Once you're past the bridge, in front of you is the Carbon Glacier, the lowest-elevation glacier in the contiguous United States. If you haven't seen a glacier up close before, you might be really surprised to see that it's not brilliant white but rather a moving brown and

A hiker with a tiny pack cruises across the Carbon River suspension bridge.

FAY FULLER: A GAL WITH MOXIE

In 1887, the world was an interesting place. The Statue of Liberty had been dedicated in New York Harbor the previous fall, Coca-Cola had just been conceived by a pharmacist from Atlanta, and the ballpoint pen had not been invented yet. Grover Cleveland was president, Anne Sullivan had just begun teaching Helen Keller, and the first official Groundhog Day was celebrated. Things were changing rapidly in the United States, but the sweet spots for women's liberation were far off. It would be another thirty years before women received the right to vote or were elected to the US Senate, and just shy of a hundred years before the first female Supreme Court justice was sworn into office. Yet that same year, a seventeen-year-old girl saw Mount Rainier for the first time and decided she wanted to climb it. It wouldn't be easy to convince the powers that be that she was capable, but she was determined.

Three years later, twenty-year-old Fay Fuller, now a teacher and journalist living in Yelm, Washington, was granted permission to join a climbing party. On August 9, 1890, Fuller donned her climbing getup, which consisted of thick flannel underwear, a heavy flannel bloomer suit (immodest at the time), a straw hat, woolen hose, and heavy calfskin boys' shoes with caulks (sharp spikes) on the soles. She painted her face with charcoal and strapped on a pair of goggles to deter the sun. No doubt she looked in a mirror and thought she was foxy.

That day, her climbing party made it to Camp Muir and then, on August 10 at half past four in the morning, they set out for the summit. Strong willed with plenty of moxie and guts, she refused gentle assistance from the men in her group, determined to reach the summit on her own. At 4 PM, they reached the top, and Fay became the first woman in recorded history to successfully stand on Mount Rainier's summit. Because it was late, they spent the night at the summit in an ice cave near the steam vents and descended the following day.

Fay Fuller would continue her work in the outdoor industry as a women's champion and climbing advocate. Her leadership helped create the Washington Alpine Club, as well as the Portland-based Mazamas. She was eighty-eight years old when she passed away in 1958, leaving a legend behind her. Strong, determined, and unphased by societal norms, she persevered in attaining her goals. Imagine what she could have done if she had been alive during the age of energy drinks.

Fay Peak, southeast of Mowich Lake, bears her namesake. Give it a wink when you walk by.

gray mess of ice, snow, rock, and sand around 700 feet deep. As you stand looking for a minute or two, you'll likely hear stones rolling around and falling from the glacier's moraine into the dirty Carbon River below. During the summer, a small cave often forms where the ice melts into the water below. Stay on the trail and do not explore anywhere by the glacier's snout, even though the cave is tempting. Glaciers are unpredictable, the water is swift and bitter cold, and rockfall is always imminent.

The Carbon River presents a challenge for park officials as it constantly changes course. Bridges you cross in any given year may not last through the next winter.

The trail climbs upward, skirting the rocky hill above the Carbon Glacier. If you didn't get your fill of views at the bottom, rest assured they keep getting better. Use caution with your footing and when passing other backpackers and hikers in this area. High above you, the Northern Crags flaunt their strong, granite cliff faces. On warm days, the exposure and rock in this area make for a hot and exhausting climb. Shade can't come fast enough! Erosion from a trail washout years ago may still be evident; the hillside was washed away completely. The new trail crosses a scree slope above the old trail.

A mile after leaving the Carbon River Suspension Bridge, reach Dick Creek Camp, which appears almost out of nowhere. Stop and give accolades to those who were creative enough to design this two-site camp on the somewhat exposed hillside (there is no group site here). A privy and a few level spots with shade make this a good place to stop for a breather or a snack. If you need water, Dick Creek is a grand place to fill up before continuing your climb to Mystic Camp.

Spray Park Trail: The Alternate Route

One-way distance: 8.6 miles (from Mowich Lake, through Spray Park, back to Wonderland)
High point: 6400 feet
Elevation gain/loss: +2140/−3870 feet

JUST 0.3 MILE SOUTH OF Mowich Lake, find the intersection for the Spray Park Trail. The Spray Park and Seattle Park areas are unquestionably some of the most beautiful and unforgettable places in Mount Rainier National Park. You can follow this alternate route in lieu of the Wonderland Trail proper, arriving in the Carbon River valley and reconnecting with the Wonderland Trail at the Carbon River Suspension Bridge.

Follow the Spray Park Trail (see the Mowich Lake to Dick Creek map) under a forested canopy and along a fairly gentle series of ups and downs for about 1.5 miles to an outcropping with a view of Eagle Cliff. The views are somewhat overgrown, but from this angle Rainier shows her *mowich,* or "deer face," and curious hikers may want a look. Use caution with your footing. Eagle Cliff below you was once the site of the North Mowich Glacier Mine, which had small ore cars, a small railroad track, two tunnels, high flumes, water pipes, and heavy machinery. The mine was abandoned in 1908 and the mountain has taken back any evidence of the operation.

In another 0.3 mile, find Eagles Roost Camp on the southern hillside. If Eagles Roost is home for the night, proceed 0.1 mile farther along the main trail to a stream crossing to fill up with water before setting up camp. Eagles Roost is a surprisingly large camp ingeniously located on a crazy-steep hillside deep in the forest. There are seven individual campsites but no group site. If you arrive here and think that all the sites are taken, you might be mistaken. Follow the signs toward the toilet to find another campsite even farther downhill. Going "out" to get water, or hopping back up on the main trail, gives the legs a bonus burn.

Leave Eagles Roost and continue to an intersection with a side trail on the right leading to Spray Falls. Spray Falls is a misty waterfall that tumbles about 400 feet down andesite rock. It's worth a look and is also a nice place for a packs-off break and snack. The side trip out and back adds only 0.5 mile to your day.

On the main trail, start your climb to Spray Park. About 0.5 mile from the Spray Falls trail intersection, the way starts breaking out into meadows and open clearings. This is the start of Spray Park, even though you're still climbing. Views start to take your breath away as you work your way up the erosion-preventing stairs. Wildflowers and subalpine firs make a fine foreground for shutterbugs. Hessong Rock shows up to the northwest, with its rocky, fortresslike crown.

The vista from Eagle Cliff Viewpoint along the Spray Park Trail offers jaw-dropping scenery.

The climb continues, eventually cresting between the boundary of Spray Park and Seattle Park, which is a fuzzy line. A gradual descent leads to some big rocks on which to stretch out and enjoy the view. Marmots also enjoy sunning themselves on these rocks, so keep an eye out when choosing your seat.

While this area looks like a killer place to pitch a tent and spend the night, camping is prohibited. Off-trail travel is discouraged, even though small footpaths run in every direction. The short growing season makes it almost impossible for the trampled vegetation on these little paths to regenerate.

A bit farther on, permanent snowfields abound; use caution when crossing them. Painted rocks, cairns, and snow wands are all common trail markers. As talus and pumice stones take over the trail, the terrain becomes barren but still incredibly scenic. The rocks and stone give way to meadows as you begin your descent into Cataract Valley, and views of Rainier become more distant.

Follow the trail across the appropriately named Marmot Creek. Wildflowers play hopscotch with subalpine firs until the trail ducks back into the woods at roughly 1.5 miles

The setting sun illuminates Mount Rainier while Observation Rock looks over Spray Park's lush meadows.

from the intersection with the Spray Falls spur. At 4.7 miles from the Spray Falls intersection, arrive at heavily forested Cataract Valley Camp. The camp has six individual sites and one group site. There are three water sources; the most reliable is a creek near the center of the camp area.

Cairns near Seattle Park help hikers find their way through snow and talus fields.

Leave Cataract Valley Camp and begin the seemingly long descent of 1.6 miles to the Carbon River below. Arrive at an intersection with the trail to Carbon River Camp. This camp has a rough history of the Carbon River trying to wash it away. The Park Service has rebuilt it nicely, but it still has some evidence of debris and consequently isn't the most beautiful camp in the park. Regardless, it serves you well, offering fresh, flowing water from Cataract Creek, four individual campsites, and one group site. If you aren't staying at Carbon River Camp, you may still want to take the opportunity to fill your water bottles at Cataract Creek, down the spur trail toward the camp. The next reliable opportunity for fresh, flowing water is another 1.2 miles away at Dick Creek Camp.

Ahead of you to the east, look for the Carbon River Suspension Bridge. This bridge is not nearly as tall as the Tahoma Creek Suspension Bridge on the mountain's west side, but it's equally impressive in length. Cross the river on the swaying bridge and arrive at the other side, your feet firmly planted again on the Wonderland Trail.

Dick Creek to Mystic Camp

One-way distance: 3.6 miles
High point: 6000 feet
Elevation gain/loss: +1700/−300 feet

WATER IS PLENTIFUL AT DICK Creek Camp, so feel free to load up if you need more before climbing onward through a forested hillside and a series of long switchbacks. About 1.5 miles after leaving Dick Creek, the trail starts to tease you, breaking out into small meadows with wildflowers and trickling creeks before weaving back into trees, all the while

Splendid Spray Falls is definitely worth the short walk on the spur trail.

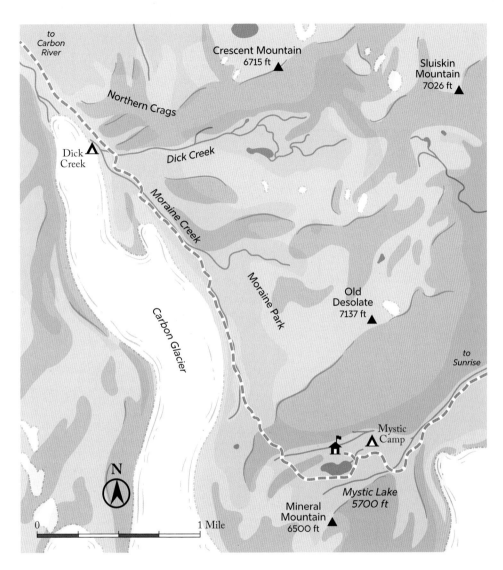

climbing upward. Heather abounds here in the summertime, and wildflowers splendidly decorate the entryway to Moraine Park, which is about 2.5 miles from Dick Creek.

Once you hit a fairly level meadow, you've arrived at Moraine Park. Marmots used to sun themselves on nearly every rock here, but within the past decade, they've moved on. This marmot relocation mystery most likely has to do with these furry creatures adapting to changing landscapes and their need to survive as the climate shifts. But wildflowers still pop in every direction, and nature feels vibrantly alive in this special place. Resist the

Moraine Park provides a relatively flat respite in between climbs.

temptation to walk through meadows to find a rocky perch—there will be plenty of options once you continue uphill, including the crème de la crème of all sitting rocks, a third of the way up on your left (east) as you're climbing Old Desolate's shoulder.

After Moraine Park's somewhat short reprieve from climbing, continue gaining elevation on the shoulder of Old Desolate (to your left). The climb gives way to a saddle and a good, level resting spot. To your right, a boot-beaten trail leads the way to a climbing path up Curtis Ridge. On this same trail, a beautiful tarn only a few hundred yards away makes a great reflection photo if conditions permit. To your left is a scramble up to the top of Old Desolate. This trail is unmarked and may be nearly impossible to find. Don't attempt

Paintbrush offers a brilliant magenta blaze to the meadows between Moraine Park and Mystic Lake.

A spotted sandpiper peeps in an attempt to keep hikers away from its ground nest near Mystic Lake.

to head this way unless you're a skilled mountaineer, as the rock is loose and the climbing steep and hazardous.

Carry on with your journey, following ups and downs through busy, buzzing meadows. Marmots scramble underfoot and butterflies dance in the air. Keep a watchful eye out for bears in this area, as they are known to frequent Mystic Lake in the summer. As the mountain reveals itself from this angle, see if you can spot one of its most popular and hazardous climbing routes: Liberty Ridge. To find it, look center-right of the view.

At 3.6 miles from Dick Creek Camp, arrive at beautiful Mystic Lake and a spur to the patrol cabin. In summer, there's frequently a ranger stationed here, and the patrol cabin has a decent mountain view from its porch. The patrol cabin can be tough to locate—it's farther away from the Wonderland than you'd expect, roughly 0.4 mile down the spur trail. When you hike down the spur, stay right and head away from the lake. The cabin is tucked deep in the woods.

Back on the main trail, find Mystic Camp downhill from the lake. A playful creek runs nearby, providing a fresh, flowing water source. The group site here is one of the best on the Wonderland. You can find it farther along the Wonderland, some distance away from the other camps, at the former location of Mystic's patrol cabin. The group site is private and even has its own privy. In contrast, the individual camp area has one of the worst privies on the trail: it lacks privacy, and on warm days you can find it by following the odor and the hum of bugs. Despite the poor privy, the seven individual campsites are wooded, peaceful,

A frontal system moves in over the peaceful backcountry.

and a short walk away from the water source. What they lack in privacy, they make up for in entertainment. Deer and bear have both come through camp on some of my recent trips—neither was a bother or hazard, just an amazing treat for the eyes. 🐾 On a clear night, backtrack up to the lake and stand or sit on the trail for a great star-gazing spot. Refrain from sitting or walking on foliage near the lake's edge, as the Park Service has worked very hard to recover those fragile areas.

Mystic Lake used to be a hustling and bustling horse camp back in the early 1900s, filled with people making summit bids on the mountain's north side. The meadows around the lake were trampled by feet and hooves and marred by campfires, destroying and polluting this pristine, fragile area. Gone are the days of hubbub and the evidence of meadow damage. The lake was named by two of the mountain's most enthusiastic explorers in the early 1900s. They chose "Mystic" on account of a mysterious, temporary whirlpool seen near the lake's outlet. My guess is the moonshine must have been pretty strong that night (and I don't mean the earth's lunar satellite). A mystic whirlpool has never revealed itself on any of my adventures, though there have been plenty of mosquitoes and amphibians near the water's edge.

Mystic Camp to Sunrise Camp

One-way distance: 8.9 miles
High point: 6700 feet
Elevation gain/loss: +2400/−1900 feet

LEAVE MYSTIC CAMP AND DESCEND past the group site into the forest below. Less than a mile after leaving camp, come to the first water crossing of the West Fork White River. In 2006, this area was destroyed by flooding. Dead trees stand here as if frozen in fear, and volunteers have created a "trail" by using rock borders. Years ago, the washout was so bad that the Wonderland Trail took an unfortunate detour, requiring backpackers to scramble up steep tree roots using both hands and feet for balance. Be grateful for the hours spent repairing this section of trail, and cross your fingers it doesn't wash out again any time soon.

Follow several footbridges over glacial debris, admiring the power of the volcano. Walking through this rocky wasteland, you may feel at times as if you are on the moon. In just under 2 miles, the Winthrop Glacier starts showing its brown, slowly churning face. As you did near the Carbon Glacier, stop, look, and listen. What is technically lifeless is alive with noise, falling rock, and melting ice.

The trail crosses yet another disturbed river valley near the Winthrop Glacier.

Winthrop Glacier was named after the mountain's first known tourist, Theodore Winthrop. In 1852 he traveled with Native people by canoe from Port Townsend to Nisqually; later, he rode his horse north from near the Oregon border, going through the Cascades to visit Mount Rainier. Sadly, he was killed a few years later in a Civil War battle.

When you're done admiring the glacier, cross a swift waterway on a sturdy bridge and take a snack break if you want at the waterfall on the other side. Garda Falls is directly above you, falling 200 to 300 feet; it was named after Garda Fogg, a beautiful, bold, mountaineer from Tacoma who actively participated in adventures with The Mountaineers Club in the early twentieth

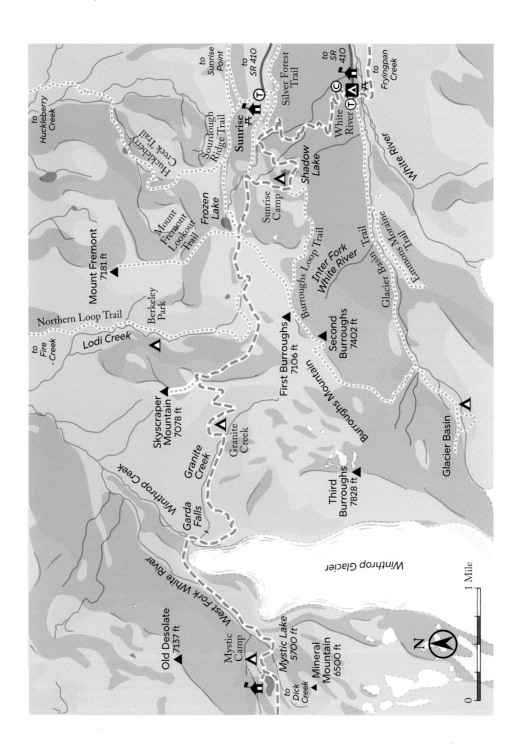

A wet bridge over the churning, milky Winthrop Creek is testament to the water's power.

century. She collected photos and wrote of her outings, including one in July 1919 through Mount Rainier National Park. Known for being independent, Fogg was not one to follow rules and strayed from social norms to exhibit her zest for life. A historical picture of her in 1915 shows her smiling widely with wind blowing through her long, dark hair as she dances beachside in a grass skirt. She lived to the ripe old age of ninety-one, passing away in 1976, proving that the time spent in the mountains keeps you young.

After Garda Falls, the climbing begins again as you head away from Winthrop Glacier. Trees and brush give way to a few last good glacier views. Watch your footing on the loose stones here. Ducking back into the forest, the way turns steep and alternates between dense forest and brushy creeks and marshes as you continue your uphill quest. Cross Granite Creek on a small footbridge and arrive at Granite Creek Camp, 4.6 miles from Mystic Lake.

On a hillside, Granite Creek Camp has three individual campsites and one group site, located across the trail to the north. Granite Creek flows to the west of camp, providing a crystal-clear, year-round water source. If you camp here and still feel like you have some gumption, take a sunset hike up Skyscraper Mountain (see Blue Ribbon Area sidebar).

From Granite Creek Camp, make your way through woods and then meadows as you head to the ridgeline 1.3 miles above camp, known as Skyscraper Pass. Once there, enjoy the spectacular views all around you. It's here that you might be inspired to summit Skyscraper Mountain, north of the trail. Around the corner, the trail continues through a giant, deceiving cirque—it seems much shorter than it really is! The park concessions and gift shop are now roughly 3 miles away.

Continue hiking along gentle, rolling ups and downs to a junction 1.2 miles from the ridgeline. A trail leads left (north) to the Berkeley Park area and the Northern Loop Trail. Make a mental note to come back and do the Northern Loop, as it has much to offer (see The Northern Loop in chapter 8 for details). For now, stay on the Wonderland. Climb a bit and in 0.8 mile arrive at a junction with the Mount Fremont Lookout Trail and the Burroughs Loop Trail; from this junction, you have the option of either going toward Frozen Lake and Sunrise or staying on the Wonderland toward Sunrise Camp.

Things get interesting here. First, remember that Sunrise Camp and Sunrise are two different things: Sunrise Camp is the wilderness camp for the Wonderland Trail, while Sunrise is the visitor center and concessions area. Sunrise Camp is about 1.5 miles from Sunrise concessionaires. If your goal is to stay the night at Sunrise Camp (or to avoid the concessions area), continue on the Wonderland, following signs toward Sunrise Camp and the Wonderland Trail. If you want to head to the snack bar for ice cream or hot dogs, follow

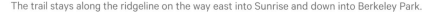

The trail stays along the ridgeline on the way east into Sunrise and down into Berkeley Park.

BLUE RIBBON AREA: SKYSCRAPER MOUNTAIN

If you're camped at Granite Creek, you might want to hit the gorgeous sunset views of Skyscraper Mountain, but you can also summit this peak when the Wonderland guides you by this spot. Located 1.3 miles east of Granite Creek Camp and roughly 3 miles west of Sunrise Camp, the boot-beaten, unofficial path to Skyscraper Mountain takes off from subalpine landscape and is easy to see and follow.

When you arrive at a relatively level ridgeline area known as Skyscraper Pass, head north on the obvious, rocky and loose dirt trail as it zigzags up to the top. From the pass, this peak looks steeper and more difficult to climb than it really is—you'll be amazed when, in just shy of 0.5 mile and only 400 feet of elevation gain, you find yourself standing on the summit. Still have doubts? Watch other people climb up and see how quickly it goes for them.

From the summit, you have views of the vast Grand Park to the trail's north, along with the West Fork White River purring along in the valley below you. Mount Fremont stands to the east, with Berkeley Park's emerald vegetation and trickling waterways tucked into the neighboring basin. Peaks all around you beckon to be identified, such as Sluiskin, Redstone, and Old Desolate. Behind you to the southwest, Mount Rainier looms so large that you feel like you can reach out and touch the glaciers. You may even witness (or at least hear) rockfall and avalanches on a warm summer day.

The wildlife in this area is fun to find. Near Skyscraper Pass, look for marmots posing shamelessly for cameras as they watch the hikers go by. Bears often roam the hills deep down in Berkeley Park; you can sometimes spot them with the naked eye, using binoculars or a zoom on a camera to confirm the sighting. 🐾 A band of mountain goats frequently roams the hills adjacent to Mount Fremont—they appear like white dots from this perch. Chipmunks scamper around the summit, their sweet, striped faces hunting for leftover crumbs. All of it makes for a perfect Wonderland bonus trip.

You'll want to stay all day, but sooner or later the pointy rocks at the top will start to hurt your rear and you'll decide you'd better head back down. Thankfully, the downhill goes quickly too.

Hiker Joe enjoys the views of Mount Rainier from near the summit of Skyscraper Mountain.

A small bear crosses the trail near Sunrise Camp.

the signs toward Frozen Lake, Sourdough Ridge, and Sunrise. Trails lead in every direction here and the signs can be confusing.

Because Sunrise Camp is about 1.5 miles from Sunrise, you may want to set up camp first before heading to the snack bar. All concessions, and the ranger station, have limited hours that vary by season. Sunrise has a nice bathroom with running water—head here for a refreshing face splash—and the exhibits at the visitor center are also worth a look. Ditch your trash here in the frontcountry or wait until you arrive at the White River Campground—both places have bear-resistant trash cans. The mountain views are spectacular and get even better as you continue toward Summerland and Indian Bar. Sunrise boasts views of the Tatoosh Range to the south, and you may even glimpse Mount Adams, the second-highest volcano in the state. The peak on Rainier's southern shoulder is Little Tahoma, a volcanic remnant popular among climbers. If it were freestanding, it would be the third-highest peak in the state.

Whichever way you go—Sunrise or Sunrise Camp—the area is sure to be filled with fresh-smelling day hikers, laughing children, loud voices, and the noise of cars coming and going. It may take some time for your senses to readjust to the sights and sounds of civilization. Sunrise offers no hotels or motels, so the visitors usually disappear at sundown.

Sunrise Camp, 1 mile from the Fremont and Burroughs trail junction, is a big camp in the woods; because it's high in elevation, it can be very cold and windy, even in the heart of summer. It hosts eight individual campsites and two large group sites, all of which have a decent amount of privacy. The water source is the outlet of Shadow Lake, 0.5 mile along the Wonderland Trail toward White River Campground. The Sunrise Camp privy is an actual outhouse that gets used constantly, what with all the day hikers and backpackers. This camp's proximity to the parking lot makes it a fantastic first-time backcountry destination for kiddos. If you find you've camped next door to a crying baby, do your best to have patience and understand that everyone has to start camping somewhere.

When I recently hiked the Wonderland again, I chatted trailside with a reader named Joe who suggested I include his favorite dinner and breakfast spot in this book—a lovely idea! If you are staying at Sunrise Camp and want a superb mountain view, a change of

Marmots share inside jokes as they watch hikers from their rocky perch near Sunrise.

scenery, and usually few people if you time it right, head west (toward the mountain) on Burroughs Loop Trail. With your food and camera in tow, grunt a little as it climbs 185 feet in under 0.3 mile to an observation pullout surrounded by a protective, hip-high stone wall. The area beneath you includes the White River, Glacier Basin, and the Emmons Glacier. You will also see a gorgeous, turquoise-colored lake formed by glacial silt and debris. Emmons Glacier and Camp Schurman is one of the most popular routes to the summit, and if you stay until it's dark, you may be able to see the long row of headlamps wiggling as they make their way to the top. Thanks, Joe!

From the visitor center at Sunrise, it can be tricky to find the Wonderland Trail again. Head across the parking lot to the south and find the Silver Forest Trail or Emmons Vista. Once there, head west and you'll be back on the Wonderland in 0.5 mile.

It's hard to imagine the pristine meadows around Sunrise filled with two hundred or more canvas tents, along with horses and people everywhere—but that's exactly what it looked like in the 1930s when the Civilian Conservation Corps camped here to build roads, bridges, patrol cabins, and fire lookouts. Tourist dollars were on everyone's mind back then: some people even suggested that a golf course be installed in these meadows. In 1931, Sunrise Lodge was built; there were intentions of eventually constructing a bigger hotel, but it never came about.

Long before it was known as Sunrise, this place was called Yakima Park, or Me-yah-ah Pah, a name bestowed by the Yakima tribe meaning "place of the chief." Native people held horse races in these meadows and had an old-fashioned Olympics of sorts, where warriors exhibited their skills in all kinds of games, such as spear tosses and foot races. The meadows were also used for picking berries, hunting, and tribal dances and celebrations. These days, meadow preservation for the short growing season is in full swing. Park staffers are stationed around the meadows on weekends to remind folks to stay on trails, and a junior ranger program teaches children about the ecosystem.

CHAPTER 6

THE EAST SIDE: SUNRISE CAMP TO NICKEL CREEK

The east side of Mount Rainier is the mountain's most popular—and for good reason. Few places on Earth are more beautiful or more majestic. High cliffs graced with waterfalls reach down to lush, green meadows filled with flowers, while the mountain herself stands proudly in the background. This 21.4-mile section is also where you'll climb to the highest point on the Wonderland Trail: Panhandle Gap at 6800 feet. To soak it all in, heed my mantra of "Don't rush and take plenty of time"—it's especially true for this section.

The mountain gets more and more majestic as you climb toward Summerland.

Sunrise Camp to Summerland

One-way distance: 10.3 miles
High point: 6200 feet
Elevation gain/loss: +2100/–2400 feet

FROM SUNRISE CAMP, HEAD EAST and in less than half a mile pass Shadow Lake. The lake outlet serves as the water source for the camp and is a good place to stop and fill up for the day; water is seasonal farther along this section of trail. In 0.8 mile from camp, arrive at a junction. The Wonderland Trail makes a hard right-hand turn and heads south. Give your knees a pep talk and descend nearly 2000 feet in just 2.6 miles to the White River Campground. If you have a food or fuel cache here, follow the main campground road to the left approximately 400 feet to the ranger station.

The White River Campground is the only frontcountry car campground that the Wonderland Trail goes directly through. It's a lovely camp in a large forest, with 88 campsites, water for washing dishes, flush toilets, fire grates, and the permanent white noise of the appropriately named White River to lull you to sleep. Cars come and go, with families

Lousewort and bistort blanket the meadow near Summerland.

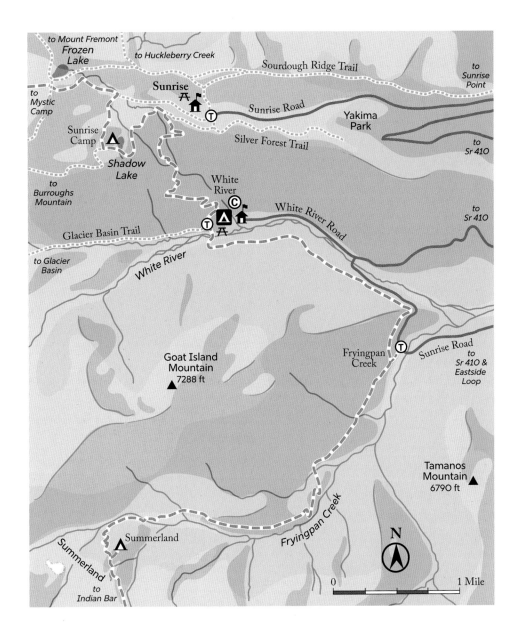

pulling food from coolers, while the trees offer some privacy. Wonderland Trail hikers are permitted to use the campground as one of their wilderness camps, free of charge. But as with all wilderness camps, it must be listed on your permit and arranged in advance. There are four campsites reserved for thru-hikers near the Wonderland Trail in a quiet area behind a historical patrol cabin. Wilderness camping rules apply, and fires are prohibited in those sites.

When you're ready to hop back on the Wonderland, walk across the road to a parking lot and the well-hidden continuation of the trail. This is also the parking lot for the Glacier Basin Trail, which leads to the second-most-popular climbing route on the mountain: the Emmons Glacier. Wish the climbers well and pop into the trees.

Cross the swift, glacial waters of the White River and pause to check out the graveyard of stone in every direction, by now a familiar river-crossing sight. Duck back into the forest and play teeter-totter with the trail, moving gently up and then gently back down, for 2.6 miles until you reach an intersection with the Fryingpan Creek Trail. This spur leads left a short ways to the Fryingpan Creek trailhead.

Continue south in an ancient forest—the smooth grade will make you wish your hiking boots were rollerblades. Gradual elevation gain takes you up the valley along the steep gorge of Fryingpan Creek. The trail flirts with this creek three times, each with a unique view of the valley and steep Tamanos Mountain above. An avalanche chute gives way to open meadows and brushy hillsides at the base of Goat Island Mountain. This area is well known for bears, and evidence of them is occasionally scattered on the trail. 🐾 Little Tahoma and Rainier's summit come into view as you make your way up along the trail. Cross a "thankful-it's-there" log bridge over a swift creek and climb a few more steep switchbacks. Soon afterward, Summerland appears so suddenly that it almost startles you.

A red-breasted nuthatch scours a snag for lunch.

Summerland is named by Major Edward S. Ingraham in 1888 for its amazing summer flower meadows. It has been a favorite place of natural beauty for many, many people for years, so pack your patience on a busy summer weekend and resist the impulse to throw trail elbows. Plan to stay at Summerland during the week, if possible, for a better shot at solitude. Throngs of day hikers flock to this area for its magnificent views. The meadow to your right (southwest) makes a fine foreground for Little Tahoma and the Fryingpan Glacier. Panhandle Gap is in the distance to the south, 1.4 trail miles away, while Emmons Glacier is up close and personal, slightly to the north. If you're lucky

Summerland was named for its wildflower bounty in summer, but its colors in fall are also quite lovely.

enough to camp at Summerland (and able to wake up in the middle of the night), try getting up around 2 AM to watch the parade of climbers' headlamps heading skyward. In good weather, the moon and stars also put on a show, as very little city light reaches into the vast wilderness. You may be dragging a little the next day, but your nighttime nature rendezvous will be a treasured memory.

Summerland has five individual campsites, and a beautiful stone shelter built by the Civilian Conservation Corps in the 1930s, which serves as the group site. The composting toilet here is perched up high like a true throne and is mostly odor-free. You can find camp water by continuing south on the trail to a small meadow and a branch of Fryingpan Creek. A ranger is often stationed at this camp during busy months to sort out permit details and remind day hikers to stay on trails.

Because of the high number of visitors who can't resist the temptation to feed small creatures—such as Townsend's chipmunks and golden-mantled ground squirrels—they are

South of Summerland, the landscape transforms abruptly from subalpine to alpine.

bold and can be aggressive. Don't let these shameless flirts entice you into giving them a nut from your gorp—they need to learn to forage! They've been known to leave "presents" behind once they've ransacked your tent in an effort to find a crumb. Keep your tent zipped up, your food stored properly, and your pack pockets wide open to keep them from chewing holes in your pockets.

Some of the most magnificent marmots on the trail are also found at Summerland. Some frolic and chase each other, while others are mellow and lazy, sunning themselves on rocks or nibbling on flowers in the open meadows. In early season, Summerland is a great place for spotting baby marmots who are learning the ropes from Mom.

Panhandle Gap is home to mountain goats. With a keen eye, you can often see them from camp as they wander in the snow patches and granite above you. Bears are also frequent visitors to Summerland, but the Park Service has done a great job of managing them, so they rarely come into camp. As you watch the sunset in the evenings, scan the hillsides in all directions for bears enjoying summer greens.

Summerland to Indian Bar

One-way distance: 4.4 miles
High point: 6800 feet
Elevation gain/loss: +900/−1800 feet

THE STRETCH FROM SUMMERLAND TO Indian Bar presents beauty and challenge. You'll climb above tree line, quickly trading lush green for stone, snow, and rock cairns. Permanent snowfields linger all year, and at times you'll feel as if you're nearing the summit of Rainier. Panhandle Gap is a chameleon, changing dramatically from week to week, month to month, and year to year; the trail can be rocky with a few snowy patches or completely covered with snow.

On one of my first Wonderland trips, my hiking partner and I encountered a man who told us a goosebump-inducing story of his handshake with death as he slid down a waterfall at Panhandle Gap. After that, we were terrified to cross the Panhandle—but when we did, we were remarkably surprised at how straightforward and soft the snow was. A different year, the story came back to haunt us as we cautiously placed our feet in icy bootprints to

Looking back toward Summerland from Panhandle Gap during a low snow year

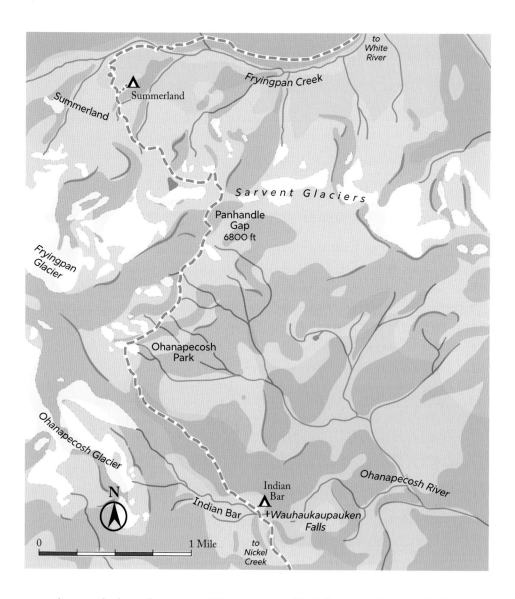

gingerly cross the hazardous slope. Other years, we dillydallied over the snowfields, taking pictures and looking for goats, with danger a million miles from our thoughts.

The fact remains that Panhandle Gap has the potential to be one of your greatest hazards on the Wonderland Trail. If possible, avoid crossing it in early morning or late evening, as snow can turn icy during those times. Do not cross Panhandle Gap in bad weather or if visibility is poor. Losing the trail or slipping can have dire consequences. Past the Panhandle,

Wildflowers add inviting colors to the edge of the trail between Summerland and Indian Bar.

Bands of mountain goats are often visible trailside near Panhandle Gap.

the trail continues to cross patches of snow. You won't be done with your slippery journey entirely until you start your descent to Indian Bar.

Despite the hazards the Panhandle presents, it's also one of the most scenic and spectacular areas in the park. Waterfalls abound on large cliffs, mountain goats graze in open meadows, and marmots scamper, ducking in and out of tunnels. Use caution and common sense and you'll arrive safely at Indian Bar with amazing photos and memories.

As you leave Summerland, you'll cross several small tributaries of Fryingpan Creek and ascend erosion-preventing stairs. Watch for curious marmots! This is their prime habitat, and you'll feel an adrenaline rush if one of the little rascals darts unexpectedly in front of your boots. One year I was taking photos of a mother marmot and her baby when the trusting mother ran off, leaving her toddler in my care. The little one quickly befriended me and tried to crawl up to investigate my camera. Marmots are very friendly in this area! Their long claws should help you remember that the animals are wild and should be treated as such. 🐾

A few switchbacks lead you away from the meadows and higher into subalpine terrain. Look back and say goodbye to Summerland in the distance, as before long it won't be visible. Log footbridges abound, seeming out of place among the granite slabs. Numerous trail markers corral you in the right direction if you wander off—look for brightly painted rocks, rock cairns, and snow wands. The trail and trail markers change as the season progresses. The Park Service works hard to find the safest route over the Panhandle, so keep a close eye out for the most recent markers, which will look freshly placed. Don't follow footprints on snow if it's not safe to do so.

The trail crosses through the Sarvent Glaciers, dotting both sides of the trail, and Fryingpan Glacier is high above you on the flanks of Rainier. Seasonally, a nameless lake filled with radiant, turquoise-colored glacier runoff is present on the west side of the trail. Stop and take a few pictures here, but save some shots for higher up, as the water shines like a blue diamond when you start to climb.

Keep climbing through snow patches, using caution as you traverse to the top. You're almost to Panhandle Gap! One final traverse puts you squarely on top, just 1.4 miles from Summerland. Take a break and grab a snack as a reward. You are not done climbing and crossing snow patches, so grab some gumption, too, and then continue. This is mountain-goat country, and it's not uncommon to see bands of twenty or thirty goats at a time. 🐾

Gently descend to more snow crossings, watching for snow wands and trail markers. Play leapfrog with snow patches and rocks until the tundra gives way to heather and grasses. Large cliffs and their trickling waterfalls begin to appear in the distance. The beauty of this place is mind-blowing—you might want your hiking partner to pinch you to make sure you aren't dreaming. Begin a gentle descent with rolling meadows as you leave the snow behind. Bears frequent this area, as well as the meadows, trees, and hillsides around Indian Bar.

Indian Bar was named by a park superintendent in 1929, in an homage to the sandbar where Native Americans frequently camped while hunting in this region of the park. Although tossing back a cold one might sound good, regrettably there is no place on the Wonderland where you can actually belly up to a full-service "bar."

COUNTERCLOCKWISE TIP

Hiking counterclockwise along the Wonderland, the hill from Indian Bar to Panhandle Gap is a decent climb with a lot of trail stairs, which makes it feel longer than it really is. Take your time and enjoy the scenery as you climb into the subalpine terrain. After Panhandle Gap, you'll be going downhill across permanent snowfields, which can be icy in the early morning and late afternoon. Use extra caution, ensure your steps are sound, and use trekking poles if you brought them.

The final descent to Indian Bar is on an impressive "staircase" built by the Park Service to prevent erosion on this steep hillside. Be kind to your knees by stopping frequently for breaks. Keep your eyes open for the Indian Bar Shelter down in the valley below, next to the large sandbar. Gradually make your way to the end of the staircase and cross a large wildflower meadow. Resist the urge to break out spinning while singing the opening song from *The Sound of Music*.

This area is the headwaters for the Ohanapecosh River, which filters underground from the Ohanapecosh Glacier and snowmelt above you. The meaning of the word Ohanapecosh has been disputed. Most people agree that it's a Native American term, but whether it means "standing on the lip of a rock," "looking down on something wonderful," or "clear stream, deep blue, and/or deep blue holes" is anyone's guess. Each translation makes sense, but the last one particularly rings true, as the water here is as cold, clear, and pristine as anywhere on Earth.

Morning light bathes the shadowed Indian Bar basin as the day wakes up.

The wilderness camp at Indian Bar is one of the most beautiful in the country; find it just after the meadow on a hillside to the east. It has four individual campsites and one group site (the shelter) located across the river. All four of the campsites are good, but some (such as site 2) have great views of the meadow below and the glaciers above. If you're lucky, you'll catch an evening parade of elk, deer, or bear in the meadow. The bridge across the river leads you over a beautiful waterfall with a tongue-twisting name: Wauhaukaupauken (wow-how-cow-pow-ken) Falls.

The Indian Bar Shelter across the river serves as the group site. Those lucky enough to stay here will find ample room for several tents in front of the building. This rustic old shelter was built by the Civilian Conservation Corps in the 1940s and features a fireplace and sleeping platforms suspended by aging, rusted chains. The nonfunctioning fireplace is filled

Waterfalls flowing over steep cliffs serve as the headwaters of the Ohanapecosh River near Indian Bar.

Built in the 1940s, the Indian Bar group shelter sits in a spectacular meadow.

with stone for ambiance and safety. The sleeping platforms are still functional—but use them at your own risk. Mr. and Mrs. Snugglemouse have set up a household with a large family under the shelter and might be happy to find some warmth near your toes.

Be sure to check out the toilet perched high up on the hillside behind the shelter, which is the best view from a privy on the whole Wonderland Trail—perhaps the best in the whole state. Don't wait until nature's call is a scream before you set out to use it though. The walk is enough to make your calves, lungs, and bladder peeved.

Indian Bar to Nickel Creek

One-way distance: 6.7 miles
High point: 5930 feet
Elevation gain/loss: +930/−2530 feet

LEAVE INDIAN BAR AND IMMEDIATELY start your ascent toward the Cowlitz Divide. Be prepared for more eye-popping scenery as you climb up and out of the Indian Bar valley and into

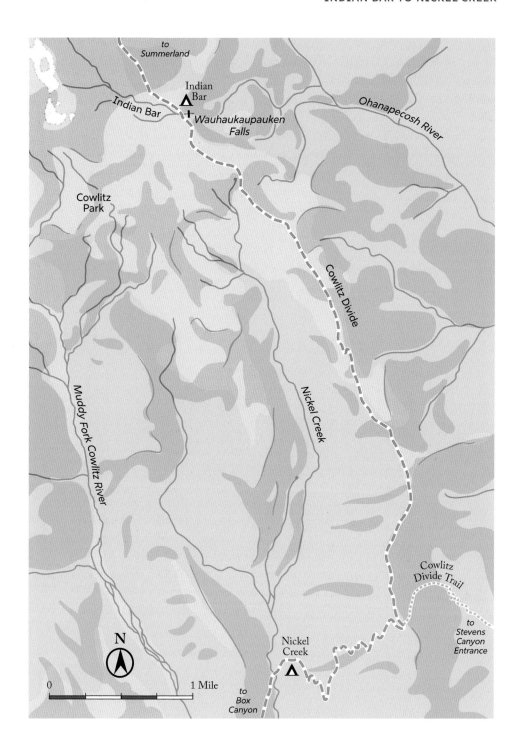

to
Summerland

Indian
Bar

Indian Bar

Wauhaukaupauken
Falls

Ohanapecosh River

Cowlitz
Park

Cowlitz Divide

Muddy Fork Cowlitz River

Nickel Creek

Cowlitz
Divide Trail

to
Stevens
Canyon
Entrance

N

Nickel
Creek

to
Box
Canyon

0   1 Mile

the surrounding hills. Keep your eyes out for bears and stop often to let the view permeate your spirit.  Glance back to watch the Indian Bar Shelter fade out of sight. Fragile meadows filled with wildflowers are in every direction as you climb, climb, climb. Behind you, Little Tahoma pops up into the sky and the Rainier summit comes back into view.

At 1.9 miles from Indian Bar, views continue to increase as you wander through a fairly level meadow. This meadow, at 5930 feet, is the stuff of postcards when it's in bloom. Flowers abound in every direction, the mountain stands strong and clear in the background, and the hum of bugs makes up the soundtrack. To the south stand the jagged teeth of the Tatoosh Range and, farther beyond, the Mount Adams and Mount Saint Helens volcanoes are visible.

A few ups and downs play tag through the next few meadows, until the downs finally win and you abruptly start to descend along the spine of the ridgeline. Berries tempt you in

Backpackers make their way high above the Indian Bar valley.

BLUE RIBBON AREA: COWLITZ DIVIDE

When people ask me about my favorite spot on the Wonderland Trail, the Cowlitz Divide is right up there, if not first in line. Located 1.9 miles south of Indian Bar and 2 miles north of Nickel Creek Camp, a fairly level meadow replete with rainbows of wildflowers and purr-worthy views sits at roughly 5960 feet. It's the place I visit repeatedly in my mind whenever I have to endure painful dental work or someone cuts me off in traffic.

To the west, Mount Rainier looms large, with Little Tahoma—a volcanic remnant eroded away from Rainier's flanks—front and center. The headwaters of both the Ohanapecosh River and Nickel Creek are visible from this area, as are verdant meadows tucked high up on hillsides, good for the occasional bear or mountain goat sighting. Lupine, beargrass, arnica, lousewort, bistort, Sitka valerian, and other wildflowers scent the breeze and attract a soundtrack of pollinating insects. There is no shortage of soul food, and magic seeps in through your pores. It truly is one of the most beautiful places on the Wonderland Trail—enjoy every minute when you get there.

Mount Rainier hides behind puffs of clouds near the Cowlitz Divide.

The setting sun shines brightly near Indian Bar.

the sunny areas. Enter the forest and before long come to a junction with the Cowlitz Divide Trail to the east, 4.7 miles from Indian Bar.

Continue on the Wonderland under dense forest canopy with the familiar sight of Oregon grape, vanilla leaf, and ferns at your feet. Switchback a fairly steep and seemingly endless descent to arrive at Nickel Creek, 2 miles from the Cowlitz Divide Trail junction (and 4.8 miles from the fairly level meadow at the top of the Cowlitz Divide).

If you're using an older map, you might find that Nickel Creek Camp has moved slightly to the north from the old location. Be grateful, as the old camp was directly beside the trail and had little privacy. The new, forested camp has three individual campsites and one very large group site. Water for Nickel Creek Camp is plentiful year-round but requires a 0.2-mile walk farther along the Wonderland to a crossing of Nickel Creek.

COUNTERCLOCKWISE TIP

Gaining the Cowlitz Divide from Nickel Creek involves an elevation gain of over 2500 feet. The climb starts off moderately, in the trees, but because the scenery doesn't change much, it can feel a bit grueling. At 2 miles, arrive at a junction with the Cowlitz Divide Trail, a good place for a much-needed break and/or snack. From here, the Wonderland continues climbing and gains the ridgeline. The path is fairly steep and direct at times, but views start to change, foreshadowing things to come. Pass meadows dotted with trees as the way rolls up and down for a bit before you make your final push to the top, at 5930 feet. The meadow here is spectacular when in bloom and features eye-popping Rainier views. From here, gently drop into the Indian Bar area roughly 1000 feet below you.

CHAPTER 7

THE SOUTH SIDE: NICKEL CREEK TO LONGMIRE

If your itinerary takes you to the south side of the mountain last, you'll probably be less impressed than you were in other sections of the Wonderland. The views from the other sides of Rainier are superior in many ways to those the south side has to offer. But what the south side lacks in views, it makes up for in water features. Waterfalls abound along the 13.3 miles from Nickel Creek Camp to Longmire, as do clear streams and riparian forests. If you're experiencing this area as your first taste of the Wonderland, it's a fine appetizer for the main course!

An abundance of vanilla leaf hugs some forested
stretches of the Wonderland Trail.

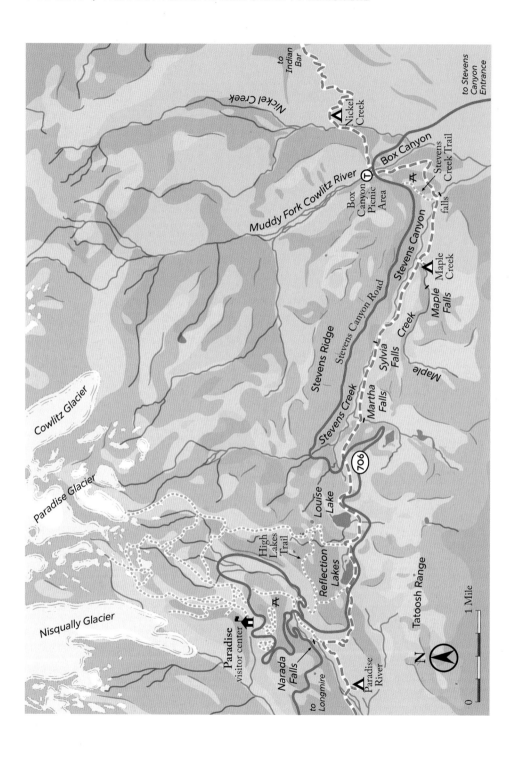

Nickel Creek to Paradise River

One-way distance: 9.5 miles
High point: 4850 feet
Elevation gain/loss: +2250/–1850 feet

LEAVE NICKEL CREEK CAMP AND head downhill on a gentle grade through lowland forest. In 0.8 mile, arrive at the Box Canyon area and Stevens Canyon Road. Box Canyon attracts a fair number of visitors, including car-traveling sightseers. Port-a-potties are the only restrooms; the permanent ones have been closed for a few years. Hopefully they will reopen before your visit, but if not, you can cross the road to use the facilities.

The Wonderland Trail continues on the north side of Stevens Canyon Road, not far from where it just spit you out. Cross over the pedestrian bridge at Box Canyon and feast your eyes on the deep slot, carved over eons by the milky waters of the rowdy Muddy Fork Cowlitz River far below. Named Box Canyon for its shape, the whole canyon forms a narrow, rectangular box that's 25 to 40 feet wide, 180 feet deep, and 0.25 mile long.

Stevens Creek, where warm pine meets playful water, is magical.

BLUE RIBBON AREA: MARTHA FALLS

If this is your last hurrah with the Wonderland Trail, you might be only marginally impressed because you've seen so much incredible beauty, but Martha Falls deserves more than just a passing nod.

Its entire height is a magnificent 670 feet, though you'd need to be in a helicopter or airplane to see it all. Near the Wonderland, it cascades down a series of tiers that range from 35 to 50 feet, sliding and shimmering until it eventually drops again. This time, it crosses the Wonderland and free-falls near Stevens Creek, dropping over 120 feet. Ferns and tall evergreens edge the cascading whitewater with emerald hues. Since the Wonderland Trail crosses near one of its plunge pools, you can snap a memorable photo of you and your hiking buddies as you stand on the banks with the falls behind you.

And remember that guy James Longmire (see "Who Was This Longmire Dude, Anyway?" sidebar in chapter 3) who built the Longmire Springs Hotel and today still has a park area named after him? Remember how he had a son named Elcaine? Well, Martha was Elcaine's wife (James Longmire's daughter-in-law for those with trail brain). One of their sons, Ben, named the falls after his mother.

Martha was born in April 1850 and died in 1932, just before her eighty-second birthday. She married Elcaine at age sixteen and had her first baby at seventeen; their last child was born

when she was forty-two. Park historical photos show Martha wearing ankle-length dark dresses, often with ruching or adornment across the bodice and a belt at her waistline. Her hair was parted in the middle and pulled back into a bun on the top of her head. With twelve children, it's a wonder she even had time to get dressed at all.

Elcaine was all beard up to his temples, save for a nose and some eyes peeking out behind the wiry hairs. Together they were part of park history. It's fun to let your mind wander back in time and to imagine that at some point, they probably stood in the same spot you're standing in now.

Fun fact: One of Elcaine and Martha's youngest kids, Martha (her mother's namesake), lived to be 107 years old, passing away in 1999. The Longmire family still has grandkids, great-grandkids, and the like living in the Puget Sound region, although today, they wear much more practical outfits.

Martha Falls drops right next to the Wonderland.

Follow the signs toward Maple Creek camp in a forested valley.

After the Box Canyon bridge, the Wonderland Trail begins to lose elevation slightly while paralleling the Muddy Fork Cowlitz River. In 1.5 miles from the bridge, the trail reaches a junction on your right with the Stevens Creek Trail, which leads back to Stevens Canyon Road (and to the Box Canyon picnic area). From the junction, begin your official westward march toward Longmire.

Cross Stevens Creek over a sturdy bridge downstream of an unnamed waterfall rushing below you. The brushy river plants and gentle walking are a change of scenery and pace from the Wonderland's dramatic subalpine zones. In 0.8 mile from the unnamed waterfall, reach Maple Creek Camp, which sits on the south side of the trail. Maple Creek Camp has four individual campsites, one group site, and a composting toilet. It's a nice lowland river camp but can be buggy in high season.

From the camp, begin a gradual ascent of the valley floor, following Stevens Creek. Cross several footbridges and listen for the rushing waters of Sylvia Falls on the north side of the

This sketchy section of trail in Stevens Canyon will have you walking gingerly.

trail, a few footsteps off the Wonderland. This picturesque waterfall sits deep in the trees, framed by mossy forest. Use caution as you take photos, as it's easy to get carried away and get too close to the hillside's edge.

After Sylvia Falls, the trail begins climbing more steeply, and Stevens Canyon Road is visible across the valley. In a short distance, arrive at a sketchy trail section, a casualty of landslides produced by the floods of 2006. This section of trail had plagued the Park Service for years, but the 2006 event closed it completely for a while.

The mastermind of the current solution was former trail foreman Carl Fabiani, who crawled all over this area after the floods, looking up and down for a way to reroute the Wonderland after it was destroyed. A proposed alternative route would have added an extra mile to this section. Since the landslide that obliterated the trail was only approximately 100 yards across, an extra mile was not a good solution. Fabiani directed his crew of volunteers and Park Service employees to cut what he hoped would become a permanent trail into the side of the hill. Sadly, this section of trail has become more hazardous with each passing year. Rumor has it that this stretch will be rerouted soon, which may add some distance and elevation. In the meantime, use extra care when navigating the precarious dirt and pebbles.

In just shy of 2 miles from Maple Creek Camp, cross beneath Martha Falls on a log bridge and ascend a nicely constructed trail staircase.

Continue climbing, and at 2.6 miles from Maple Creek, arrive at a crossing of Stevens Canyon Road. After you cross the road, continue climbing another 0.7 mile until you reach the first and largest of the Reflection Lakes: Louise Lake. You are only a few feet from the road, and civilization isn't far off.

In another 0.6 mile, reach a junction with the High Lakes Trail, only steps from the road. Follow the Wonderland up to the roadway and the sound of motors; this is the only section of the Wonderland Trail where you must walk on the road's shoulder. Duck onto the walking path along Reflection Lakes, an area usually teeming with visitors snapping pictures of the scenic vista. Pass the cars and commotion and walk along the lakes for 0.6 mile. At the west end of the last lake, cross to the south side of Stevens Canyon Road to find the continuation of the Wonderland Trail.

The trail parallels the road for approximately a half mile before descending on a series of gentle switchbacks. In another 0.7 mile, reach a trail junction that leads north to Narada Falls. If you haven't seen enough waterfalls yet, hike 0.2 mile to the viewpoint; Narada Falls drops from approximately 170 feet above you.

If you're all waterfalled out, or are simply dreaming of real food at Longmire, continue your descent another 0.7 mile to reach Paradise River Camp. The camp is forested and sits along the Paradise River—a fresh, year-round water source. The three individual campsites

Sturdy stairs guide hikers up the embankment near Martha Falls.

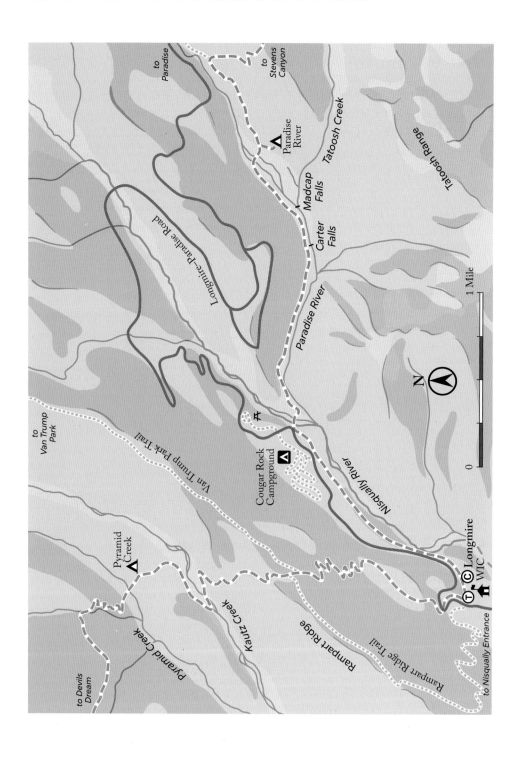

and one group site are all equally pleasing, and there are plenty of berries in season, whether you're camping here or just passing through.

Several years ago, Paradise River Camp was closed due to some northern spotted owls who decided a tree in the camp made a fine place to nest and raise their young. The owlets fledged, Mama and Papa Owl moved on, and the Park Service reopened the camp. Mount Rainier has one of the largest, relatively undisturbed populations of northern spotted owls in the western Washington Cascades. Because these spectacular birds are a threatened species, with numbers in decline, protecting them is a priority for park and state biologists. The Paradise River area is the perfect habitat for spotted owls—they rely on older forests with high tree canopies for nesting, foraging, and plenty of flying room. Studies have shown that the home ranges of spotted owls are larger where flying squirrels are the predominate prey. Keep a close eye on the forest canopy above you for a real-life nature show!

Paradise River to Longmire

One-way distance: 3.8 miles
High point: 3800 feet
Elevation gain/loss: Negligible/−1025 feet

FROM THE PARADISE RIVER CAMP, the way descends gradually. A large, curious wooden penstock pipe soon appears on the north side of the trail. It is the relic of a power plant that used to exist on the Paradise River, upstream from its junction with the Nisqually River. Water flowing through this pipe provided water pressure to the power plant's generator. Almost nothing remains of the power plant except this pipe.

Just over 0.7 mile from Paradise River Camp, arrive at Madcap Falls, followed by Carter Falls 0.2 mile farther along the trail. At both of these scenic falls, the water gracefully and powerfully flows over stone in a hypnotic rhythm. Carter Falls plunges 55 feet in a rather symmetrical fashion, making for iconic photos. It was named after Henry Carter, a local mountain guide, employee of James Longmire, and trail builder who constructed early trails in the Paradise area.

From Carter Falls, the trail becomes wide and flat, making for smooth sailing. At 1.1 miles from Carter Falls, cross the Nisqually

A relic of a power plant on the Paradise River, a penstock pipe remains trailside near Longmire.

Deep forest welcomes hikers near Paradise River.

River on log bridges and arrive at a junction with the Longmire–Paradise Road.

Just across the road is Cougar Rock Campground, a frontcountry camp. Unlike White River Campground, the Wonderland Trail does not go through Cougar Rock, and a separate system for staying in the car campground applies (sites are first-come, first-served, but a portion of sites are reservable through recreation.gov). Though Cougar Rock Campground is not part of the Wonderland's permit system, it's the only place near the trail where you're permitted to enjoy a warm campfire in a designated fire pit, unless you decide to pay for a car campsite at White River Campground.

If you're not staying at Cougar Rock, continue on the trail on the south side of the road. Enjoy the wide, flat tread—you and your companions can spread out elbow to elbow and feel the soft evergreen needles beneath your feet. Day hikers pop up like daisies on a hot summer day as you approach the Longmire Wilderness Information Center and other facilities, just 1.8 miles from Cougar Rock Campground.

Congratulations! This is your shining moment. You are one of the few people in the world who have hiked the full circumference of the Wonderland Trail. Celebrate by skipping into the National Park Inn dining room for a burger and some cobbler before you head home.

CHAPTER 8

SAMPLING THE WONDERLAND TRAIL

If you're excited to see the Wonderland Trail but you can't arrange an extended backpacking trip, there are plenty of ways you can sample the trail. Section hiking allows you to enjoy the Wonderland's many features without having to hike it all at once, the perfect sampler platter! Additionally, two other trails intersecting the Wonderland can be done as shorter loops, showcasing some of the finest backcountry scenery to be found at Mount Rainier: the Northern Loop and the Eastside Loop. Whichever way you choose to tour the park, rest assured that you will find beauty and solitude in all directions.

The sun sets in mid-September over
the tranquil Northern Loop.

SECTION HIKING THE WONDERLAND

Because the Wonderland Trail meets up with the road in several places, it's easy to hike smaller sections of the trail. Of course, you'll need to arrange transportation if you want to hike these sections one-way, trailhead to trailhead, instead of out and back.

The permit system is the same for section-hiking overnighters as it is for Wonderland Trail thru-hikers. Be sure to secure your permit either by the reservation system or the walk-up system (see Getting Your Permit in chapter 2). Also be sure to check park regulations, just as you would if you were hiking the entire trail. For instance, while all wilderness camps currently provide bear poles for hanging food, mandatory bear-proof canisters are probably in the park's future. (For park contact information, see Resources at the back of this book.)

Now comes a difficult question: Which section to hike? They all have their unique charm and beauty, so what you choose depends on what you most want to see and how much time you have. I outline a few suggestions briefly below. All are described in the clockwise direction, though you can choose to hike them counterclockwise as well.

Upland ground birds like this grouse are frequently spotted in meadows.

For a high suspension bridge, wildflowers, challenging hiking, and the most "remote" feeling: Start at Longmire, end at Mowich Lake, for a one-way trip of 34 miles, with +9755/−7600 feet of elevation gain and loss. Allow 3–4 days.

For waterfalls, easier hiking, and river valleys: Start at Box Canyon, end at Longmire, for a one-way trip of 12.5 miles, with +2250/−2480 feet of elevation gain and loss. Allow 1–2 days.

For glaciers, marmots, Rainier views, and big trees: Start at Mowich Lake, end at the Sunrise Visitor Center, for a one-way trip of 21.9 miles, with +6370/−4900 feet of elevation gain and loss. Allow 3–4 days.

For wildflowers, snowfields, marmots, more-challenging hiking, and Rainier views: Start at the White River Campground, end at Box Canyon, for a one-way trip of 18.8 miles, with +3930/−5230 feet of elevation gain and loss. Allow 2–3 days.

A trailside tarn near Windy Gap is a peaceful place to stop and catch your breath.

THE NORTHERN LOOP

Loop distance: 34 miles (from Sunrise), 44.8 miles (from Carbon River Entrance)
High point: 6800 feet (from Sunrise), 6700 feet (from Carbon River Entrance)
Elevation gain/loss: +8960/−8960 feet
Hiking time: Allow 4–5 days
Map: Green Trails Mount Rainier Wonderland Map No. 269S

IF YOUR BACKPACKING GOALS INCLUDE finding serenity and fewer bootprints, consider a few days on the Northern Loop. On the north side of the mountain, this spectacular trail

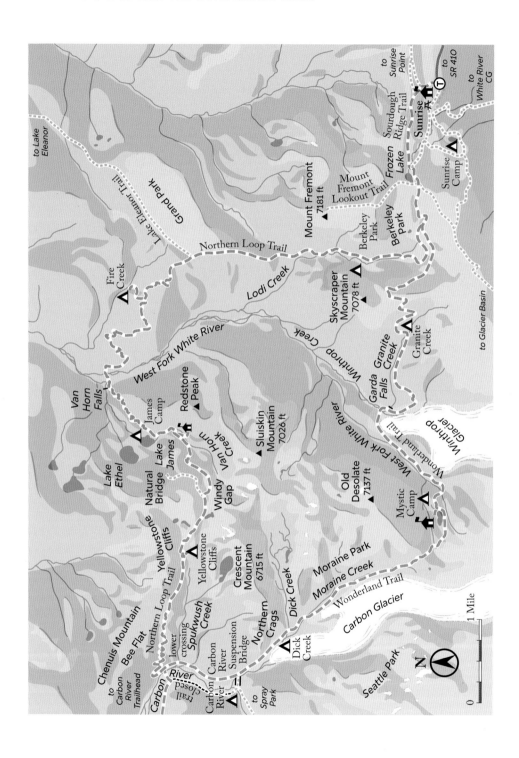

takes you through wilderness with a high mountain pass, a natural bridge, and frequent opportunities for bear sightings. It passes through several subalpine zones before it meets back up with the Wonderland Trail to complete a full loop.

The Northern Loop follows a typical Rainier trail pattern, with challenging ups and downs that lead to rewarding views—followed by even more challenging ups and downs. The only relatively flat parts of the loop are near Grand Park (on the east side of the loop), near Windy Gap (on the north side), and Moraine Park (on the west side). You'll earn your reward as your heart, lungs, and legs get in tip-top shape and your soul gets lifted by grandeur.

Your total trail distance depends on where you choose to camp and what you choose to see. Camping at Fire Creek adds an extra mile to the trip, and a visit to the Lake James Patrol Cabin adds 0.8 mile. You won't want to miss Natural Bridge on your way from Lake James to Windy Gap; the side trip to this amazing feature adds 1.8 miles roundtrip.

You can start your trip from one of two locations: either Sunrise or the Carbon River Entrance. Sunrise is perhaps the more desirable, so that's the starting point the following trail description uses. The Carbon River Road's washout adds an extra 10.8 miles of walking (or biking) on abandoned roadway to complete the trek. The loop can be hiked either clockwise or counterclockwise, which gives you some flexibility in securing your permit.

DRIVING DIRECTIONS. To get to Sunrise from Enumclaw, drive State Route 410 southbound for 43 miles to the park's northeast corner. Turn right (west) onto the Sunrise Road and find the White River Entrance in just over 1 mile. Continue on the Sunrise Road for another 16 miles to its end.

To reach the Carbon River trailhead from Puyallup, drive SR 410 to the town of Buckley. From Buckley, head south on SR 165 through the towns of Carbonado and Wilkeson. Continue on SR 165 and cross the Fairfax Bridge. At the Mowich Lake/Carbon River junction bear left (northeast) onto Carbon River Road. The road is now closed and gated at the ranger station. Park on the side of the road.

AS WITH ALL WILDERNESS CAMPING at Mount Rainier, the Northern Loop requires a permit (see Getting Your Permit in chapter 2). If you start at Sunrise, stop by the White River Wilderness Information Center as you enter the park to pick up your permit (whether reserved or walk-up). Ask the ranger about water crossings and bridges, especially the bridge over the White River between Fire Creek and James Camp. If you start at Carbon River, you can pick up your permit at the Carbon River Ranger Station, near the park's Carbon River Entrance.

Sunrise to Berkeley Park

One-way distance: 3.1 miles
High point: 6800 feet
Elevation gain/loss: +400/−1600 feet

AT SUNRISE, FIND THE TRAILHEAD to the right (east) of the restrooms. Start climbing in the high meadows of Sunrise up to the Sourdough Ridge Trail, not far from the parking area. Head west on the Sourdough Ridge Trail, working your way toward Frozen Lake. Sunrise has a maze of trails that often aren't well marked, and many of them lead to the Frozen Lake intersection. The shortest route out of Sunrise is the Sourdough Ridge Trail. If you get turned around, look for signs to Frozen Lake and follow the day hikers.

Just west of Frozen Lake, hop on the Wonderland Trail and follow it through tundra and subalpine flowers until the green of Berkeley Park appears below you. You've reached the Northern Loop junction, just 0.8 mile from the Frozen Lake junction. Gold star!

Drop into the green, fragrant meadows of Berkeley Park, snacking on Cascade blueberries (*Vaccinium deliciosum*) in season. There are plenty of green areas in Mount Rainer National Park, but this cirque feels special. Streams crisscross this meadow and water is abundant. Look for marmots feeding on meadow greens and playing tag in the fields. 🐾

Drop 800 feet in just 1.2 miles to the Berkeley Park Camp below, 3.1 miles away from your start at Sunrise. This somewhat forested camp has two individual campsites and one group site. Lodi Creek, to the west of camp, is your water source. The camp latrine can be buggy and somewhat undesirable at certain times of the year, due to heavy traffic from both backpackers and day hikers. Hold your nose if you must use it, and then try to repress the memory.

Berkeley Park and the area surrounding it are known for bears. 🐾 Even if you don't see an actual bear while you're here, you'll no doubt see plenty of bear signs in the form of scat and claw marks on trees. Practice safe bear etiquette as you move about.

If you face a long drive to the park, Berkeley Park wilderness camp is a good place to start your hike.

A lenticular cloud over the summit, seen from the Northern Loop Trail, signifies changing weather.

Berkeley Park to Fire Creek Camp Trail Junction

One-way distance: 4.2 miles
High point: 5763 feet
Elevation gain/loss: +260/–960 feet

LEAVE BERKELEY PARK AND ENJOY the relatively level trail. At 0.5 mile from camp, cross Lodi Creek and stop for water if needed. Unless you're staying at Fire Creek, this is the last water available until you reach the West Fork White River, approximately 6.3 miles away.

After a small switchback, enter the wide, flat area of Grand Park. The vast meadows of Grand Park spreading to the northeast are popular with elk, deer, and bear, so keep an eye out for wildlife. 🐾

About a half mile after leaving Grand Park, come to a viewpoint. Be sure to stop, as the pictures you take here won't live up to what the eye can enjoy in person. A 270-degree panoramic view unfolds, with the White River valley, Natural Bridge, Windy Gap, Redstone Peak, Berkeley Park, and Mount Fremont all visible. Stretch out your legs and give your quads a pep talk, as they're in for a long haul.

The descent from the Grand Park area into the West Fork White River basin is long and filled with seemingly endless switchbacks—a true challenge for the quads. Take it slow and be sure to indulge in the ridiculous amount of late-season Cascade blueberries as you head downhill.

About a third of the way down to the valley below, find the turnoff for Fire Creek Camp on your right (to the north, 4.2 miles from Berkeley Park Camp). The camp is 0.5 mile down this spur trail. If this is home for the night, or if you're low on water, head on down. Fire Creek Camp is a pretty and private little camp located, as are most Rainier camps, in the woods. It rarely gets much traffic, and it has three individual campsites and one group site. Fire Creek flows year-round nearby, although it can slow to just a trickle in late summer. Years ago, a ranger station was located here, but it has since been removed.

Fire Creek Camp Trail Junction to James Camp

One-way distance: 5 miles
High point: 4900 feet
Elevation gain/loss: +1420/−1700 feet

FROM THE TRAIL JUNCTION TO Fire Creek Camp, continue to descend, following switchbacks under the deep forest canopy. Try to remind yourself that there is a flat-bottomed end to this slope down there somewhere. In 2.6 miles, arrive at the West Fork White River and cross it using the footbridges. The Park Service does a fairly good job of keeping these bridges safe for crossings, but use caution with your footing. Remember, look at the log or the opposite bank—not down at the water!

Just past the river crossing is Van Horn Falls to the north. Be sure to head down the short spur trail to check it out. Several summers ago, I sat and watched river otters frolicking playfully, rolling around and jumping in the water pockets just below the mist. Water is plentiful year-round, so fill up your water bottles and rest those tired feet and quads. As you know, on Mount Rainier trails, what goes down must go back up.

Back on the main loop, climb, climb, climb, and then climb some more. Take plenty of breaks, as this section is tough on the lungs and heart and seems to have more switchbacks than a zebra has stripes. Your memories of this section are more likely to be of your huffing and puffing than of the deep forest, so take time to look around. The trail guides you through roots, rocks, and soft evergreen needles as you continue climbing 1420 feet up to the Lake James area.

James Camp is 2.4 miles from the crossing of the West Fork White River and sits on a small hill in deep forest. There are only a couple of peekaboo views of the lake. James Camp's location is far superior to the old Redstone Camp, which was west of the lake and closer to the patrol cabin. Note that the old camp still shows up on some maps.

James Camp has three individual campsites and one group site. The water source is not Lake James but rather Van Horn Creek, located between the camp and the lake. Lake James is not as impressive as some of the other lakes in the park: although it's decent-sized and forested, it's surrounded by big trees and is difficult to see. The Park Service has deemed its shoreline a restoration area, as years of boots have put pressure on the lake's ecosystem. Tread lightly and respect closed areas.

To reach the patrol cabin, hike 0.4 mile farther along the main loop trail and then another 0.4 mile down a spur trail to your left. Occasionally, rangers are stationed here, but it's not staffed on a regular basis.

Van Horn Falls is an enchanting vision after a rainstorm.

The Lake James Ranger Station features plenty of history, making it an interesting site to visit.

This patrol cabin has an interesting story. Years ago, now-retired trails foreman Carl Fabiani and a coworker headed out to the cabin for an overnight trip in early spring. The snow on the trail had melted just enough for routefinding, but they were the first ones to visit the area after a long winter. The day was misty and cold, and they eagerly anticipated the warmth of the cabin's woodstove. But when they arrived, they couldn't believe their eyes: at some point during the offseason, a bear had used the cabin as its crash pad.

Someone had mistakenly left food there the previous fall, and apparently there was no stopping the hungry bruin from getting at it. Instead of knocking down the door, the bear crawled up on the roof, ripping off shingles to create a bear-sized hole. Once inside, he made a huge mess of the place, partying it up and tearing everything to bits. The bear must have panicked as he tried to get out afterwards: it looked like he had climbed the walls and continued ripping away at the roof until half of it was gone. When Fabiani and his coworker came upon the cabin, it was in shambles. Thankfully, the furry, frenzied villain had moved on. With no bear scare in sight, they scooted the cabin's interior furnishings to dry spots under the remaining shingles and spent a cold, damp night huddled under half a roof. The cabin has long since been repaired.

James Camp to Yellowstone Cliffs

One-way distance: 3.6 miles
High point: 5800 feet
Elevation gain/loss: +1120/–600 feet

FROM JAMES CAMP, HIKE THE 0.4 mile to the patrol cabin spur and then continue on the main loop, climbing gradually for approximately 1.5 miles to the gentle, meandering meadows of Windy Gap. Bursting with a rainbow of wildflowers in season, Windy Gap opens to amazing vistas of Sluiskin Mountain and Crescent Mountain.

In another 0.2 mile, arrive at a side trail on your right (north) leading to Natural Bridge. Time permitting, be sure to catch this awesome natural attraction. The Natural Bridge is a stone arch formed from eroded andesite lava over a small canyon. The view from the end of the spur trail has a clear view of the bridge and looks down into the Lake Ethel and Lake James basin. The bridge is stable enough for the brave and the daring to sit or stand upon—but exercise caution. The Grim Reaper is on standby; there is no margin for error here. This side trip adds 1.8 miles roundtrip and 300 feet of elevation gain and loss to your overall loop. The trail to the Natural Bridge area is also a great place to see bears. They love the berries on the hillside and the solitude afforded by the infrequent travelers. Savor the peace that they enjoy as you hike to and from the bridge.

Leave the Natural Bridge trail junction and suck up tremendous views in the Windy Gap area. Although Mount Rainier is not visible, your eyes can take in the surrounding peaks, boulder fields, and meadows. A bit farther along the trail, reach an unnamed tarn with seasonal water, big rocks, and perfect places to sit for a packs-off break or snack. Rest your legs, enjoy the quiet, and prepare for the descent to the Carbon River valley, 3100 feet below. Mountain goats love the rocks in this area, so keep your eyes open for visitors.

The Natural Bridge on the Northern Loop is a must-see natural feature.

From Windy Gap, head down through subalpine scenery to views of Tyee Peak to the north and the jagged stone teeth of the Yellowstone Cliffs just above you. Whoever named these cliffs was either color-blind, lost, or just had a great sense of humor. The cliffs aren't yellow at all; they're mostly orange.

At 1.5 miles (and 600 feet of elevation loss) from the Natural Bridge trail junction, arrive at a trail heading left (south) to the Yellowstone Cliffs Camp. If this is home for the night, follow the spur trail to a small camp in the trees with views of the cliffs and meadows. The two individual campsites use the babbling Spukwush Creek as a water source. There is no group site.

Yellowstone Cliffs to Dick Creek

One-way distance: 5.5 miles
High point: 5200 feet
Elevation gain/loss: +1600/−2500 feet

LEAVE THE YELLOWSTONE CLIFFS CAMP and give your quads another pep talk. They'll need strength, encouragement, and plenty of power to crank down the next 3.4 miles. The trail descending to the Carbon River is steep and lined with umpteen switchbacks (after twenty, I lost count). Be gentle to your knees and go easy on your body by taking plenty of breaks, resting whenever you feel fatigued. Remember, exhaustion is often the first step to injury.

A backpacker makes his way toward the Yellowstone Cliffs.

When you arrive at the lower Carbon River crossing, send up a cheer! Feel the flat ground under your feet and revel in the sensation. Head south, hiking along the river for 1.1 miles. You are walking in one of the last standing examples of a true temperate rainforest in the Cascade Mountains.

Arrive at the Carbon River Suspension Bridge; you can cross it for amusement and pictures if you want, but you don't actually need to. Instead, connect with the Wonderland Trail and continue south another mile, heading uphill to Dick Creek Camp, 5.5 miles from Yellowstone Cliffs Camp.

You can continue your Northern Loop adventure by reading the trail descriptions in chapter 5, starting with Dick Creek to Mystic Camp. From Dick Creek Camp, you have two more camp options (Mystic and Granite Creek Camps) and 12.6 miles to go to reach your car at Sunrise.

THE EASTSIDE LOOP

Loop distance: 36 miles
High point: 6800 feet
Elevation gain/loss: +7430/−6610 feet
Hiking time: Allow 3–4 days
Map: Green Trails Mount Rainier Wonderland Map No. 269S

THIS LOOP ON THE EAST side of the park takes you through a picturesque, rugged landscape as you sample one of the most scenic sections of the Wonderland Trail. Although you won't get views of Rainier on the first part of the Eastside Loop, you'll be treated to the rugged peaks of the Cowlitz Chimneys and the cliffs of Governors Ridge. And because of the lack of Rainier views, this first section of trail, going south from the Owyhigh Lakes trailhead, is one of the least used trails in the park, dispensing a peaceful dose of solitude. Other backpackers arrive as you meet the Wonderland section of this loop, where the views of Rainier are postcard worthy. But even with the added company, peace will settle over you as you traipse through the high meadows of Cowlitz Divide and beneath the large cliffs of the Ohanapecosh headwaters. As a mid-loop bonus, you can take a great side trip to the Grove of the Patriarchs, a stand of impressive old-growth trees. Before you do, double check it's accessibility. As of this book's publication, the suspension bridge to this exhibit was damaged and the area is closed.

Because the Eastside Loop touches the road (or comes close) in many locations, your starting trailhead options are plentiful. Going clockwise from north to south, you can

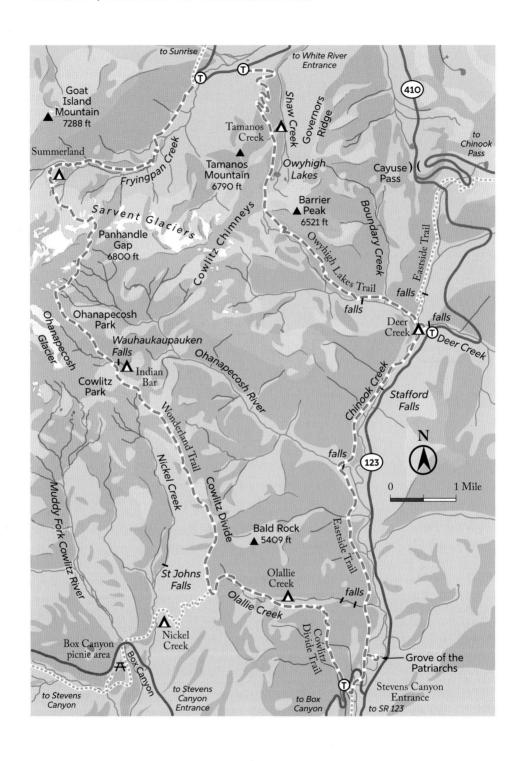

to Sunrise

to White River
Entrance

410

Goat
Island
Mountain
7288 ft

Shaw Creek

Governors Ridge

to Chinook
Pass

Tamanos
Creek

Summerland

Tamanos
Mountain
6790 ft

Owyhigh
Lakes

Cayuse
Pass

Fryingpan Creek

Sarvent Glaciers

Cowlitz Chimneys

Barrier
Peak
6521 ft

Owyhigh Lakes Trail

Boundary Creek

Eastside Trail

Panhandle
Gap
6800 ft

falls

falls

falls

Ohanapecosh
Park

Ohanapecosh Glacier

Wauhaukaupauken
Falls

Ohanapecosh River

Deer
Creek

T

falls

Deer Creek

Indian
Bar

Cowlitz
Park

Chinook Creek

Stafford
Falls

Wonderland Trail

Nickel Creek

Cowlitz Divide

N

Muddy Fork Cowlitz River

falls

123

0   1 Mile

Bald Rock
5409 ft

Eastside Trail

St Johns
Falls

Olallie
Creek

falls

Olallie Creek

Nickel
Creek

Cowlitz Divide Trail

Box Canyon
picnic area

Box Canyon

Grove of the
Patriarchs

to Stevens
Canyon

to Stevens
Canyon
Entrance

to Box
Canyon

T

Stevens Canyon
Entrance
to SR 123

start at the Sunrise Road trailheads, the Deer Creek trailhead off State Route 123, or the Cowlitz Divide trailhead off Stevens Canyon Road.

The following trail description starts at the Owyhigh Lakes trailhead—one of two Sunrise Road trailhead options. If you need a walk-up permit, starting here and traveling clockwise increases your odds of securing a night at the popular Indian Bar or Summerland Camps, since they'll fall a day or two into your trip instead of at the beginning.

> **DRIVING DIRECTIONS.** To get to the Owyhigh Lakes trailhead, take State Route 410, driving either from the north or the south, and follow the Sunrise Road turnoff. Drive about 3 miles to the trailhead parking area on your right; the parking lot isn't huge, so keep an eye out. There is room for several cars. Look for the trailhead on the left (south) side of the road.

AS WITH ALL WILDERNESS CAMPING at Mount Rainier, the Eastside Loop requires a permit (see Getting Your Permit in chapter 2). On your way to the trailhead, stop and pick up your permit (whether reserved or walk-up) at the wilderness information center at the White River Entrance. Ask the ranger about trail conditions, such as any issues with water crossings or bridges, especially in early season. Most bridges on the Eastside Loop are large and sturdy, but there are a few vulnerable log bridges in the mix.

Owyhigh Lakes Trailhead to Deer Creek

One-way distance: 9.4 miles
High point: 5300 feet
Elevation gain/loss: +1600/−2240 feet

FROM THE PARKING AREA ON the north side of the road, cross to the trailhead on the south side and start out on the Owyhigh Lakes Trail. Climb gradually at first and then a bit more steadily. At the first switchback, you'll hear Shaw Creek, which sings to you as you continue to switchback steadily up through forest on the northeastern side of Tamanos Mountain.

At 3.8 miles from the trailhead, cross a footbridge over Tamanos Creek and arrive at Tamanos Creek Camp. Nicely tucked away in the woods, the camp boasts four flat, private campsites and one group site. Its water source, Tamanos Creek, can dry up late in the summer or in low snowpack years. Carry extra "just in case" water if you plan to camp here in late summer or early fall.

As you continue on the trail, you're rewarded for all that climbing with some nice, flat travel on the side of Tamanos Mountain, named for the Chinook Jargon word for "spirit."

Shallow Owyhigh Lakes sit in a peaceful, grassy meadow below Governors Ridge.

This place is hauntingly beautiful. The trail offers peekaboo views until you pop out into an open meadow with views of Owyhigh Lakes, along with Governors Ridge and Barrier Peak to the east. Cascade blueberries (*Vaccinium deliciosum*) abound in late season.

The Owyhigh Lakes are very shallow, and the trail does not lead to their shoreline but rather cruises along above them. If you need water, there's a small bootpath down to the lakes. Wildflowers are abundant in the lake basin, and you're likely to spot wildlife since this is one of the least visited areas of the park. 🐾 Look for mountain goats on the cliffs surrounding you, and keep your eyes out for elk or bear in the meadows. Legend has it that these shallow lakes were named for Chief Owhi of the Yakama Tribe after he loaned his horses to Theodore Winthrop (namesake of Winthrop Glacier) in the mid-1850s to aid in exploration of this area.

After the lakes, continue through even more meadows with rainbows of wildflowers and flowing creeks. In the fall, this place explodes with bright-orange and yellow foliage. A snooze here is tempting if the sun is shining. The Cowlitz Chimneys, to the west, bare their jagged teeth as you wander through the sweeping views. The trail pops in and out of meadows along hillsides before leading you back into thick forest. Practice good bear etiquette. 🐾 Sightings are common in this area, especially in late season due to an abundance of Cascade blueberries.

Continue descending, first on a series of gentle switchbacks and then on a gentle grade. Several small bridges take you over seasonal tributaries and creeks, including the largest, Boundary Creek.

At 4.7 miles from the Owyhigh Lakes, arrive at a junction with the Eastside Trail (not to be confused with the Eastside Loop as described here). The Eastside Trail heads north (left) from this junction.

Stay on the Owyhigh Lakes Trail, and in 0.1 mile arrive at another junction; from here, trails fan out in three directions. A gentle creek greets you as you scratch your head trying to figure out which way to go. The park signs here are confusing, as nothing officially points you to Deer Creek Camp. Luckily, someone took the time to scratch in the words "Deer Creek," along with a helpful arrow. Turn right (south) at the junction and hop onto the Eastside Trail, heading south along the waters of Chinook Creek. If you end up at State Route 123—or start climbing uphill—you made a mistake and missed the turn. Consult your map if you get confused.

After walking along the Eastside Trail for a few paces, find Deer Creek Camp on the left (east) side of the trail, 9.4 miles from the Owyhigh Lakes trailhead. Reward yourself with a big ol' fat treat from your food bag for a job well done! If this is home for the night, settle in at this pretty campsite in the woods, with rushing Chinook Creek nearby. Deer Creek Camp has two individual campsites, plus a backcountry toilet perched on a hillside behind camp.

Deer Creek to Olallie Creek

One-way distance: 10.3 miles
High point: 3800 feet
Elevation gain/loss: +1760/−200 feet

FROM DEER CREEK CAMP, HEAD south on a nearly level section of the Eastside Trail. In about 1 mile, cross Chinook Creek on a sturdy bridge and enjoy the pretty canyon and falls nearby. Waterfalls abound here, with one beauty following another. Keep your camera at your fingertips.

In 6.3 miles from Deer Creek Camp, arrive at an intersection with the Grove of the Patriarchs spur trail. Sadly in November 2021, floods closed the Grove of the Patriarchs, and as of this printing, it has yet to reopen. When it does, it adds only 0.6 mile roundtrip to your day and is worth exploring. The Grove of the Patriarchs showcases some of the largest and oldest trees still living in the Cascades. Lying among them are some of their fallen compatriots—deceased giant trees displaying impressive root systems as they give themselves up as nurse logs for new seedlings. Cross over a fun little suspension bridge and loop around the displays. The 2006 floods also damaged this area quite a lot, and it is still recovering. Stay on designated trails to help this fragile area rebound.

Back on the main loop, continue heading south on the Eastside Trail for 0.4 mile to the parking area for the Grove of the Patriarchs on Stevens Canyon Road. A real restroom awaits! Additionally, you can toss your garbage in the trash cans here to lighten your load.

Cross Stevens Canyon Road and find the trail on the other side. In another 0.5 mile, park signs point in various directions as if intent on confusing even the most experienced navigator. This is the top of the Silver Falls Loop Trail, which connects with the frontcountry Ohanapecosh Campground. Your goal here is to find the Cowlitz Divide Trail, located uphill on your right, heading northwest.

Give yourself a round of applause for your navigation skills, and head up the Cowlitz Divide Trail for 0.3 mile to another crossing of Stevens Canyon Road. Cross the road to find the continuation of the trail. With all the road crossings and challenging routefinding now out of the way, grab a snack, stretch, and prepare for your climb. The Cowlitz Divide Trail ascends steeply for about 1 mile before giving you a bit of reprieve, changing to a moderate grade.

The Eastside Trail after Deer Creek Camp is waterfall heaven.

At 2.8 miles from your last road crossing, arrive at a small spur trail on your right (north), which leads to Olallie Creek Camp. This camp is deep in the heart of the forest, surrounded by berries and accompanied by small, seasonal Olallie Creek. Rarely does the creek dry up completely, but during hot summers it can become a tiny trickle. There is a true sense of wilderness at this camp, which is far less used than many others in the area. Owls roost in trees above while Douglas squirrels scamper around below. Bears frequent the area, but they have plenty of food of their own to forage, so sleep well and rest up for your big day ahead. 🐾

Water playfully dances down rocky protusions on the way to a plunge pool near Deer Creek Camp.

Olallie Creek to Indian Bar

One-way distance: 6.2 miles
High point: 5930 feet
Elevation gain/loss: +2130/–930 feet

FROM OLALLIE CREEK CAMP, CONTINUE climbing on the Cowlitz Divide Trail along a moderate incline. The forest feels large and mysterious around each turn. About 0.7 mile from camp, climb a small set of switchbacks and then continue gaining elevation gently.

At 1.5 miles from camp (including 1000 feet of climbing), arrive at a junction with the Wonderland Trail. Prepare your mind and your camera for what lies ahead, as this section of the Wonderland Trail will make your head spin.

Head right (north) at the intersection and make your way up the spine of the Cowlitz Divide. The climbing is tough and steep but you will have previews of coming attractions as you wander from tree line to flowers and then back. While you gain elevation overall,

the ups and downs start to make you wonder if you'll ever reach the top of this climb. Use extra caution with footing in early season, as a slip and slide on snow in certain areas could mean the end of a great day or even a great life. The scenery keeps getting better. The giant view of Rainier will make you wish you had an extra-wide wide-angle lens and several more days to soak it all in.

At 2.8 miles from the junction of the Cowlitz Divide and Wonderland Trail, finally arrive at the "top," the high point of this trail section at 5930 feet. The trail skirts a meadow showing off an outstanding display of wildflowers of all colors and varieties. In front of you, Mount Rainier and Little Tahoma stand guard over the great valleys and waterfalls of Ohanapecosh Park. Glaciers rise above it all, hanging precariously on the giant slopes. From here to Indian Bar, it feels like you're walking through a movie set.

As you descend into the Ohanapecosh valley, keep a sharp eye out for the Indian Bar Shelter in the meadow, just off the sandbar to the trail's west. This rustic shelter was built in the 1940s by the Civilian Conservation Corps and now serves as a group campsite. Watch it get larger and larger until you reach Indian Bar Camp, just 1.9 miles from the top of the ridge.

The camp is located past the bridge over Wauhaukaupauken (wow-how-cow-pow-ken) Falls. It has four individual campsites and one group site (the shelter). Site 2 has great views down to the meadow below and the glaciers above. And the most beautiful view you've ever seen from a backcountry privy can be found on the hillside behind the group shelter. Get your water from the creek between the group shelter and the main camp.

Indian Bar to Summerland

One-way distance: 4.4 miles
High point: 6800 feet
Elevation gain/loss: +1800/−900 feet

TRY TO RESIST THE URGE to stay in the Indian Bar area forever, as plenty of impressive scenery still lies ahead. Back on the trail, cross a large, fragrant meadow and start your ascent to Panhandle Gap, the highest point on the Wonderland Trail at 6800 feet. Erosion-preventing stair steps, built by the Park Service, guide you higher and higher upward into valley views.

Approximately 1.5 miles from Indian Bar Camp, the trail levels off a little and leads you into a subalpine adventure. Mountain goats in herds of twenty or more frequent the area all the way to Summerland. If they're on the actual trail, use caution when passing; or better

The mossy edges of the Eastside Trail draw you forward like a magnet.

yet, wait until they decide to move on. Resist the urge to strap your pack onto a goat's back, even though it might seem like a fine idea at this point.

Follow a series of ups and downs over talus, permanent snowfields, and tundralike tread for 1.5 miles until you reach Panhandle Gap. Permanent snowfields linger here all year, and at times you'll feel as if you're nearing the summit of Rainier itself. Use caution with footing and routefinding. Do not cross Panhandle Gap in bad weather or if visibility is poor, as a fall could have ugly consequences. If possible, avoid crossing the gap in early morning or late evening—the snow can turn icy during those times. Snow wands, painted rocks, and cairns help you find your way through the tricky spots.

As you head down into the basin, stop to look around. The Fryingpan Glacier is high above you to the west as the Sarvent Glaciers glisten on either side of the trail. A sea-

In early fall, the meadows on the way to Indian Bar light up with autumn foliage.

sonal lake to the west, formed by glacial runoff, shines turquoise in the sun. Follow the trail as it snakes near the lake and then continues through the rocky terrain. There's Summerland in the distance! Cross a small branch of Fryingpan Creek, the Summerland Camp's water source, and find the camp on the hillside to the east of the trail, 4.4 miles from Indian Bar.

Summerland's fanciful name came from Major Edward S. Ingraham, who named it as an homage to the gorgeous flower show this area puts on in the summer. The camp has five individual campsites and one group site—a stone shelter built by the Civilian Conservation Corps. The composting toilet is perched high on the hill behind the shelter.

Keep an eye out for the marmots of Summerland, lazily sunning themselves on rocks or nibbling on flowers. They love the meadows here!

Enjoying the view from your campsite at Indian Bar is one of the pleasures of the Eastside Loop.

Summerland to Owyhigh Lakes Trailhead

One-way distance: 5.7 miles
High point: 5900 feet
Elevation gain/loss: Negligible/–2220 feet

SAY GOODBYE TO SUMMERLAND AND descend the valley between Goat Island Mountain and Tamanos Mountain. A few switchbacks give way to a brushy hillside and an avalanche chute. This area is well known for bears—they're often spotted on Goat Island Mountain to the northwest. Be bear aware, especially in late season, as it would be easy to startle one in the high brush.

Cross a log bridge over a swift creek and continue descending, playing peekaboo with Fryingpan Creek to the east. The descent gives way to a gentle grade through deep old-growth forest.

At 4.3 miles from Summerland, arrive at a junction with a trail to the Fryingpan Creek trailhead, just slightly to your right. Leave the Wonderland Trail and head toward the trailhead, reaching it and Sunrise Road in approximately 0.1 mile.

Unfortunately, there's no trail for this final section of the Eastside Loop; walking the road is the only way to return to your car at the Owyhigh Lakes trailhead. Luckily, the speed limit is fairly low here, so your odds of becoming a hood ornament are small. Enjoy the final 1.3 miles of your hike on the relatively level roadway, reaching your vehicle and celebrating the completion of a great trip.

THE MOTHER MOUNTAIN LOOP

Loop distance: 17.8 miles
High point: 6380 feet
Elevation gain/loss: +5090 / –5045 feet
Hiking time: Allow 2–3 days, or 1 very long day
Map: Green Trails Mount Rainier Wonderland Map No. 269S
Notes: Contact a wilderness information center to ensure the Carbon River bridges are in place and safe to cross. If they are not, do not cross the river, and make this hike as an out-and-back instead.

IF YOU ONLY HAVE a weekend to spare, this is a great way to see part of the Wonderland Trail and the gorgeous Spray Park area. If you're in great shape, you could also do this loop as a trail run or a seriously long day hike. The distance is somewhere between 15.5 miles and 20 miles, depending on which GPS data you consult and how many side trips you take to waterfalls and vistas. With the annual reroute of the Carbon River after the winter storms, it can also vary from year to year.

While Mowich Lake is the best place to start (and thus how this trail description is written), you could theoretically park at the former Carbon River Road and walk (or bike) the now-defunct road to Ipsut Creek Campground. Starting at Ipsut Creek adds another 10-plus miles to the trip. If you do this, be advised that bicycles are allowed on the old road but not on the park trails. There are bike racks, but you'll most likely want to bring a lock.

The elevation gains and losses come in big, challenging hills instead of being spread out, and can challenge even the fittest knees and quads. Hikers coming up the hill from Ipsut

The last rays of the day's sunlight drop behind Puget Sound, as seen from Spray Park.

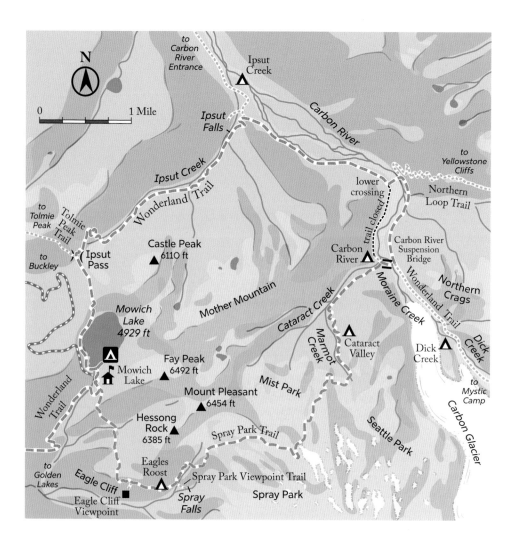

Pass often wear looks of misery. Having a lightweight pack and a set of ultralight trekking poles makes a big difference.

You can go either direction on the loop; you won't miss anything no matter which you choose. Both ways have big climbs and descents and stellar views of the mountain, so go whichever direction makes you happy. Some say the hill going up to Ipsut Pass (counterclockwise) is steeper and more grueling than the one going up to Spray Park (clockwise), and I would have to agree, but you'll work for your steps either way. I've written this description in counterclockwise detail, but the main features remain the same no matter which direction you choose.

Spray Park is the cherry on the sundae, so you might want to hit it first if you are champing at the bit for views. Or you could save the best for last. If you have a walk-up permit, you might want to plan to be in Spray Park during the best weather day. As the sun sets low in Spray Park, alpenglow lights up the mountain.

There are five camps along this route; all require backcountry permits except Mowich Lake, where both backcountry and frontcountry (walk-in car camping) options are available.

1. **Mowich Lake Campground:** This is our starting destination, so you could stay the night here before or after your romp. No reservations are needed for walk-in car camping, but they are required for the backcountry section and wilderness camps, which is clearly signed. The sites are very close together with little privacy, so you may want to forego camping here, or just suck it up and know that you'll have a lot of other folks to visit with come evening. Stoves are allowed but campfires are prohibited. Amenities include pit toilets, picnic tables, a frequently staffed patrol cabin, and a gorgeous lake.

2. **Eagle's Roost Camp:** This one is located along the Spray Park Trail just a couple miles away from Mowich Lake. You could forego Mowich Lake Campground and stay here instead, either before or after your mountain romp, direction dependent.

3. **Cataract Valley Camp:** Staying here is a great option for this hike. It's on the northern side of Spray Park, perfect if you get a late start going counterclockwise and want to take in the sunset on the mountain. Going counterclockwise, this camp is on the downhill portion, just under 7 miles from Mowich Lake. Alternatively, if you get an early start going clockwise, this camp is a great option for the end of the day, and you'll save the best for last, hitting Spray Park before heading home.

4. **Carbon River Camp:** Another fantastic option, this camp falls at the base of the big hill going up to (or down from) Spray Park, just prior to (or after) the Carbon River Suspension Bridge. It's not the most aesthetically pleasing camp, as it's sustained damage over the years—but the sites themselves are flat and worthy, and once your head hits the camp pillow, you'll be none the wiser.

5. **Ipsut Creek Campground:** Less than 6 miles from Mowich Lake, this camp can make a fantastic end to the night in either direction. Since it sits at the base of both big hills (Spray Park and Ipsut Pass), you'll likely be tired from the descent and ready to crash before heading uphill again. Previously a car campground, it's now a wilderness camp due to the washed-out former road, but it has all the luxuries you'd

expect: pit toilets, picnic tables, and plenty of room for multiple tents in each site. It has a patrol cabin, too, but it's rarely staffed. As with all wilderness camps, stoves are allowed but campfires are prohibited.

Mowich Lake to Cataract Valley Camp

One-way distance: 6.8 miles
High point: 6380 feet
Elevation gain/loss: +1910 / −2360 feet

FROM MOWICH LAKE, HEAD SOUTH toward the pit toilets and locate the trail dropping quickly down the hill not far from them.

Clockwise hikers should head toward Mowich Lake and then follow the Wonderland to the left (north) around the lake's edge for 1.5 miles, passing the Tolmie Peak Trail to reach Ipsut Pass. Then prep your quads for the big drop down to Ipsut Creek.

Alpenglow illuminates the mountain as a hiker makes his way through Spray Park.

Going counterclockwise, follow the Wonderland Trail as it makes its way steeply down the hillside. At 0.3 mile from Mowich Lake, arrive at an intersection with the Spray Park Trail and head left (south). Follow the Spray Park Trail under forest canopy and around a couple of talus fields to a signed viewpoint known as Eagle Cliff. If time permits, a short jaunt down to see the mountain is well worth your while; it's just a couple hundred feet roundtrip. In another 0.3 mile, the signed turnoff for Eagle's Roost Camp pops up on the right.

Next up is Spray Falls, with a sign directing you down to the viewpoint. Again, it's a short side trip, less than a half mile roundtrip, to visit one of the most gorgeous waterfalls in the park. With a drop of 354 feet, the waterfall's veiling horsetail pleasingly cascades down the steep cliff face. The best views can be attained by rock hopping across the outlet stream—just use extreme care in early season or after rainfall, as the water can be fast and the rocks slippery.

Up until now, the hiking has ebbed and flowed with gentle ups and downs, but now the real climbing begins. Thankfully, the switchbacks aren't too grueling, and you'll huff and puff your way up to Spray Park before you know it. Spray Park isn't exactly level, so you'll get there as you are still heading up. As you climb through the subalpine trail stairs, wildflowers such as lupine, paintbrush, and beargrass greet you. The mountain starts to look like a beacon in the sky, and the views are so grand that you'll want to watch them instead of your feet. Don't trip, Kip.

Keep your eyes out for bears, as they are abundant in this area and are frequently seen grazing in meadows or on hillsides. 🐾 Goats are seen here, too, often hanging out on cliff bands above Spray Park. Marmots used to be more prevalent than they are now, but you might see one or two on rocks or hear their distant alert whistle.

Eventually, the trail levels out in sublime meadows for a short distance before it begins a descent into an area known as Seattle Park. Here, the path is rocky and truly more alpine with less vegetation. You will likely cross snow patches that linger throughout the year, and routefinding can be tough. Keep your eyes open for cairns (rock stacks) and the occasional tag of paint on rocks to guide you through the maze.

After passing through the alpine zone, the way hits vegetation again and makes a sometimes steep descent to Cataract Valley Camp, just shy of 7 miles from Mowich Lake. If this is camp for the night, enjoy the squeaking pikas that live in the talus fields nearby. They are excruciatingly cute and seem somewhat excited to pose for you.

Cataract Valley Camp to Ipsut Creek Campground

One-way distance: 5.6 miles
High point: 4490 feet
Elevation gain/loss: +640/-2775 feet

FROM CATARACT VALLEY CAMP, DESCEND for 1.6 miles, reaching the turnoff for the Carbon River Camp. Water is available via Cataract Creek, a short jaunt down the spur trail to the camp should you need to fill a bottle.

In 0.2 mile from the Carbon River Camp turnoff, reach one of the best artificial features along the trail—the Carbon River Suspension Bridge. This bridge is equally as impressive in length as its cousin, the Tahoma Creek Suspension Bridge on the Wonderland's west side, but it's not nearly as high. It sways, groans, and wiggles as you walk across its planks

The author crosses the Carbon River Suspension bridge on her way to toward Cataract Valley Camp.

over the rushing Carbon River. Use care when sliding your hands across the metal wiring of the bridge's sides, as it has started unravelling in places and can cut or poke skin.

From the suspension bridge, turn left and begin a descent to the Carbon River. A couple of washed-out areas give you a sneak preview of what's to come. Follow the flags and cairns in places where the trail disappears. This area is forested, but water careens down the hillsides near here and often makes a mess of things.

In just over a mile from the suspension bridge, arrive at a crossing of the Carbon River. Every year, this area changes, depending on the severity of seasonal floods. It can be quite confusing and sometimes dicey. Do not attempt to cross the Carbon River if the bridges are out. It can be deadly—turn back instead! Most years, the Park Service reroutes this area and a sturdy log bridge is in place over the rushing, milky water. You'll need to stay vigilant to find the path through the river valley, as it's often not obvious. Look for orange or pink flagging tape and cairns. Footprints are not always your friends; those hiking before you could have been lost and their prints might be taking you the wrong way.

Once across, climb the steep bank back up to the remnants of the Wonderland Trail and follow it to the right as it winds its way gently downslope through the evergreens and riparian brush. Another washout follows and, depending on the year, possibly even another after that. Stick with it—the navigation is challenging, but also fun. Once again, follow the flagging tape and cairns until you are back on what is a normal-looking trail.

In approximately 1.7 miles from the Carbon River crossing, reach a signed junction. If you are staying at Ipsut Creek Campground for the night, follow the spur trail another 0.3 mile to reach it. Even if you aren't staying at the camp, you'll likely want to follow the signed spur trail to Ipsut Creek Campground for about 400 feet to reach a signed intersection for Ipsut Falls. This trail jogs left a few steps to reach a gorgeous viewpoint of the spectacular waterfall—well worth the extra steps. Ipsut Creek runs gorgeously clear and cold here and is a great place to get water, especially if you have reservations at the camp.

Ipsut Creek Campground to Mowich Lake

One-way distance: 5.4 miles
High point: 5110 feet
Elevation gain/loss: +2825/-260 feet

FROM THE IPSUT CREEK CAMPGROUND spur trail, continue on the Wonderland Trail and begin the climb to Ipsut Pass. The top of this climb is arduous and will squeeze all the joy out of your face, so push against the GHS (Grumpy Hiker Scowl) and fight the urge to growl. You got this! The scenery is beautiful and makes a good excuse to stop often. The trail climbs through a gorgeous old-growth forest harboring one of the world's largest Alaska yellow cedars. Thanks to its perfect microclimate, this area has not been hit with fires and other natural disturbances like other areas of the park, and most of the trees are happy as pigs in a puddle.

In 3.4 miles, arrive at the top of Ipsut Pass; it's actually somewhat flat—what a treat! A junction with the Tolmie Peak Trail scoots off to the right as you follow the gentle ups and down of the wide, forested Wonderland Trail. Roughly 1 mile from Ipsut Pass, return to your start by the gorgeous, lapping shoreline of Mowich Lake. Take a bow! And for the love of all things living and good, treat yourself to a delicious meal on the way home.

ACKNOWLEDGMENTS

IT'S BEEN OVER A DECADE since the first edition of this book hit store shelves, and I scratch my head in wonder at where the time has gone. You, my wonderful readers, are to thank for its success and for affectionately nicknaming it "the Wonderland Bible"—I didn't see that coming and I'm humbly honored. What an absolute pleasure it's been meeting so many of you, both in person and online. Your questions, comments, and kind words continued to warm my heart and kept me inspired as I moved forward with this new edition. Mount Rainier is magical, and it's been so much fun watching all of you fall under the same spell that captivated me enough to write this guide in the first place. Here's to us—the dreamers, the planners, the hopefuls, and the adventurers who seek to see it all in our lifetimes. Check this one off your bucket list!

Thank you for tolerating my cheesy, dad-joke-esque wisecracks. Hopefully the jokes gave you a giggle along with the quintessential eye roll. This book is meant to be read cover to cover; I hope you read up on every camp, dream about the jaw-dropping views, and submerge yourself in the honeymoon phase of trip-planning. You can also take the e-book version of this guide with you on the trail to experience the route chapter by chapter. Some of you burly beasts have even carried the paperback version with you around the mountain!

High above the Indian Bar basin, the trail meanders through sublime scenery.

Twice I've caught readers flipping through it trailside, leading to fast friendships. I spend a fair amount of time in Mount Rainier National Park and would love to meet you, so please say hi should our paths cross.

As from the very beginning, I wish to thank my close personal friends and family who have been so supportive of my writing career. You've joined me on hikes, listened to my backcountry babblings, cheered me up while sipping lattes on bad days, and watched my life transform into one of complete passion for wild places and the creatures that dwell there.

Special thanks to my husband, Vilnis, who has stood by my side, encouraged my dreams, and even shared the occasional freeze-dried mac and cheese with me near our tent on cold nights. Your eternal optimism and enthusiasm for life make this journey of ours a wonderful adventure. Wind beneath my wings? No—you are my wings.

Many of the park's personnel who helped me are now retired; they are incredible humans who seem to have superpowers. They let stress roll off them like water off a duck's back and are patient and resourceful when park visitors need help. Special thanks to Ranger Pigeon who knew all the answers to my barrage of questions and then some—knowledge is your superpower. Ranger Mildice, your boundless love for the park and its visitors is an example for us all. For all the volunteers, donors, and other park staff who work hard to keep things running smoothly, thank you endlessly.

The sleepy beast that was at my feet as I wrote the first edition of this book more than a decade ago, a German Shepherd named Summit, is now resting in peace under a beautiful cherry tree that holds his collar in its branches. He was a beautiful soul and would no doubt love his brother, a rough collie named Scout. Though Scout isn't allowed on the park trails, coming home to him after hiking is like walking into a victory parade. His whole body moves from side to side with elation and my heart swells with happiness.

Lastly, thank you, Mount Rainier. You are an icon on the Seattle skyline, representing change with strength and grace. You allow us to walk up close along your shoulders and marinate in your spectacular beauty, and we are better people for it. May we never take your generosity for granted.

You, my amazing readers, are the purpose of this book. May its pages lead you to places where your soul can find rest. Happy trails!

APPENDIX A

CLOCKWISE ITINERARIES

Most backpackers travel the Wonderland Trail clockwise, and that's how the descriptions in this book read. Following are itineraries starting from the more popular trailheads and lasting from seven to thirteen days. More days on the trail equals shorter camp-to-camp mileage and more time to enjoy the sights and side trips. Taking ten to twelve days to complete the trail generally gives you plenty of time to smell the lupine and spend the night in the most desirable locations.

Please note: The seven-day itineraries are very difficult and are only recommended for very strong backpackers. While the mileage may seem manageable, the elevation gain and loss make for very long, demanding days. Only attempt a seven-day schedule if you are a superhuman hiker—or if you like to defy the Beast of Ultimate Challenge by looking deep into his pitiless eyes.

LONGMIRE TRAILHEAD

7 days

DAY 1	Longmire to South Puyallup River	12.0 miles
DAY 2	South Puyallup River to Golden Lakes	12.5 miles
DAY 3	Golden Lakes to Ipsut Creek	14.9 miles
DAY 4	Ipsut Creek to Granite Creek	12.7 miles
DAY 5	Granite Creek to Summerland	14.6 miles
DAY 6	Summerland to Nickel Creek	11.1 miles
DAY 7	Nickel Creek to Longmire	13.3 miles

Alternate route through Spray Park

| DAY 3 | Golden Lakes to Cataract Valley | 15.7 miles |
| DAY 4 | Cataract Valley to Granite Creek | 11.0 miles |

8 days

DAY 1	Longmire to South Puyallup River	12.0 miles
DAY 2	South Puyallup River to Golden Lakes	12.5 miles
DAY 3	Golden Lakes to Mowich Lake	9.5 miles
DAY 4	Mowich Lake to Dick Creek via Ipsut Pass	9.3 miles
DAY 5	Dick Creek to Sunrise Camp	12.5 miles

Hikers enjoy meadows covered with subalpine buttercup on Emerald Ridge.

243

DAY 6	Sunrise Camp to Summerland	10.3 miles
DAY 7	Summerland to Maple Creek	14.2 miles
DAY 8	Maple Creek to Longmire	10.2 miles

Alternate route through Spray Park

DAY 3	Golden Lakes to Eagles Roost	11.0 miles
DAY 4	Eagles Roost to Mystic Camp	11.1 miles
DAY 5	Mystic Camp to Sunrise Camp	8.9 miles

9 days

DAY 1	Longmire to Devils Dream	5.5 miles
DAY 2	Devils Dream to Klapatche Park	11.2 miles
DAY 3	Klapatche Park to Golden Lakes	7.8 miles
DAY 4	Golden Lakes to Mowich Lake	9.5 miles
DAY 5	Mowich Lake to Dick Creek via Ipsut Pass	9.3 miles
DAY 6	Dick Creek to Sunrise Camp	12.5 miles
DAY 7	Sunrise Camp to Summerland	10.3 miles
DAY 8	Summerland to Maple Creek	14.2 miles
DAY 9	Maple Creek to Longmire	10.2 miles

Alternate route through Spray Park

DAY 4	Golden Lakes to Eagles Roost	11.0 miles
DAY 5	Eagles Roost to Mystic Camp	11.1 miles
DAY 6	Mystic Camp to Sunrise Camp	8.9 miles

10 days

DAY 1	Longmire to Devils Dream	5.5 miles
DAY 2	Devils Dream to Klapatche Park	11.2 miles
DAY 3	Klapatche Park to Golden Lakes	7.8 miles
DAY 4	Golden Lakes to Mowich Lake	9.5 miles
DAY 5	Mowich Lake to Dick Creek via Ipsut Pass	9.3 miles
DAY 6	Dick Creek to Sunrise Camp	12.5 miles
DAY 7	Sunrise Camp to Summerland	10.3 miles
DAY 8	Summerland to Indian Bar	4.4 miles
DAY 9	Indian Bar to Maple Creek	9.8 miles
DAY 10	Maple Creek to Longmire	10.2 miles

Alternate route through Spray Park

DAY 4	Golden Lakes to Eagles Roost	11.0 miles
DAY 5	Eagles Roost to Mystic Camp	11.1 miles
DAY 6	Mystic Camp to Sunrise Camp	8.9 miles

11 days

DAY 1	Longmire to Devils Dream	5.5 miles
DAY 2	Devils Dream to South Puyallup River	6.5 miles
DAY 3	South Puyallup River to Klapatche Park	4.7 miles
DAY 4	Klapatche Park to Golden Lakes	7.8 miles
DAY 5	Golden Lakes to Mowich Lake	9.5 miles

DAY 6	Mowich Lake to Dick Creek via Ipsut Pass	9.3 miles
DAY 7	Dick Creek to Sunrise Camp	12.5 miles
DAY 8	Sunrise Camp to Summerland	10.3 miles
DAY 9	Summerland to Indian Bar	4.4 miles
DAY 10	Indian Bar to Maple Creek	9.8 miles
DAY 11	Maple Creek to Longmire	10.2 miles

Alternate route through Spray Park

DAY 5	Golden Lakes to Eagles Roost	11.0 miles
DAY 6	Eagles Roost to Mystic Camp	11.1 miles
DAY 7	Mystic Camp to Sunrise Camp	8.9 miles

12 days

DAY 1	Longmire to Devils Dream	5.5 miles
DAY 2	Devils Dream to South Puyallup River	6.5 miles
DAY 3	South Puyallup River to Klapatche Park	4.7 miles
DAY 4	Klapatche Park to Golden Lakes	7.8 miles
DAY 5	Golden Lakes to South Mowich River	5.3 miles
DAY 6	South Mowich River to Ipsut Creek	9.6 miles
DAY 7	Ipsut Creek to Mystic Camp	8.1 miles
DAY 8	Mystic Camp to Sunrise Camp	8.9 miles
DAY 9	Sunrise Camp to Summerland	10.3 miles
DAY 10	Summerland to Indian Bar	4.4 miles
DAY 11	Indian Bar to Maple Creek	9.8 miles
DAY 12	Maple Creek to Longmire	10.2 miles

Alternate route through Spray Park

| DAY 6 | South Mowich River to Cataract Valley | 10.4 miles |
| DAY 7 | Cataract Valley to Mystic Camp | 6.4 miles |

13 days

DAY 1	Longmire to Devils Dream	5.5 miles
DAY 2	Devils Dream to South Puyallup River	6.5 miles
DAY 3	South Puyallup River to Klapatche Park	4.7 miles
DAY 4	Klapatche Park to Golden Lakes	7.8 miles
DAY 5	Golden Lakes to South Mowich River	5.3 miles
DAY 6	South Mowich River to Ipsut Creek	9.6 miles
DAY 7	Ipsut Creek to Mystic Camp	8.1 miles
DAY 8	Mystic Camp to Granite Creek	4.6 miles
DAY 9	Granite Creek to Sunrise	4.3 miles
DAY 10	Sunrise to Summerland	10.3 miles
DAY 11	Summerland to Indian Bar	4.4 miles
DAY 12	Indian Bar to Maple Creek	9.8 miles
DAY 13	Maple Creek to Longmire	10.2 miles

Alternate route through Spray Park

| DAY 6 | South Mowich River to Cataract Valley | 10.4 miles |
| DAY 7 | Cataract Valley to Mystic Camp | 6.4 miles |

SUNRISE TRAILHEAD

7 days

DAY 1	Sunrise trailhead to Summerland	10.0 miles
DAY 2	Summerland to Maple Creek	14.2 miles
DAY 3	Maple Creek to Pyramid Creek	13.7 miles
DAY 4	Pyramid Creek to Klapatche Park	13.2 miles
DAY 5	Klapatche Park to South Mowich River	13.1 miles
DAY 6	South Mowich River to Dick Creek via Ipsut Pass	13.5 miles
DAY 7	Dick Creek to Sunrise trailhead	13.8 miles

Alternate route through Spray Park

DAY 6	South Mowich River to Dick Creek	13.2 miles

8 days

DAY 1	Sunrise trailhead to Summerland	10.0 miles
DAY 2	Summerland to Maple Creek	14.2 miles
DAY 3	Maple Creek to Pyramid Creek	13.7 miles
DAY 4	Pyramid Creek to Klapatche Park	13.2 miles
DAY 5	Klapatche Park to South Mowich River	13.1 miles
DAY 6	South Mowich River to Ipsut Creek	9.6 miles
DAY 7	Ipsut Creek to Mystic Camp	8.1 miles
DAY 8	Mystic Camp to Sunrise trailhead	10.2 miles

Alternate route through Spray Park

DAY 6	South Mowich River to Cataract Valley	10.4 miles
DAY 7	Cataract Valley to Mystic Camp	6.4 miles

9 days

DAY 1	Sunrise trailhead to Summerland	10.0 miles
DAY 2	Summerland to Indian Bar	4.4 miles
DAY 3	Indian Bar to Maple Creek	9.8 miles
DAY 4	Maple Creek to Pyramid Creek	13.7 miles
DAY 5	Pyramid Creek to Klapatche Park	13.2 miles
DAY 6	Klapatche Park to South Mowich River	13.1 miles
DAY 7	South Mowich River to Ipsut Creek	9.6 miles
DAY 8	Ipsut Creek to Mystic Camp	8.1 miles
DAY 9	Mystic Camp to Sunrise trailhead	10.2 miles

Alternate route through Spray Park

DAY 7	South Mowich River to Cataract Valley	10.4 miles
DAY 8	Cataract Valley to Mystic Camp	6.4 miles

10 days

DAY 1	Sunrise trailhead to Summerland	10.0 miles
DAY 2	Summerland to Indian Bar	4.4 miles
DAY 3	Indian Bar to Maple Creek	9.8 miles
DAY 4	Maple Creek to Pyramid Creek	13.7 miles

DAY 5	Pyramid Creek to South Puyallup River	8.5 miles
DAY 6	South Puyallup River to Klapatche Park	4.7 miles
DAY 7	Klapatche Park to Golden Lakes	7.8 miles
DAY 8	Golden Lakes to Mowich Lake	9.5 miles
DAY 9	Mowich Lake to Mystic Camp via Ipsut Pass	12.9 miles
DAY 10	Mystic Camp to Sunrise trailhead	10.2 miles

Alternate route through Spray Park

| DAY 8 | Golden Lakes to Eagles Roost | 11.0 miles |
| DAY 9 | Eagles Roost to Mystic Camp | 11.1 miles |

11 days

DAY 1	Sunrise trailhead to Summerland	10.0 miles
DAY 2	Summerland to Indian Bar	4.4 miles
DAY 3	Indian Bar to Maple Creek	9.8 miles
DAY 4	Maple Creek to Pyramid Creek	13.7 miles
DAY 5	Pyramid Creek to South Puyallup River	8.5 miles
DAY 6	South Puyallup River to Klapatche Park	4.7 miles
DAY 7	Klapatche Park to Golden Lakes	7.8 miles
DAY 8	Golden Lakes to Mowich Lake	9.5 miles
DAY 9	Mowich Lake to Ipsut Creek	5.4 miles
DAY 10	Ipsut Creek to Mystic Camp	8.1 miles
DAY 11	Mystic Camp to Sunrise trailhead	10.2 miles

Alternate route through Spray Park

| DAY 9 | Mowich Lake to Cataract Valley | 6.8 miles |
| DAY 10 | Cataract Valley to Mystic Camp | 6.4 miles |

12 days

DAY 1	Sunrise trailhead to Summerland	10.0 miles
DAY 2	Summerland to Indian Bar	4.4 miles
DAY 3	Indian Bar to Nickel Creek	6.7 miles
DAY 4	Nickel Creek to Paradise River	9.5 miles
DAY 5	Paradise River to Devils Dream	9.3 miles
DAY 6	Devils Dream to South Puyallup River	6.5 miles
DAY 7	South Puyallup River to Klapatche Park	4.7 miles
DAY 8	Klapatche Park to Golden Lakes	7.8 miles
DAY 9	Golden Lakes to Mowich Lake	9.5 miles
DAY 10	Mowich Lake to Carbon River via Ipsut Pass	8.5 miles
DAY 11	Carbon River to Mystic Camp	4.8 miles
DAY 12	Mystic Camp to Sunrise trailhead	10.2 miles

Alternate route through Spray Park

| DAY 10 | Mowich Lake to Cataract Valley | 6.8 miles |
| DAY 11 | Cataract Valley to Mystic Camp | 6.4 miles |

13 days

DAY 1	Sunrise trailhead to Summerland	10.0 miles
DAY 2	Summerland to Indian Bar	4.4 miles
DAY 3	Indian Bar to Nickel Creek	6.7 miles
DAY 4	Nickel Creek to Paradise River	9.5 miles
DAY 5	Paradise River to Pyramid Creek	7.3 miles
DAY 6	Pyramid Creek to South Puyallup River	8.5 miles
DAY 7	South Puyallup River to Klapatche Park	4.7 miles
DAY 8	Klapatche Park to Golden Lakes	7.8 miles
DAY 9	Golden Lakes to Mowich Lake	9.5 miles
DAY 10	Mowich Lake to Carbon River via Ipsut Pass	8.5 miles
DAY 11	Carbon River to Mystic Camp	4.8 miles
DAY 12	Mystic Camp to Granite Creek	4.6 miles
DAY 13	Granite Creek to Sunrise trailhead	5.6 miles

Alternate route through Spray Park

| DAY 10 | Mowich Lake to Cataract Valley | 6.8 miles |
| DAY 11 | Cataract Valley to Mystic Camp | 6.4 miles |

MOWICH LAKE TRAILHEAD

7 days

DAY 1	Mowich Lake to Mystic Camp via Ipsut Pass	12.9 miles
DAY 2	Mystic Camp to White River Campground	12.3 miles
DAY 3	White River Campground to Indian Bar	11.3 miles
DAY 4	Indian Bar to Paradise River	16.2 miles
DAY 5	Paradise River to South Puyallup River	15.8 miles
DAY 6	South Puyallup River to Golden Lakes	12.5 miles
DAY 7	Golden Lakes to Mowich Lake	9.5 miles

Alternate route through Spray Park

| DAY 1 | Mowich Lake to Mystic Camp | 13.2 miles |

8 days

DAY 1	Mowich Lake to Dick Creek via Ipsut Pass	9.3 miles
DAY 2	Dick Creek to Sunrise Camp	12.5 miles
DAY 3	Sunrise Camp to Summerland	10.3 miles
DAY 4	Summerland to Maple Creek	14.2 miles
DAY 5	Maple Creek to Pyramid Creek	13.7 miles
DAY 6	Pyramid Creek to South Puyallup River	8.5 miles
DAY 7	South Puyallup River to Golden Lakes	12.5 miles
DAY 8	Golden Lakes to Mowich Lake	9.5 miles

Alternate route through Spray Park

| DAY 1 | Mowich Lake to Dick Creek | 9.6 miles |

Shaggy mane mushrooms, along with many other varieties of fungi, flourish in the park.

9 days

DAY 1	Mowich Lake to Ipsut Creek	5.4 miles
DAY 2	Ipsut Creek to Mystic Camp	8.1 miles
DAY 3	Mystic Camp to White River Campground	12.3 miles
DAY 4	White River Campground to Indian Bar	11.3 miles
DAY 5	Indian Bar to Maple Creek	9.8 miles
DAY 6	Maple Creek to Pyramid Creek	13.7 miles
DAY 7	Pyramid Creek to South Puyallup River	8.5 miles
DAY 8	South Puyallup River to Golden Lakes	12.5 miles
DAY 9	Golden Lakes to Mowich Lake	9.5 miles

Alternate route through Spray Park

| DAY 1 | Mowich Lake to Cataract Valley | 6.8 miles |
| DAY 2 | Cataract Valley to Mystic Camp | 6.4 miles |

10 days

DAY 1	Mowich Lake to Ipsut Creek	5.4 miles
DAY 2	Ipsut Creek to Mystic Camp	8.1 miles
DAY 3	Mystic Camp to Sunrise Camp	8.9 miles
DAY 4	Sunrise Camp to Summerland	10.3 miles
DAY 5	Summerland to Nickel Creek	11.1 miles
DAY 6	Nickel Creek to Paradise River	9.5 miles
DAY 7	Paradise River to Devils Dream	9.3 miles
DAY 8	Devils Dream to Klapatche Park	11.2 miles
DAY 9	Klapatche Park to Golden Lakes	7.8 miles
DAY 10	Golden Lakes to Mowich Lake	9.5 miles

Alternate route through Spray Park

| DAY 1 | Mowich Lake to Cataract Valley | 6.8 miles |
| DAY 2 | Cataract Valley to Mystic Camp | 6.4 miles |

11 days

DAY 1	Mowich Lake to Ipsut Creek	5.4 miles
DAY 2	Ipsut Creek to Mystic Camp	8.1 miles
DAY 3	Mystic Camp to Sunrise Camp	8.9 miles
DAY 4	Sunrise Camp to Summerland	10.3 miles
DAY 5	Summerland to Indian Bar	4.4 miles
DAY 6	Indian Bar to Maple Creek	9.8 miles
DAY 7	Maple Creek to Paradise River	6.4 miles
DAY 8	Paradise River to Devils Dream	9.3 miles
DAY 9	Devils Dream to Klapatche Park	11.2 miles
DAY 10	Klapatche Park to Golden Lakes	7.8 miles
DAY 11	Golden Lakes to Mowich Lake	9.5 miles

Alternate route through Spray Park

| DAY 1 | Mowich Lake to Cataract Valley | 6.8 miles |
| DAY 2 | Cataract Valley to Mystic Camp | 6.4 miles |

12 days

DAY 1	Mowich Lake to Ipsut Creek	5.4 miles
DAY 2	Ipsut Creek to Mystic Camp	8.1 miles
DAY 3	Mystic Camp to Sunrise Camp	8.9 miles
DAY 4	Sunrise Camp to Summerland	10.3 miles
DAY 5	Summerland to Indian Bar	4.4 miles
DAY 6	Indian Bar to Maple Creek	9.8 miles
DAY 7	Maple Creek to Paradise River	6.4 miles
DAY 8	Paradise River to Devils Dream	9.3 miles
DAY 9	Devils Dream to South Puyallup River	6.5 miles
DAY 10	South Puyallup River to Klapatche Park	4.7 miles
DAY 11	Klapatche Park to Golden Lakes	7.8 miles
DAY 12	Golden Lakes to Mowich Lake	9.5 miles

Alternate route through Spray Park

| DAY 1 | Mowich Lake to Cataract Valley | 6.8 miles |
| DAY 2 | Cataract Valley to Mystic Camp | 6.4 miles |

13 days

DAY 1	Mowich Lake to Ipsut Creek	5.4 miles
DAY 2	Ipsut Creek to Mystic Camp	8.1 miles
DAY 3	Mystic Camp to Granite Creek	4.6 miles
DAY 4	Granite Creek to Sunrise Camp	4.3 miles
DAY 5	Sunrise Camp to Summerland	10.3 miles
DAY 6	Summerland to Indian Bar	4.4 miles
DAY 7	Indian Bar to Nickel Creek	6.7 miles
DAY 8	Nickel Creek to Paradise River	9.5 miles
DAY 9	Paradise River to Pyramid Creek	7.3 miles
DAY 10	Pyramid Creek to South Puyallup River	8.5 miles
DAY 11	South Puyallup River to Klapatche Park	4.7 miles
DAY 12	Klapatche Park to Golden Lakes	7.8 miles
DAY 13	Golden Lakes to Mowich Lake	9.5 miles

Alternate route through Spray Park

| DAY 1 | Mowich Lake to Cataract Valley | 6.8 miles |
| DAY 2 | Cataract Valley to Mystic Camp | 6.4 miles |

APPENDIX B

COUNTERCLOCKWISE ITINERARIES

If you are someone who dreads steep, knee-creaking downhills, you may be a good candidate for starting your trip in the counterclockwise direction. Going counterclockwise, the hills are steeper, but the downhills are more gentle. While the uphills might make you wish you'd pushed yourself harder during your Jane Fonda or Richard Simmons workouts, reducing the downhill wear and tear on your knees and ankles means more-relaxed joints, tendons, and ligaments—and a happier you. Since clockwise is the more popular direction, you'll likely find yourself a bunch of new friends in camp each night, instead of going around the mountain with the same itinerary as everyone else. Going in either direction, solitude is not hard to find on the trail during the day.

Please note: Seven-day itineraries are very difficult and only recommended for very strong backpackers.

LONGMIRE TRAILHEAD

7 days

DAY 1	Longmire to Nickel Creek	13.3 miles
DAY 2	Nickel Creek to Summerland	11.1 miles
DAY 3	Summerland to Granite Creek	14.6 miles
DAY 4	Granite Creek to Ipsut Creek	12.7 miles
DAY 5	Ipsut Creek to Golden Lakes	14.9 miles
DAY 6	Golden Lakes to South Puyallup River	12.5 miles
DAY 7	South Puyallup River to Longmire	12.0 miles

Alternate route through Spray Park

DAY 4	Granite Creek to Eagles Roost	15.7 miles
DAY 5	Eagles Roost to Golden Lakes	11.0 miles

8 days

DAY 1	Longmire to Nickel Creek	13.3 miles
DAY 2	Nickel Creek to Summerland	11.1 miles

252

DAY 3	Summerland to Sunrise Camp	10.3 miles
DAY 4	Sunrise Camp to Mystic Camp	8.9 miles
DAY 5	Mystic Camp to Mowich Lake via Ipsut Pass	12.9 miles
DAY 6	Mowich Lake to Golden Lakes	9.5 miles
DAY 7	Golden Lakes to South Puyallup River	12.5 miles
DAY 8	South Puyallup River to Longmire	12.0 miles

Alternate route through Spray Park

| DAY 5 | Mystic Camp to Eagles Roost | 11.1 miles |
| DAY 6 | Eagles Roost to Golden Lakes | 11.0 miles |

9 days

DAY 1	Longmire to Maple Creek	10.2 miles
DAY 2	Maple Creek to Indian Bar	9.8 miles
DAY 3	Indian Bar to Summerland	4.4 miles
DAY 4	Summerland to Sunrise Camp	10.3 miles
DAY 5	Sunrise Camp to Mystic Camp	8.9 miles
DAY 6	Mystic Camp to Mowich Lake via Ipsut Pass	12.9 miles
DAY 7	Mowich Lake to Golden Lakes	9.5 miles
DAY 8	Golden Lakes to South Puyallup River	12.5 miles
DAY 9	South Puyallup River to Longmire	12.0 miles

Alternate route through Spray Park

| DAY 6 | Mystic Camp to Mowich Lake | 13.2 miles |

Alternate route through Spray Park

| DAY 6 | Mystic Camp to Eagles Roost | 11.1 miles |
| DAY 7 | Eagles Roost to Golden Lakes | 11.0 miles |

10 days

DAY 1	Longmire to Maple Creek	10.2 miles
DAY 2	Maple Creek to Indian Bar	9.8 miles
DAY 3	Indian Bar to Summerland	4.4 miles
DAY 4	Summerland to Sunrise Camp	10.3 miles
DAY 5	Sunrise Camp to Mystic Camp	8.9 miles
DAY 6	Mystic Camp to Ipsut Creek	8.1 miles
DAY 7	Ipsut Creek to South Mowich River	9.6 miles
DAY 8	South Mowich River to North Puyallup River	10.3 miles
DAY 9	North Puyallup River to South Puyallup River	7.5 miles
DAY 10	South Puyallup River to Longmire	12.0 miles

Alternate route through Spray Park

| DAY 6 | Mystic Camp to Cataract Valley | 6.4 miles |
| DAY 7 | Cataract Valley to South Mowich River | 10.4 miles |

11 days

| DAY 1 | Longmire to Maple Creek | 10.2 miles |
| DAY 2 | Maple Creek to Indian Bar | 9.8 miles |

DAY 3	Indian Bar to Summerland	4.4 miles
DAY 4	Summerland to Sunrise Camp	10.3 miles
DAY 5	Sunrise Camp to Mystic Camp	8.9 miles
DAY 6	Mystic Camp to Ipsut Creek	8.1 miles
DAY 7	Ipsut Creek to South Mowich River	9.6 miles
DAY 8	South Mowich River to Golden Lakes	5.3 miles
DAY 9	Golden Lakes to Klapatche Park	7.8 miles
DAY 10	Klapatche Park to Devils Dream	11.2 miles
DAY 11	Devils Dream to Longmire	5.5 miles

Alternate route through Spray Park

| DAY 6 | Mystic Camp to Cataract Valley | 6.4 miles |
| DAY 7 | Cataract Valley to South Mowich River | 10.4 miles |

12 days

DAY 1	Longmire to Maple Creek	10.2 miles
DAY 2	Maple Creek to Indian Bar	9.8 miles
DAY 3	Indian Bar to Summerland	4.4 miles
DAY 4	Summerland to Sunrise Camp	10.3 miles
DAY 5	Sunrise Camp to Mystic Camp	8.9 miles
DAY 6	Mystic Camp to Ipsut Creek	8.1 miles
DAY 7	Ipsut Creek to South Mowich River	9.6 miles
DAY 8	South Mowich River to Golden Lakes	5.3 miles
DAY 9	Golden Lakes to Klapatche Park	7.8 miles
DAY 10	Klapatche Park to South Puyallup River	4.7 miles
DAY 11	South Puyallup River to Devils Dream	6.5 miles
DAY 12	Devils Dream to Longmire	5.5 miles

Alternate route through Spray Park

| DAY 7 | Mystic Camp to Cataract Valley | 6.4 miles |
| DAY 8 | Cataract Valley to South Mowich River | 10.4 miles |

13 days

DAY 1	Longmire to Paradise River	3.8 miles
DAY 2	Paradise River to Nickel Creek	9.5 miles
DAY 3	Nickel Creek to Indian Bar	6.7 miles
DAY 4	Indian Bar to Summerland	4.4 miles
DAY 5	Summerland to Sunrise Camp	10.3 miles
DAY 6	Sunrise Camp to Mystic Camp	8.9 miles
DAY 7	Mystic Camp to Ipsut Creek	8.1 miles
DAY 8	Ipsut Creek to South Mowich River	9.6 miles
DAY 9	South Mowich River to Golden Lakes	5.3 miles
DAY 10	Golden Lakes to Klapatche Park	7.8 miles
DAY 11	Klapatche Park to South Puyallup River	4.7 miles
DAY 12	South Puyallup River to Devils Dream	6.5 miles
DAY 13	Devils Dream to Longmire	5.5 miles

Alternate route through Spray Park
DAY 7	Mystic Camp to Cataract Valley	6.4 miles
DAY 8	Cataract Valley to South Mowich River	10.4 miles

SUNRISE TRAILHEAD

7 days
DAY 1	Sunrise trailhead to Dick Creek	13.8 miles
DAY 2	Dick Creek to South Mowich River via Ipsut Pass	13.5 miles
DAY 3	South Mowich River to Klapatche Park	13.1 miles
DAY 4	Klapatche Park to Pyramid Creek	13.2 miles
DAY 5	Pyramid Creek to Maple Creek	13.7 miles
DAY 6	Maple Creek to Indian Bar	9.8 miles
DAY 7	Indian Bar to Sunrise trailhead	14.4 miles

Alternate route through Spray Park
DAY 2	Dick Creek to South Mowich River	13.2 miles

8 days
DAY 1	Sunrise trailhead to Mystic Camp	10.2 miles
DAY 2	Mystic Camp to Mowich Lake via Ipsut Pass	12.9 miles
DAY 3	Mowich Lake to Golden Lakes	9.5 miles
DAY 4	Golden Lakes to South Puyallup River	12.5 miles
DAY 5	South Puyallup River to Pyramid Creek	8.5 miles
DAY 6	Pyramid Creek to Maple Creek	13.7 miles
DAY 7	Maple Creek to Indian Bar	9.8 miles
DAY 8	Indian Bar to Sunrise trailhead	14.4 miles

Alternate route through Spray Park
DAY 2	Mystic Camp to Eagles Roost	11.1 miles
DAY 3	Eagles Roost to Golden Lakes	11.0 miles

9 days
DAY 1	Sunrise trailhead to Mystic Camp	10.2 miles
DAY 2	Mystic Camp to Mowich Lake via Ipsut Pass	12.9 miles
DAY 3	Mowich Lake to Golden Lakes	9.5 miles
DAY 4	Golden Lakes to Klapatche Park	7.8 miles
DAY 5	Klapatche Park to Devils Dream	11.2 miles
DAY 6	Devils Dream to Paradise River	9.3 miles
DAY 7	Paradise River to Nickel Creek	9.5 miles
DAY 8	Nickel Creek to Summerland	11.1 miles
DAY 9	Summerland to Sunrise trailhead	10.0 miles

Alternate route through Spray Park
DAY 2	Mystic Camp to Eagles Roost	11.1 miles
DAY 3	Eagles Roost to Golden Lakes	11.0 miles

10 days

DAY 1	Sunrise trailhead to Mystic Camp	10.2 miles
DAY 2	Mystic Camp to Mowich Lake via Ipsut Pass	12.9 miles
DAY 3	Mowich Lake to Golden Lakes	9.5 miles
DAY 4	Golden Lakes to Klapatche Park	7.8 miles
DAY 5	Klapatche Park to Devils Dream	11.2 miles
DAY 6	Devils Dream to Paradise River	9.3 miles
DAY 7	Paradise River to Nickel Creek	9.5 miles
DAY 8	Nickel Creek to Indian Bar	6.7 miles
DAY 9	Indian Bar to Summerland	4.4 miles
DAY 10	Summerland to Sunrise trailhead	10.0 miles

Alternate route through Spray Park

| DAY 2 | Mystic Camp to Eagles Roost | 11.1 miles |
| DAY 3 | Eagles Roost to Golden Lakes | 11.0 miles |

11 days

DAY 1	Sunrise trailhead to Mystic Camp	10.2 miles
DAY 2	Mystic Camp to Ipsut Creek	8.1 miles
DAY 3	Ipsut Creek to South Mowich River	9.6 miles
DAY 4	South Mowich River to Golden Lakes	5.3 miles
DAY 5	Golden Lakes to Klapatche Park	7.8 miles
DAY 6	Klapatche Park to Devils Dream	11.2 miles
DAY 7	Devils Dream to Paradise River	9.3 miles
DAY 8	Paradise River to Nickel Creek	9.5 miles
DAY 9	Nickel Creek to Indian Bar	6.7 miles
DAY 10	Indian Bar to Summerland	4.4 miles
DAY 11	Summerland to Sunrise trailhead	10.0 miles

Alternate route through Spray Park

| DAY 2 | Mystic Camp to Cataract Valley | 6.4 miles |
| DAY 3 | Cataract Valley to South Mowich River | 10.4 miles |

12 days

DAY 1	Sunrise trailhead to Granite Creek	5.6 miles
DAY 2	Granite Creek to Mystic Camp	4.6 miles
DAY 3	Mystic Camp to Ipsut Creek	8.1 miles
DAY 4	Ipsut Creek to South Mowich River	9.6 miles
DAY 5	South Mowich River to Golden Lakes	5.3 miles
DAY 6	Golden Lakes to Klapatche Park	7.8 miles
DAY 7	Klapatche Park to Devils Dream	11.2 miles
DAY 8	Devils Dream to Paradise River	9.3 miles
DAY 9	Paradise River to Nickel Creek	9.5 miles
DAY 10	Nickel Creek to Indian Bar	6.7 miles
DAY 11	Indian Bar to Summerland	4.4 miles
DAY 12	Summerland to Sunrise trailhead	10.0 miles

A herd of mountain goats grazes alongside the trail near Sunrise.

Alternate route through Spray Park

DAY 3	Mystic Camp to Cataract Valley	6.4 miles
DAY 4	Cataract Valley to South Mowich River	10.4 miles

13 days

DAY 1	Sunrise trailhead to Granite Creek	5.6 miles
DAY 2	Granite Creek to Mystic Camp	4.6 miles
DAY 3	Mystic Camp to Ipsut Creek	8.1 miles
DAY 4	Ipsut Creek to South Mowich River	9.6 miles
DAY 5	South Mowich River to Golden Lakes	5.3 miles
DAY 6	Golden Lakes to Klapatche Park	7.8 miles
DAY 7	Klapatche Park to South Puyallup River	4.7 miles
DAY 8	South Puyallup River to Devils Dream	6.5 miles
DAY 9	Devils Dream to Paradise River	9.3 miles
DAY 10	Paradise River to Nickel Creek	9.5 miles
DAY 11	Nickel Creek to Indian Bar	6.7 miles
DAY 12	Indian Bar to Summerland	4.4 miles
DAY 13	Summerland to Sunrise trailhead	10.0 miles

Alternate route through Spray Park

DAY 3	Mystic Camp to Cataract Valley	6.4 miles
DAY 4	Cataract Valley to South Mowich River	10.4 miles

MOWICH LAKE TRAILHEAD

7 days

DAY 1	Mowich Lake to Golden Lakes	9.5 miles
DAY 2	Golden Lakes to South Puyallup River	12.5 miles
DAY 3	South Puyallup River to Paradise River	15.8 miles
DAY 4	Paradise River to Indian Bar	16.2 miles
DAY 5	Indian Bar to White River Campground	11.3 miles
DAY 6	White River Campground to Mystic Camp	12.3 miles
DAY 7	Mystic Camp to Mowich Lake via Ipsut Pass	12.9 miles

Alternate route through Spray Park

DAY 7	Mystic Camp to Mowich Lake	13.2 miles

8 days

DAY 1	Mowich Lake to Golden Lakes	9.5 miles
DAY 2	Golden Lakes to South Puyallup River	12.5 miles
DAY 3	South Puyallup River to Paradise River	15.8 miles
DAY 4	Paradise River to Nickel Creek	9.5 miles
DAY 5	Nickel Creek to Summerland	11.1 miles
DAY 6	Summerland to Sunrise Camp	10.3 miles
DAY 7	Sunrise Camp to Mystic Camp	8.9 miles
DAY 8	Mystic Camp to Mowich Lake via Ipsut Pass	12.9 miles

Alternate route through Spray Park

DAY 8	Mystic Camp to Mowich Lake	13.2 miles

9 days

DAY 1	Mowich Lake to Golden Lakes	9.5 miles
DAY 2	Golden Lakes to Klapatche Park	7.8 miles
DAY 3	Klapatche Park to Devils Dream	11.2 miles
DAY 4	Devils Dream to Paradise River	9.3 miles
DAY 5	Paradise River to Nickel Creek	9.5 miles
DAY 6	Nickel Creek to Summerland	11.1 miles
DAY 7	Summerland to Sunrise Camp	10.3 miles
DAY 8	Sunrise Camp to Mystic Camp	8.9 miles
DAY 9	Mystic Camp to Mowich Lake via Ipsut Pass	12.9 miles

Alternate route through Spray Park

DAY 9	Mystic Camp to Mowich Lake	13.2 miles

10 days

DAY 1	Mowich Lake to Golden Lakes	9.5 miles
DAY 2	Golden Lakes to Klapatche Park	7.8 miles
DAY 3	Klapatche Park to Devils Dream	11.2 miles
DAY 4	Devils Dream to Paradise River	9.3 miles
DAY 5	Paradise River to Nickel Creek	9.5 miles
DAY 6	Nickel Creek to Indian Bar	6.7 miles
DAY 7	Indian Bar to Summerland	4.4 miles
DAY 8	Summerland to Sunrise Camp	10.3 miles
DAY 9	Sunrise Camp to Mystic Camp	8.9 miles
DAY 10	Mystic Camp to Mowich Lake via Ipsut Pass	12.9 miles

Alternate route through Spray Park

DAY 10	Mystic Camp to Mowich Lake	13.2 miles

11 days

DAY 1	Mowich Lake to Golden Lakes	9.5 miles
DAY 2	Golden Lakes to Klapatche Park	7.8 miles
DAY 3	Klapatche Park to Devils Dream	11.2 miles
DAY 4	Devils Dream to Paradise River	9.3 miles
DAY 5	Paradise River to Nickel Creek	9.5 miles
DAY 6	Nickel Creek to Indian Bar	6.7 miles
DAY 7	Indian Bar to Summerland	4.4 miles
DAY 8	Summerland to Sunrise Camp	10.3 miles
DAY 9	Sunrise Camp to Mystic Camp	8.9 miles
DAY 10	Mystic Camp to Ipsut Creek	8.1 miles
DAY 11	Ipsut Creek to Mowich Lake	5.4 miles

Alternate route through Spray Park

DAY 10	Mystic Camp to Cataract Valley	6.4 miles
DAY 11	Cataract Valley to Mowich Lake	6.8 miles

12 days

DAY 1	Mowich Lake to South Mowich River	4.2 miles
DAY 2	South Mowich River to Golden Lakes	5.3 miles
DAY 3	Golden Lakes to Klapatche Park	7.8 miles
DAY 4	Klapatche Park to Devils Dream	11.2 miles
DAY 5	Devils Dream to Paradise River	9.3 miles
DAY 6	Paradise River to Nickel Creek	9.5 miles
DAY 7	Nickel Creek to Indian Bar	6.7 miles
DAY 8	Indian Bar to Summerland	4.4 miles
DAY 9	Summerland to Sunrise Camp	10.3 miles
DAY 10	Sunrise Camp to Mystic Camp	8.9 miles
DAY 11	Mystic Camp to Ipsut Creek	8.1 miles
DAY 12	Ipsut Creek to Mowich Lake	5.4 miles

Alternate route through Spray Park

DAY 11	Mystic Camp to Cataract Valley	6.4 miles
DAY 12	Cataract Valley to Mowich Lake	6.8 miles

13 days

DAY 1	Mowich Lake to South Mowich River	4.2 miles
DAY 2	South Mowich River to Golden Lakes	5.3 miles
DAY 3	Golden Lakes to Klapatche Park	7.8 miles
DAY 4	Klapatche Park to South Puyallup River	4.7 miles
DAY 5	South Puyallup River to Devils Dream	6.5 miles
DAY 6	Devils Dream to Paradise River	9.3 miles
DAY 7	Paradise River to Nickel Creek	9.5 miles
DAY 8	Nickel Creek to Indian Bar	6.7 miles
DAY 9	Indian Bar to Summerland	4.4 miles
DAY 10	Summerland to Sunrise Camp	10.3 miles
DAY 11	Sunrise Camp to Mystic Camp	8.9 miles
DAY 12	Mystic Camp to Ipsut Creek	8.1 miles
DAY 13	Ipsut Creek to Mowich Lake	5.4 miles

Alternate route through Spray Park

DAY 12	Mystic Camp to Cataract Valley	6.4 miles
DAY 13	Cataract Valley to Mowich Lake	6.8 miles

APPENDIX C

CAMP-TO-CAMP ELEVATION GAIN AND LOSS

CAMP TO CAMP (or intersection)	DISTANCE (in miles)	GAIN	LOSS
Longmire Trailhead to Pyramid Creek	3.5	1125 FT.	220 FT.
Pyramid Creek to Devils Dream	2.0	1380 FT.	NEGLIGIBLE
Devils Dream to South Puyallup River	6.5	1620 FT.	2480 FT.
South Puyallup River to Klapatche Park	4.7	1800 FT.	500 FT.
Klapatche Park to North Puyallup River	2.8	NEGLIGIBLE	1800 FT.
North Puyallup River to Golden Lakes	5.0	1500 FT.	300 FT.
Golden Lakes to South Mowich River	5.3	NEGLIGIBLE	2300 FT.
South Mowich River to Spray Park Trail Intersection	3.9	2300 FT.	0 FT.
Spray Park Trail Intersection to Mowich Lake	0.3	30 FT.	0 FT.
Spray Park Trail			
Mowich Lake to Eagles Roost	2.1	560 FT.	590 FT.
Eagles Roost to Cataract Valley	4.7	1540 FT.	1775 FT.
Cataract Valley to Carbon River	1.6	NEGLIGIBLE	1505 FT.
Carbon River to Wonderland Trail Intersection	0.2	40 FT.	0 FT.

CAMP TO CAMP (or intersection)	DISTANCE (in miles)	GAIN	LOSS
Mowich Lake to Ipsut Creek	5.4	170 FT.	2700 FT.
Ipsut Creek to Dick Creek (with trail detour)	4.5	1900 FT.	0 FT.
Dick Creek to Mystic Camp	3.6	1700 FT.	300 FT.
Mystic Camp to Granite Creek	4.6	1200 FT.	1100 FT.
Granite Creek to Sunrise Camp	4.3	1200 FT.	800 FT.
Sunrise Camp to White River Campground	3.4	NEGLIGIBLE	1900 FT.
White River Campground to Fryingpan Creek Trail Intersection	2.6	100 FT.	500 FT.
Fryingpan Creek Trail Intersection to Summerland	4.4	2000 FT.	0 FT.
Summerland to Indian Bar	4.4	900 FT.	1800 FT.
Indian Bar to Nickel Creek	6.7	930 FT.	2530 FT.
Nickel Creek to Box Canyon Intersection	0.8	NEGLIGIBLE	400 FT.
Box Canyon Intersection to Maple Creek	2.3	200 FT.	400 FT.
Maple Creek to Paradise River	6.4	2055 FT.	1055 FT.
Paradise River to Longmire Trailhead	3.8	NEGLIGIBLE	1025 FT.

APPENDIX D

CAMPS

KEY: WT = Wonderland Trail; SPT = Spray Park Trail; NL = Northern Loop; EL = Eastside Loop.

CAMP	INDIVIDUAL SITES	GROUP SITES
Berkeley Park (NL)	2	1
Carbon River (SPT, WT)	4	1
Cataract Valley (SPT)	6	1
Deer Creek (EL)	2	0
Devils Dream (WT)	7	1
Dick Creek (WT, NL)	2	0
Eagles Roost (SPT)	7	0
Fire Creek (NL)	3	1
Golden Lakes (WT)	5	1
Granite Creek (WT, NL)	3	1
Indian Bar (WT, EL)	4	1
Ipsut Creek (WT)	12	1
James Camp (NL)	3	1
Klapatche Park (WT)	4	0

CAMP	INDIVIDUAL SITES	GROUP SITES
Maple Creek (WT)	4	1
Mowich Lake (WT)	12	0
Mystic Camp (WT, NL)	7	1
Nickel Creek (WT)	3	1
North Puyallup River (WT)	3	1
Olallie Creek (EL)	2	1
Paradise River (WT)	3	1
Pyramid Creek (WT)	3	0
South Mowich River (WT)	4	1
South Puyallup River (WT)	4	1
Summerland (WT, EL)	5	1
Sunrise Camp (WT)	8	2
Tamanos Creek (EL)	4	1
White River (WT)	4	0
Yellowstone Cliffs (NL)	2	0

NOTE: Mowich Lake Campground is a walk-in frontcountry campground. White River Campground is a drive-in car campground. Both are part of the Wonderland Trail permit system and have special areas designated for wilderness permit holders.

RESOURCES

TRAIL AND PARK RESOURCES
Mount Rainier National Park
(360) 569-6575, www.nps.gov/mora

TRANSPORTATION
Shuttle Express: (425) 981-7000, www.shuttleexpress.com
Pierce County Transit to Graham, Washington: www.piercetransit.org

LODGING
Mount Rainier Guest Services (for National Park Inn and Paradise Inn): 1-855-755-2275,
    www.mtrainierguestservices.com

CAMPGROUNDS
Cougar Rock; Ohanapecosh; White River: www.recreation.gov

WILDERNESS INFORMATION CENTERS
www.nps.gov/mora/planyourvisit/hours.htm
Longmire Wilderness Information Center: (360) 569-6650
Carbon River Ranger Station: (360) 829-9639
White River Wilderness Information Center: (360) 569-6670
Park Headquarters: (360) 569-2211

PERMITS AND REGULATIONS
www.nps.gov/mora/planyourvisit/wilderness-camping-and-hiking.htm

CACHING FOOD AND FUEL
www.nps.gov/mora/planyourvisit/caching-food-and-fuel.htm
Longmire food cache address: (via UPS or FedEx only) Mount Rainier National Park, 1 NPS Warehouse,
    Longmire, WA 98397, ATTN: Longmire WIC
White River food cache address: (via USPS, UPS, or FedEx) Mount Rainier National Park, White River
    WIC, 70002 SR 410 East, Enumclaw, WA 98022

Mowich Lake Patrol Cabin food cache address: (via UPS or FedEx) Mount Rainier National Park, Carbon River Ranger Station, 35415 Fairfax Forest Reserve Road East, Carbonado, WA 98323; (via USPS) Mount Rainier National Park, Carbon River Ranger Station, PO Box 423, Wilkeson, WA 98396

RECOMMENDED READING

Asars, Tami. *Day Hiking Mount Rainier*, 2nd ed. Seattle: Mountaineers Books, 2018.

Anderson, Kristi, ed. *Wilderness Basics: Get the Most from Your Hiking, Backpacking, and Camping Adventures*, 4th ed. Seattle: Mountaineers Books, 2013.

Colver, John, and M. Nicole Nazzaro. *Fit by Nature*. Seattle: Mountaineers Books, 2011.

Filley, Bette. *The Big Fact Book About Mount Rainier*. Issaquah, WA: Dunamis House, 1996.

Gauthier, Mike. *Mount Rainier: A Climbing Guide*. 3rd edition. Seattle: Mountaineers Books, 2017.

Kirk, Ruth. *Sunrise to Paradise*. Seattle: University of Washington Press, 1999.

Kirkconnell, Sarah Svien. *Freezer Bag Cooking: Trail Food Made Simple*. Seattle: Bay Street Publishing, 2005.

Loewen, Bree. *Pickets and Dead Men: Seasons on Rainier*. Seattle: Mountaineers Books, 2009.

Meany, Edmond. *Mount Rainier: A Record of Exploration*. Whitefish, MT: Kessinger Publishing, 2010.

Molenaar, Dee. *The Challenge of Rainier*. 4th ed. Seattle: Mountaineers Books, 2011.

Smith, Allan H. *Takhoma*. Pullman: Washington State University Press, 2006.

Van Tilburg, Christopher. *Don't Die Out There Deck*. Seattle: Mountaineers Books, 2007.

Williams, John H. *The Mountain That Was God*. 2nd ed. New York: G. P. Putnam's Son, 1911.

INDEX

ABOUT THE AUTHOR

Tami Asars grew up in western Washington playing in the foothills and mountains of the North Cascades, where hiking and backpacking was a way of life for her family. Asars has completed the Pacific Crest Trail, the Continental Divide Trail, and the Appalachian Trail—making her a Triple Crowner. She has tackled many other long-distance trails as well, including the Colorado Trail, the Arizona Trail, the Tahoe Rim Trail, the West Coast Trail, and of course, the Wonderland Trail—still her favorite by far, after twelve trips around the mountain.

Asars has served as a professional backpacking guide on the Northern Loop Trail in Mount Rainier National Park and in numerous backcountry locations in Washington State. She teaches classes on outdoor pursuits, one of which is focused entirely on the Wonderland Trail, and dedicates her time to outdoor writing and photography in support of the areas she loves so much. Asars is a full-time freelance writer who has authored several books for Mountaineers Books, including *Day Hiking: Mount Rainier*; *Day Hiking: Mount Adams and Goat Rocks*; *Fall Color Hikes: Washington*; and *Hiking the Pacific Crest Trail: Washington*. She has contributed to countless magazines including *Washington*, *City Dog*, *Mountaineer*, and *Alaska Airlines*.

She lives in the Cascade foothills with her husband, Vilnis, and their rough collie, Scout. To learn more about her, visit www.tamiasars.com.

MOUNTAINEERS BOOKS

recreation • lifestyle • conservation

MOUNTAINEERS BOOKS, including its two imprints, Skipstone and Braided River, is a leading publisher of quality outdoor recreation, sustainability, and conservation titles. As a 501(c)(3) nonprofit, we are committed to supporting the environmental and educational goals of our organization by providing expert information on human-powered adventure, sustainable practices at home and on the trail, and preservation of wilderness.

Our publications are made possible through the generosity of donors, and through sales of 700 titles on outdoor recreation, sustainable lifestyle, and conservation. To donate, purchase books, or learn more, visit us online:

MOUNTAINEERS BOOKS

1001 SW Klickitat Way, Suite 201 • Seattle, WA 98134

800-553-4453 • mbooks@mountaineersbooks.org • www.mountaineersbooks.org

An independent nonprofit publisher since 1960

Mountaineers Books is proud to support the Leave No Trace Center for Outdoor Ethics, whose mission is to promote and inspire responsible outdoor recreation through education, research, and partnerships. The Leave No Trace program is focused specifically on human-powered (nonmotorized) recreation. For more information, visit www.lnt.org.

YOU MAY ALSO LIKE

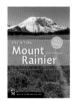

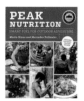